GOOD NEWS TO THE POOR

Good News to the Poor

John Wesley's Evangelical Economics

Theodore W. Jennings, Jr.

Abingdon Press
Nashville

GOOD NEWS TO THE POOR: John Wesley's Evangelical Economics

Library of Congress Cataloging-in-Publication Data

Good News to the poor / Theodore W. Jennnings, Jr.
　　p.　cm.
Includes bibliographical references.
ISBN 0-687-15528-2 (alk. paper)
　　1. Economics—Religious aspects—Methodist Church—History of doctrines—18th century. 2. Methodist Church—Great Britain—Doctrines—History—18th century. 3. Wesley, John, 1703-1791—Ethics. 5. Christian ethics—History—18th century. 6. Social ethics—History—18th century. I. Title.
BR115.E3J45　　1990
261.8'5'092—dc20　　　　　　　　　　　　　　　　　　　　90-39782
　　　　　　　　　　　　　　　　　　　　　　　　　　　　　　　CIP

00 01 02 03 04–10 9 8 7 6

MANUFACTURED IN THE UNITED STATES OF AMERICA

For
Theodore H. Runyon, Jr.,
who opened the way

and for
my students at the Seminario Metodista de México,
companions on the journey

CONTENTS

PREFACE

I t may be of some help to the reader to know how I came to write on John Wesley and, in particular, on the subject of Wesley's social ethic. Although I am a Methodist and a descendent of one of the earliest circuit riders, although my middle name is Wesley, I confess to having contracted an antipathy to the study of Wesley. Indeed I avoided courses on that and related subjects even in seminary despite the fact (or because?) they were required of those who, like myself, sought to be ordained as ministers in The United Methodist Church. The truth is that I found the whole business of eighteenth-century Christianity unspeakably boring and the preoccupations of the founder of Methodism tedious in the extreme. I had imbibed the legends of Susannah Wesley and the Aldersgate experience from infancy. I outgrew them as I outgrew a taste for pabulum. I have little enough taste for hagiography as it is. But the life of Wesley is definitely not the stuff dreams are made of. This is all the more true when you consider that the name of Wesley is associated, not without reason, with the sort of disciplined life that had little appeal to a young sophisticate in the heady days of the mid 1960s. Besides, I was interested in theology, and everyone knows that, whatever else he may have been, Wesley was *not* a theologian.

In the course of time I became a theologian, even a Methodist theologian—at least in the sense that I was teaching in a Methodist seminary. But I would still greet with horror the suggestion that I offer a course (one of those dreadful required ones) on the theology of John Wesley. I managed to fend off those suggestions. When Ted Runyon told me he was working on an essay on the relation between Wesley and Marx with the aim of showing the relevance of Wesley for contemporary liberation theology, I must admit that I greeted the idea with considerable skepticism. It seemed just another way of trying to sell a worn out product by putting a fancy label on it. Even when I read the essay and had to admit not only that it was wonderfully written but also that it seemed to make a surprisingly strong case, I did not run right out to buy a copy of Wesley's *Works*. Seven thousand pages of eighteenth-century hortatory theology still seemed something of a crucifixion of the intellect, a flagellation of the spirit, a Chinese water torture of tedium. While my respect for Wesley and those who studied him had grown, I did not feel called upon to (deny myself and) take up that study myself.

Through an improbable chain of circumstances, I found myself teaching theology and Bible in the Methodist Seminary of Mexico in the center of Mexico City. About the time my Spanish was good enough to say "Buenos dias" without consulting my notes, I was entreated by the director to offer a yearlong required course on Wesley's sermons. There was no escape. Having so far avoided the study of Wesley, I was now condemned to reading and teaching Wesley in Spanish—rather like finding oneself on the inside of a tale by Borges! Late twentieth-century Mexico City does not at first seem a hospitable environment to the study of an eighteenth-century apostle of common sense and reason. But much to my astonishment that course became one of the most exciting I have ever taught.

Partly this had to do with a community of interest that improbably joined the old Oxford logician with the adolescent evangelists who populated the seminary. These students were entirely innocent of academic pretensions. Their driving desire was to be Christians and to help others to be Christians. They found in Wesley a kindred spirit. Moreover they had a hunger to know what it might mean to be a Methodist, which made the study of Wesley particularly appealing to them. For the rather blasé world of triumphant Protestantism in which I grew up, ecumenism comes naturally, and the preoccupation with denominational particularity seems a bit of egregious bad taste. But in a context where Protestants are a tiny minority and Methodists one of a gaggle of minuscule sects within that minority the question of identity is a rather pressing one. This is especially true if one cannot really be satisfied with the purely negative identity of "not Catholic" (even if one has learned the defensive stratagem of giving to Catholicism the negative identity of "not-Christian").

But this encounter with Wesley had an unexpected result. The students found themselves confronting their own situation in a new way on the basis of the study of Wesley. Many of them had supposed that there was an inherent contradiction between evangelical piety and social action. Others had appropriated the gospel of wealth and success, which encourages a contempt for the poor and a self-contempt among the poor. They were not impressed by liberation theology, which was often viewed as a Catholic plot or (worse) an Argentine import! And the weight of tradition, in the form of sermons heard all their lives, made a fresh appropriation of biblical themes of justice and liberation quite difficult. But to find something like this in Wesley, that was another matter. Here was one who clearly shared their own concern for the gospel, for evangelization, for the new life in Christ. And he sometimes sounded like one of those liberation theologians!

The more I worked on Wesley, and the more experience I had of the grassroots church in Mexico, the more apparent it became that Wesley provided an opening to engagement with the staggering reality of life in modern Mexico not otherwise available to the church. The temptations of the church to fall back into a sectarian ghetto, to heed the siren call of the gospel of wealth and success, to separate the spiritual from the economic reality of the overwhelming majority of their fellow Mexicans—all of these proved well nigh irresistible, until confronted with the example and teaching of Wesley. What had seemed to me to be Wesley's weakness—his concentration on the personal life of faith and the unsystematic and popular character of his theologizing—proved to be his strength. It was this that made him "relevant" and provocative and even liberating in the context of the Methodist Church in Mexico.

My experience with the Methodist Church in Mexico, then, provides the point of view for this study. It is not my aim to show that Wesley had already figured out everything the liberation theologians are trying to teach us, or that Wesley was one of the great theological ethicists of all time, or even that he was the most socially aware man of his age. I still have no appetite for hagiography. But I do want to show that Wesley can provide a point of entry for the discussion of the meaning of faithful Christian witness in the midst of the calamitous economic crisis of our planet.

Far from emphasizing the significance of Wesley as the founder of Methodism, it will emerge that Methodism has from the beginning been characterized as a rejection of Wesley's most deeply held convictions about what I will call evangelical economics. But that is getting ahead of the story.

I would not have undertaken this sort of study had it not been for the ground-breaking essays of Theodore H. Runyon, Jr., and José Míguez Bonino. To this was added the encouraging response of my students at the Seminario Metodista de México to my initial attempts at presenting the thought of John Wesley. This response was then confirmed in a number of church settings at various levels of the Methodist Church in Mexico. My mother-in-law made it possible for me to acquire the computer without which the mysteries of word-processing would have forever been beyond my reach and this book but a dream. I am also grateful to Theodore H. Runyon, Jr., for helpful suggestions made at several points in the work on this study, and to my editor, Rex D. Matthews, without whose encouragement this manuscript would never have been completed or published. My wife's commitment to the poor has extended to being willing to support my theological habit and to try out some of my ideas in the church of which she is the pastor.

CHAPTER ONE

INTRODUCTION

B efore launching into the study of Wesley's economic ethics, it will be helpful to make clear how I go about reading Wesley, the problems that are encountered in such a reading, and the aim or intent of such a reading.

FROM POLITICAL TO ECONOMIC ISSUES

The study of Wesley's social ethics is frequently rendered difficult by the apparently reactionary character of Wesley's politics. Questions of political organization and institutional justice are those that many of us have on our minds when we ask about social ethics. The real questions, we suppose, are political ones. And the beginning set of assumptions with which we approach this set of issues has to do with the self-evidence of putatively democratic forms of government. Insofar as this is our starting point, the political views of Wesley provide an immediate obstacle to any attempt to take anything else he has to say seriously. Wesley was not only an apologist for the king (to the extent that some of his enemies assumed he was on the king's payroll), but he was persuaded that democracy was wholly unworkable and decidedly impious. The point is not to argue whether Wesley was right or wrong about this. It is to say that his operating assumptions are so at variance from our own as to render his views apparently irrelevant to any attempt to wrestle with issues of any importance to us.

This is important to remember when we encounter those who attempt to use Wesley's conservative political stance to legitimate their own desire to maintain the status quo as unquestionable, for Wesley himself makes clear that the duty to honor the king is one that depends on the impossibility of democracy. If power flows from the people, then the given political institutions are not immutable or above criticism. Thus Wesley can be appealed to here only by those who agree that democracy is impossible and undesirable. Since Wesley was a critic of tyranny as well, that leaves only dedicated monarchists in a position to make an appeal to Wesley's political conservatism as in any way parallel to their own.

The supposition that political questions are primary is one that characterizes what is often called the "first world," the world of the "industrialized democracies." But for the majority of the earth's population the most pressing questions are those of economic justice. The brutal reality of murderous impoverishment, of exclusion from the abundant wealth of the planet, is the overriding problem. Each year that passes brings with it an unimaginable toll, a holocaust of victims to the economic demons that enforce a concentration of wealth in the hands of a tiny few, while consigning the rest to precarious existence and even death. In the year of our Lord 1989, fourteen million children were sacrificed to the Moloch of economic injustice. More children die of poverty (hunger and the diseases of malnutrition) every year than the total number of victims of the Nazi horror in over a decade! The victims of war and political violence are no more than a fraction of those who perish at the hands of institutionalized greed and indifference.

This is why many theologies of the Third World (or, as I prefer to say, of the *real* world) place a preferential option for the poor at the center of their reflection. In so doing they find that the Bible in general and the gospel in particular take on a fresh relevance and power. Thus a theological revolution has been launched, comparable only to that of the sixteenth-century Protestant Reformation.

Between these two reformations of Church and doctrine stands another of more limited impact and intellectual fruitfulness, but one with surprising similarities to the latest one.

It is the attempt to reform Christian life, undertaken by Wesley in the eighteenth century. Although this reform is generally supposed to have focused exclusively on individual salvation, this is in fact an anachronistic characterization more applicable to many of the nineteenth-century revivals, which appropriated the cult of the individual and of personality, so important to bourgeois culture. Wesley had in view the transformation of all of life on the basis of the gospel. And this transformation was so intimately linked to economic issues that the enterprise of scriptural Christianity could be said to succeed or fail depending on the way in which it did or did not transform the relation to wealth, property, and the poor. Thus economics has a central place in Wesley's project of transforming the nation and spreading "scriptural holiness throughout the land." And this economics is an "evangelical" economics, since it emphasizes the gospel as the basis of the theory and practice of an economics totally at variance with the regnant theory and practice of "worldly" economic relations.

WHICH TEXTS?

It is easy for us to miss the significance and scope of this evangelical economics because we are trained to look for it in the wrong places. The systematic habit of mind that we owe, perhaps, to the ghost of Hegel encourages us to look for grand and sweeping theoretical vistas, which can then be made concrete through application to, and illustration by, particular instances. Nothing could be further from Wesley's approach. In theology he does not enunciate major themes like christology or atonement, from which to draw conclusions about, say, freedom from sin. He is more likely to begin from something like gossip or backbiting and show its incompatibility with love, and in the process say something about the divine nature or the "end of Christ's coming." The same is true of his economic ethics. Wesley does not start off with a theory of actual or ideal economic relations, which is then applied to the problem of unemployment. Rather he begins with the concrete reality of his hearers or readers. They are spending money on clothes, but their neighbor has none. This then opens the way to a demonstration of the incompatibility of this with the gospel. Wesley's evangelical economics is most vigorously stated in sermonic essays on visiting the sick, on dress, and on stewardship, so that those who come at Wesley with a set of ready-made questions about class consciousness or government policy or free trade will be reduced to quarreling over scraps.

This is partly what makes the reading of Wesley seem so tedious. He seems to be endlessly preoccupied about triviality, about *adiaphora*. Unless we ask why Wesley is concerned about this or that seemingly trivial pursuit and listen attentively to what he says in reply, we will overlook his social and economic ethic entirely. The supposition that counsel about visiting the sick and not buying jewelry and abstaining from drinking tea are only "personal" ethics and so not relevant to broader social questions says more about modern alienated consciousness, with its segregation of the personal from the public, than it does about the triviality and legalism, let alone individualism, of Wesley's ethics.

In attempting to clarify Wesley's evangelical economics, then, it is important not only to pay attention to the texts that dominate the scholarly discussion of this problem—for example, Wesley's sermon "On the Uses of Money"—but also to attempt a fresh appraisal on the basis of a rereading of all the pertinent texts. It will become clear that the deficiency of many readings of Wesley is that they endlessly repeat the same set of quotations from Wesley without placing them in the context of Wesley's economic thought as a whole. Thus the supposition that Wesley contributed to the rise of a capitalist ethos, whether this is viewed positively (Warner, Semmel) or negatively (Cort, Thompson), is traceable to an arbitrary restriction in the data, to the lack of an appraisal of texts whose relevance has sometimes been obscured by the supposition that they deal not with the social question of economics but with the petty moralizing of a strictly personal ethic.

In fairness this partial reading of Wesley has been fostered by Methodist tradition itself, which has frequently sought to view Wesley in terms of the narrowest interpretation of evangelical concern for individual souls. But I will argue that this reading is mistaken. Those who seek to deflect attention from the pressing themes of social transformation by speaking of the evangelical imperative to save souls cannot find solace in Wesley's practice or thought. While Wesley did emphasize personal conversion, this was always inseparably linked to a real transformation in the form of one's life. This transformation did not simply make one a more complacent exemplar of conventional morality, but rather brought one into necessary conflict with the character of the world and its conventional wisdom. Above all it had to result in a transformation of one's relation to the world, especially as this world was instantiated in mammon, the desire of riches, the ethos of acquisition and expenditure. Those "evangelicals" who preach a conversion that does not turn us toward the poor, that does not result in a redistribution of wealth, cannot plausibly claim that there is any relation between saving persons and changing society. Rather they are offering individual salvation as a substitute for meaningful transformation either of persons or of society. Such a project receives no support from either Wesley or the gospel he sought to serve.

A THEOLOGICAL READING

There have been a number of very useful studies of the rise of Methodism within the socioeconomic and political environment of the eighteenth century. This essay does not attempt to cover that well plowed ground. Rather it has seemed important to me to attempt to reread Wesley himself. I do not mean to suggest that Wesley can be fully understood apart from the social environment within which he worked. But I am persuaded that the studies of this social environment can become truly illuminating only insofar as they are informed by a thorough reading of Wesley himself, a reading that seeks to understand the relation between the apparently diverse themes of his treatment of evangelical economics. This is not, in the first place, a historical task, but a theological one. It is an attempt to understand the internal coherence of Wesley's thought on this subject as a theme addressed also to us for theological consideration.

I approach these texts not as a historian but as a theologian, as one concerned to understand what it might mean to consider economic life as a theme for theological reflection and as one whose main concern is to address contemporary Christendom with this theme.

This reading of Wesley is, then, an attempt at what Wesley called "practical divinity." That is, it seeks to clarify a dimension of the life of the Church and of Christians on the basis of, or by means of a reading of, Wesley. This is by no means the only way to engage in such a practical theology. One may do so, as I have attempted to do, by way of an interpretation of the central acts of the life of the community, its worship.[1] Or one may seek to develop studies of ministerial function (as in many forms of pastoral theology). Or one may seek, as Wesley did, to develop clarifications of particular doctrines that bear prominently on the Christian life; themes like "the new birth" or the problem of "sin in believers." Or one may even attempt a comprehensive theological treatment of all doctrines relevant to a direct consideration of Christian existence, as for example Reinhold Niebuhr's *Nature and Destiny of Man*. But one may also attempt to clarify one or another of these issues by means of a reading of classic texts, whether biblical texts or texts produced by previous theologians in the attempt to clarify these issues for their own time. It is the latter task that this book sets for itself.

Now the aim of such an inquiry is, to a certain degree, historical—that is, it attempts to get at what the theologian in question was really after. It would be irresponsible to simply use isolated fragments of his or her thought as proof texts for one's own position. This would not only violate canons of academic inquiry, but it would also be discourteous to persons or texts that have no means of defending themselves from such misuse.

But it would be similarly inappropriate to confine one's reading of such texts to a strictly "historical" reading that relegates the text to the past, hermetically sealing it off from the possibility of illuminating any era other than its own. Too often a historical reading succeeds in producing a mound of scholarship heaped like a pyramid to cover the tomb of its subject. There is a sense in which a theological reading seeks to allow a text from the past to speak again, to become contemporary, to "live on."

Clearly it is a delicate balancing act to combine both a respect for the actual text as it was written with an insertion of that text into the different context of contemporary debate. All one can do is make oneself aware of this difficulty and seek to be responsible to both sides of the tension. This also means that one will accept the necessary differences in interpretation as a reflection not only of better and worse readings but also of the differing contexts within which the text is being read.

THE CONTEMPORARY DEBATE

Since theological readings of Wesley's texts will necessarily differ in terms of the frame of reference of the contemporary discussion in which they are read, it is important to specify in a general way what I take to be the terms of the discussion within which I read these texts of Wesley. I have already indicated in the preface of this book the autobiographical context. Here I will indicate something of the theological context.

One of the conditions for a rereading of Wesley in this connection is the move from an emphasis on political issues to an emphasis on economic issues as significant for the general theme of social ethics. This change of orientation is especially important for the development of what is generally known as "liberation theology." This reading of Wesley does not presuppose a detailed knowledge of this liberation theology; still less does it seek to introduce the reader to the growing literature on this subject. But what may be called the general point of view (as opposed to the detailed formulations) of liberation theology does provide a point of departure. To a certain degree this merely reflects the contingent fact that I began reading Wesley at the same time that I was coming to terms with some of the themes of that liberation theology (see the preface). But I have also come to be persuaded that these themes do in fact help to make clear what Wesley was getting at in his own theological reflection on evangelical economics. That is, the general themes of liberation theology serve as a point of view that can illuminate Wesley's own concerns and offer a perspective from which to consider the positive contribution of Wesley as well as suggesting ways to develop some of those themes in ways that move "beyond" Wesley.

Liberation theology begins as a commitment to the poor. It is a commitment that seeks to make the point of view of the poor determinative for theological, especially practical or pastoral, discourse. It supposes that "reality," especially social reality, looks different, depending on one's place within the social reality.

Let's take a trivial example. My doctor's office looks quite normal to me. But to someone who is wealthy and powerful it seems not only drab but also inconvenient and positively irritating; it is necessary to wait, to take one's turn, and so on. But to the woman who lives in the shelter for the homeless it looks like a place of astonishing opulence. It is also a place that she cannot afford; it represents a level of medical care beyond her reach, a place that excludes her. The same observation might be made about the church on the corner, the shopping center, and so on. The point is that these things look different and mean different things, depending on where one is in the economic, social, or political system.

This difference may be generalized to larger sets of phenomena. Thus the activity of The United Methodist Church may appear, to those who are relatively comfortable in the social and economic world, to be generous and humane. Others who fear the loss of their privileges in the social system, or who wish to further buttress this position, may regard this denomination as being under the influence of dangerous left-wingers. Meanwhile the truly poor and marginalized may see this church as either irrelevant to their needs or as systematically excluding them from meaningful participation, and as serving only to salve the conscience of affluent do-gooders while actually preventing any significant change. Similar differences may be seen in relation to issues like universal suffrage, labor unions, trade policy, and so on.

Liberation theology takes this difference seriously, but it does more. It decides that the most "true" of these points of view is the one that belongs to those who are generally excluded and marginalized—that is, those who suffer most from the existing arrangements and realities: the poor. It sides with the poor and takes as its initial point of departure their plight, their condition. This is what it means to make a "preferential option for the poor." It means to view reality from the point of view of those who suffer, who are helpless, who are victims.

Such a move is made not simply on the demographic grounds that this is the situation of the majority of people on our planet, but also on the theological grounds that this is what the gospel requires of us. Indeed much of liberation theology consists in the hermeneutical spiral by which the Bible illumines the situation of the poor and the situation of the poor illuminates the reading of the Bible. By this means it is possible to recognize in the Bible God's turning to the poor (whether as slaves in Egypt or the dispossessed of prophetic concern or the despised to whom Jesus turned and in whose plight he told his disciples he was to be found) as an analogue to what must be done in our own situation.

Of course, the point of this solidarity with the poor is to transform their condition of marginalization. It does this in part by simply making the cry of the poor heard where before it was silenced. It does this as well by enabling the poor to become not simply passive victims of the way things are but also agents for the change of society. Moreover it may do this by cooperating with other projects for the alteration of the plight of the poor and oppressed, even when these projects are governed by non-Christian perspectives. This option for the poor, then, becomes the starting point for the transformation of theological reflection, of pastoral action, and of social reality as a whole.

This multi-faceted project is developed in terms of the specific reality of the Third World, especially Latin America, and by using the available resources of social, economic, and political analysis. In Latin America especially this has meant an appropriation of some of the categories of Marxist social analysis, both because these seem to illuminate helpfully the social situation and because they are the categories in terms of which the intellectual debate of Latin American culture is carried on. However, this does not mean that these theologians make themselves subservient to a particular ideological and superpower partner, any more than Wesley's use of the categories of Deism in considering questions like civil liberty made Wesley simply a Deist.

This is a brief sketch of what I take to be the terms of debate within which it seems helpful to read Wesley. I will argue that Wesley is in many respects far closer to this liberation theology perspective than he is generally recognized to be. Conversely, I will suggest that a consideration of Wesley's refusal of the point of view of wealth and power together with his determination to make the point of view of the poor normative is illuminated by the perspective of liberation theology. In evaluating Wesley's evangelical economics I will argue that Wesley in fact has something important to offer, not only in opening us to a fresh appreciation of the themes of liberation theology, but also (perhaps) in making a contribution to the further development of liberation theology itself. It will also appear that the terms of our contemporary discussion suggest ways of "updating" Wesley's point of view so as to take into account our altered theological, as well as socioeconomic, reality.

EVANGELICAL ECONOMICS

I have explained how I intend to read Wesley in this book, but now I must explain the theme of this reading. I have identified this theme as "evangelical economics." What I mean by this is the way in which the gospel may inform our interaction with the sphere of economics, with "making a living." Economics may and should be dealt with in terms of the larger picture of the means of production and modes of trade and so on. In the modern era we have become increasingly aware of the way in which this sphere of "macroeconomics" affects our lives and those of all our fellow creatures (not only human beings, as the ecological crisis makes clear).

This larger picture is one that has really only come into view in the modern period. But the day-to-day reality of wealth and poverty, of accumulating and sharing, of gaining, spending, and giving has always been a subject of awareness. It affects all of us, and does so immediately. While in our own time it is necessary to address the larger economic picture in ways not possible for those to whom this picture was opaque, the reflections of earlier periods on the more immediate economic sphere are not without relevance for us, since they did attempt to clarify some of the basic values that pertain to human interaction in this sphere.

When we turn to earlier thinkers for help in this area, we cannot ask them what they have to say about nuclear power or labor-management relations or collective bargaining or Third World debt or the effects of industrialization, still less post-industrialization. These were issues hardly even glimpsed by the eighteenth century. What we can ask of them is whether the economic sphere is one that may be helpfully illuminated in terms of basic human values, of basic commitments generated by hearing and adhering to the gospel.

Of course, many will suppose that we are entirely on our own here, that economic reality has so drastically changed that there is no possibility of getting help from previous periods of history, still less from something so ancient as the first-century gospel. But Christians are unlikely to be fully persuaded of this. They are likely to suppose that certain basic principles apply to our own circumstances, however much altered they may be from those of the first century. The help may be only indirect, but it is nevertheless real.

This was certainly Wesley's approach. He recognized that eighteenth-century economic reality was not the same as that which obtained for first-century Palestine, or even the more cosmopolitan world of the Roman Empire. Still Wesley thought the gospel was not irrelevant to the task of clarifying the nature of an appropriate participation in the economic reality of his own time. It still spoke. That is what it means to say that Wesley developed an evangelical economics. He interpreted contemporary economic reality in terms or categories derived from the Bible generally and from the gospel in particular.

In this study, "evangelical economics" will refer to the set of notions that Wesley developed on the basis of his reading of the Bible to illuminate and to govern the activity of Christians in the world of economics. It thus refers to the interrelationship between such notions as the criticism of wealth, the forms of solidarity with the poor, the notion of stewardship, and the vision of an economic practice based on the example of the Pentecostal community. I will try to show that these are not simply a set of isolated themes, but really have an integrated and unitary character in Wesley's thought.

A consideration of Wesley's evangelical economics may suggest something of the scope of such a task for contemporary theological reflection—not that Wesley is beyond reproach in all of this, or that he provides us with a fully adequate model of Christian ethics, or that we may simply appropriate Wesley's answers to our questions. Rather, by attending to what and how Wesley thinks about economic justice, we may be provoked to do our own thinking about our own situation on the basis of the same gospel that provoked his thought and practice. This may be particularly useful for those who think of themselves as the spiritual or, at least, institutional descendants of Wesley and who find themselves perplexed about the relationship between evangelical piety and a preferential option for the poor.

SUMMARY OF THE ARGUMENT

To present Wesley's views as clearly as possible I will first indicate how it is that one who seems at first so reactionary in his political commitments can become an exponent of a radical socioeconomic ethic. While Wesley may have largely accepted the political status quo, this was not true of the economic one. His critical stance toward given economic structures, relationships, and attitudes was made possible by a demystification of wealth and power. This demystification has its basis in a view of the danger that wealth poses for faith, and leads Wesley to a critique of the Constantinian alliance between the community of faith and the forces of economic power and privilege (chap. 2).

This demystification of wealth and power, then, makes

possible what we would today call a preferential option for the poor. Wesley overcomes the danger of a merely sentimental turn toward the poor by means of an immersion in the concrete reality of the poor. This results in taking the question of the plight of the poor as the criterion of all action, including the so-called "spiritual" action of the Church (chap. 3).

With the immersion in the concrete reality of the poor comes the possibility of a transformation in standpoint or point of view, such that otherwise commonplace activities and practices are seen to be destructive of the life of the poor. Out of such a transformation of standpoint comes Wesley's protest against injustice, whether in the domestic form of exploitation or in the wider arena of oppression represented by colonialism and slavery (chap. 4).

But Wesley is not content merely to condemn injustice. He is also concerned to develop a positive ethic that will alter the given socioeconomic reality. Thus he proposes a view of stewardship that breaks the spell of "private property" and leads to a redistribution of wealth whose criterion is the welfare of the poor. This goes so far as to lead Wesley to an acceptance of the economic model of the Pentecostal community of Acts 2–4, which "had all things in common" and "made distribution to the poor," as the proper expression of a Christian faith that works by love (chap. 5).

This Pentecostal redistribution of wealth is often dismissed as an unworkable economic model. Wesley attempts to counter this objection through his own example, that of other exemplary Methodists, and the practice of at least some of the societies. At every opportunity Wesley seeks to counter other objections to the practice of an evangelical economics. Despite this it appears that the Methodists were recalcitrant. Wesley's relation to the Methodists thus becomes increasingly polemical (chap. 6).

To understand how it is that Wesley could place so much stress on evangelical economics as the criterion of the success or failure of the Methodist movement as such, it is necessary to see how the major themes of Wesley's theology of the Christian life are implicated in the theory and practice of evangelical economics. Far from being a mere addendum to his thought or a dispensable application, the transformation of relations to prosperity, to the poor, and to property itself are the necessary consequence of Wesley's view of the nature of faith and grace. This connection makes it appropriate for Wesley to suppose that the Methodist movement, whatever its incidental successes, was in danger of self-destruction (chap. 7).

But if Wesley's project of spreading scriptural holiness did fail precisely at the point of this evangelical economics, then it is important to see what are the ways in which Wesley himself contributed to this failure. This analysis is to be distinguished from the attempt to assess the impact of Wesley on his followers or of them on their age. This has been attempted by a number of historians, but usually without attending to the question of the ways in which Wesley himself may have opened the door to a misunderstanding and a misrepresentation of the key elements of his evangelical economics. Such an internal criticism of Wesley's manner of presenting his evangelical economics helps us to see some of the pitfalls that must be avoided if the project of Methodism is to be realized (chap. 8).

Finally it is necessary to ask about the relevance of Wesley's views for our own very different situation. Thus we will have to inquire about the limits and the possibilities of Wesley's thought for our own time (chap. 9).

This study then is organized in such a way as to permit the themes of Wesley's economic ethic to emerge in a coherent way. Wesley was not a deductive but an inductive thinker. Accordingly the theological basis of his evangelical economics is not presented first but as a part of the argument for the importance of the ethic (chap. 7). Instead of attempting to present all of Wesley's social ethic, I have relegated his political thought to an appendix so that the true character of his economic ethic can emerge in its full radicality.

This book is an attempt to clarify Wesley's views on their own terms through careful attention to his own texts. I have not attempted a scholarly discussion of the important secondary literature on Wesley or his movement except in notes that serve to place my argument within the framework of representative texts in that scholarship.

The text cited is Thomas Jackson's edition of *The Works of John*

Wesley, except where otherwise noted. Since this text is the most widely available and the least expensive, it is in keeping with the aim of this study to use it. That aim is to address the nonspecialist with the question of an evangelical economics by means of a reflection on the texts of John Wesley.

CHAPTER TWO

THE DEMYSTIFICATION
OF WEALTH

How is it that Wesley, who opposed democracy and seems to have believed it to be his duty to support the political status quo, could be the same Wesley who vigorously opposed injustice and dedicated himself to seek the welfare of the poor as the necessary consequence of saving faith? While Wesley always supported the monarchy, he was by no means an apologist for wealth and privilege. Indeed he saw these as the chief enemies of faith and holiness. It is because of this that he was able to break the hold of conservative political views to embrace the cause of the poor. The entry point to a consideration of Wesley's socioeconomic ethic, therefore, must be an examination of the way he was able to demystify wealth and power. Since this is also a critical task today, it may be helpful to see what is at stake in such a demystification in our own situation. In this way we will better be able to see the importance of the breakthrough that Wesley makes in this sphere.

Perhaps the most pernicious threat to the gospel of Jesus Christ is the pseudo-gospel of wealth and power. This pseudo-gospel takes many forms in the contemporary world. It is most crudely expressed in the evangelizing message of Pentecostal and fundamentalist missionaries from the United States in their penetration of the Third World. Their message is that socioeconomic upward mobility is the sign of divine approval. Those who are converted are promised that they will receive material blessings. The present poverty that some of their hearers experience is a sign of God's disapproval, a curse that conversion will speedily remove. Those who have already begun their move toward wealth are absolved of any guilt they may begin to feel about the economic distance that separates them from their family and friends. Indeed any attempt to relieve poverty directly is not only unnecessary, but it is also impious, flying in the face of God's manifest will. Far from being a scandal, the accumulation of wealth on the part of the apostles of this gospel is an appropriate consequence of their faith and is the divine seal of approval on their message and ministry. Since an obvious corollary of this message is that the immense wealth and power generated by the economic system of the United States is a special sign of divine approval, it is similarly impious to attack the policies of the United States, especially as they relate to its dealings with poorer nations. It should not be too surprising, then, if we find the groups who bring this message to be well-funded by the wealthy in the United States.[1] This pseudo-gospel of wealth and power is the grassroots movement whose mission is to combat liberation theology. Indeed, one of its basic tenets as it moves into Latin America is that liberation theology is a satanic perversion of the gospel.

While this ideology may be found in its crudest form among those who launch "evangelistic" missions to the Third World, and especially to Latin America, it is not invisible in the United States itself, as the recent scandals involving the PTL Club and others should make evident. It is noteworthy that in many circles it was not and is not felt to be scandalous that the electronic evangelists should make million dollar salaries, but only that they should do so while breaking the rules of sexual or financial conduct. Thus Wesley's comments about the willful ignoring of Jesus' prohibition of laying up treasure on earth among the Christians of his day apply with undiminished force to our own time.

There are many who will neither rob nor steal; and some who will not defraud their neighbour; nay, who will not gain either by his ignorance or necessity. But this is quite another point. Even these do not scruple the thing, but the manner of it. They do not scruple the "laying up treasures upon earth;" but the laying them up by dishonesty. They do not start at disobeying Christ, but at a branch of heathen morality. So that even these honest men do no more obey this command than a highwayman or a house-breaker. Nay, they never designed to obey it. From their youth up, it never entered into their thoughts. They were bred up by their Christian parents, masters, and friends, without any instruction at all concerning it; unless it were this,—to break it as soon and as much as they could, and to continue breaking it to their lives' end.[2]

That the only thing that scandalizes the majority of persons even today is not wealth but underhanded means of acquiring it shows that we have not yet learned all we might from Wesley.

But before pointing the finger too gleefully in the direction of the religious right, we should acknowledge that the underlying suppositions that legitimate the egregious wealth of some of its leaders are widely shared even in the religious culture of more centrist groups. There are, of course, groups that explicitly make the support of capitalism (sometimes called economic democracy) a hallmark of Christian faithfulness. But even those who would think twice about equating Christianity and capitalism would not question the assumption that upward economic mobility is consistent with Christian faith or that the increase of middle-class comforts is a divine blessing. What Protestant clergy in the United States would suppose that pastors should not receive a larger salary simply because they serve a larger or more wealthy congregation? Who supposes that there is an inherent contradiction between middle-class comfort and Christian discipleship? Thus, whether for the religious right or the religious "center," Wesley's lament of more than two centuries ago still holds:

They have read or heard these words [about laying up treasure] an hundred times, and yet never suspect that they are themselves condemned thereby, any more than by those which forbid parents to offer up their sons or daughters unto Moloch. O that God would speak to these miserable self-deceivers with his own voice, his mighty voice; that they may at last awake out of the snare of the devil, and the scales may fall from their eyes! ("Sermon on the Mount, Discourse VIII," V:366)[3]

The gospel of wealth, whether in its more egregious forms or in the subtler (or perhaps simply less consistent) acquiescence in the dominant values of a consumer society, is a persistent and widespread ideology and ethos that makes the prophetic note sounded by liberation theology in the twentieth century, or by Wesleyan theology in the eighteenth century, appear to be either a perversion of the gospel or simply an unintelligible rendition of it.

No prophetic critique of this dominant ethos or of the ideology that supports it can make much headway unless wealth and power are themselves demystified. While the demystification of wealth and power is a dominant theme of the Old and New Testaments, it has also been undertaken by some of the theologians of the Christian tradition. For those who are members of the Wesleyan movement, the work of John Wesley in this regard is or should be especially significant. The various Methodist and holiness churches that derive from Wesley's movement of evangelization may find in his thought an antidote to the poison of the pseudo-gospel of wealth and a helpful point of entry into a more authentic understanding of the biblical witness. And those who do not stand within the Wesleyan tradition may nevertheless find here a provocative wedding of evangelical fervor and radical social witness.

THE TEMPTATIONS OF WEALTH

To see the way in which Wesley develops his critique of wealth and power, it will be helpful to begin where Wesley himself often begins, with the analysis of the perils and possibilities of the personal life of faith. For Wesley the stakes in the life of faith were always high, losing one's soul or gaining the kingdom of God. It is precisely this which is at stake, he maintains, in the economic life of the Christian. For those who take for granted the values of a society committed to consumer capitalism, the words of Wesley must seem decidedly perverse:

Those who calmly desire and deliberately seek to attain [possessions], whether they do, in fact, gain the world or no, do infallibly lose their own souls. These are they that sell Him who bought them with his blood, for a few pieces of gold or silver. These enter into a covenant with death and hell; and their covenant shall stand; for they are daily making themselves meet to partake of their inheritance with the devil and his angels! ("Sermon on the Mount, Discourse VIII," V:369)

What is the basis of this harsh judgment? Here Wesley was guided by his study of the life of faith both in the direct observation provided by the annual interview with all members of his movement and the store of learning gleaned from his work in producing *The Christian Library*. Hardly before or since has any theologian had such a vast body of data and reflection at hand for the development of an understanding of the life of faith.

An illustration of the application of this wisdom to the situation of those who had acquired possessions is Wesley's sermon "On Riches" (VII:214-22), which concludes the second series of sermons published in 1788. Here Wesley maintains, not for the first time, that "it is easier for a camel to go through the eye of a needle, than for those that *have riches* not to *trust* in them" (VII:215). Here as always Wesley defines the rich as "one that has food and raiment sufficient for himself and his family, and something over" (ibid.). This definition applies to any who find themselves in what today we would call the lower middle class!

But what is the harm in wealth? How does it imperil the life of faith? Wesley tries to make the answer as concrete as possible by examining the way wealth distorts the "tempers" that are the root of holiness.

In the first place, wealth is destructive of humility. In an earlier sermon, Wesley remarked of those who had possessions: "How hard it is for them, whose every word is applauded, not to be wise in their own eyes! How hard for them not to think themselves better than the poor, base, uneducated herd of men!" ("Sermon on the Mount, Discourse VIII," V:368).

Wealth is also destructive of patience. Wesley illustrates this as follows:

> Many years ago I was sitting with a gentleman in London, who feared God greatly, and generally gave away, year by year, nine tenths of his yearly income. A servant came in and threw some coals on the fire. A puff of smoke came out. The baronet threw himself back in his chair and cried out, "O Mr. Wesley, these are the crosses I meet with daily!" Would he not have been less impatient, if he had had fifty, instead of five thousand, pounds a year? ("The Danger of Riches," VII:13; see also "On Riches," VII:220)

Even one who on Wesley's terms was in many respects an exemplary Christian was damaged by the baleful influence of wealth. And what must be the case of those who neither fear God nor give away all but a tithe of their fortune?

Wealth has the tendency not only to destroy humility and patience, but also to produce vices. Thus it produces passions

> contrary to the love of our neighbour: Contempt, for instance, particularly of inferiors, than which nothing is more contrary to love:—Resentment of any real or supposed offense; perhaps even revenge, although God claims this as his own peculiar prerogative:—At least anger; for it immediately rises in the mind of a rich man, "What! to use *me* thus! Nay, but he shall soon know better: I am able to do myself justice!" ("On Riches," VII:220)

While Wesley did not accept the popular notion that the poor were lazy, he knew that the rich were:

> You cannot deny yourself the poor pleasure of a little sleep, or of a soft bed. . . . Indeed, you "cannot go out so early in the morning; besides it is dark, nay, cold, perhaps rainy too. . . ." You did not say so when you were a poor man. You then regarded none of these things. . . . You are but the shadow of what you were! What have riches done for you? ("The Danger of Riches," VII:13)

And with the increase of pride and sloth, it is no longer felt to be appropriate to identify oneself with the poor, to minister to their needs. The one who before was willing to visit the poor is so no longer:

> What hinders? Do you fear spoiling your silken coat? Or is there another lion in the way? Are you afraid of catching vermin? And are you not afraid lest the roaring lion should catch you? Are you not afraid of Him that hath said, "Inasmuch as ye have not done it unto the least of these, ye have not done it unto me?" ("The Danger of Riches," VII:14)

As the last quotation warns, the possession of wealth tends to a forgetfulness of God, a kind of practical atheism (see also "On Riches," VII:217). Ultimately it leads to idolatry, loving the creature in place of the Creator: "But to how many species of idolatry is every rich man exposed! What continual and almost insuperable temptations is he under to 'love the world!' and that in all its branches,—the desire of the flesh, the desire of the eyes, and the pride of life" ("On Riches," VII:218).

In sermon after sermon (with titles like "On Riches," "The Danger of Riches," and "On the Danger of Increasing Riches"), Wesley hammers home the theme that the increase in possessions leads naturally to the death of religion. Wesley was not at all bashful about enforcing this message on the wealthy themselves. On several occasions in his *Journal,* Wesley reports his own attempt to carry his point directly to the rich. One illustration of this will indicate the general practice: "In the evening I was surprised to see, instead of some poor, plain people, a room full of men daubed with gold and silver. That I might not go out of their depth, I began expounding the story of Dives and Lazarus" (*Journal,* Mar. 29, 1750, II:178). Wesley was a firm believer in confrontation. Indeed, he wrote an entire sermon on the subject, entitled "The Duty of Reproving Our Neighbor" (VI:296-303).

But Wesley did not confine his reproof to the pulpit. In a letter to Mrs. Bennis, he wrote, "Some time since, when I heard brother Bennis had got very rich, I was in fear for you, lest the world should again find a way into your heart" (Dec. 1, 1773, XII:397). In much the same vein, he writes to a wealthy man:

The grand maxims which obtain in the world are, The more power, the more money, the more learning, and the more reputation a man has, the more good he will do. And whenever a Christian, pursuing the noblest ends, forms his behaviour by these maxims, he will infallibly (though perhaps by insensible degrees) decline into worldly prudence. (May 16, 1759, XII:231)

His admonition to a woman in similar circumstances is even more direct:

Riches increased; which not only led you, step by step, into more conformity to the world, but insensibly instilled self-importance, unwillingness to be contradicted, and an overbearing temper. And hence you was, of course, disgusted at those who did not yield to this temper, and blamed that conformity. . . .

Can you be too sensible, how hardly they that have riches enter into the kingdom of heaven? Yea, or into the kingdom of an inward heaven? Into the whole spirit of the Gospel? How hard it is for these (whether you do or no?) not to conform too much to the world! How hard not to be a little overbearing, especially to inferiors! (*Journal*, June 27, 1769, III:368-69; see also letter of March 20, 1759, XII:225-26)

Even on those rare occasions when the possession of wealth did not utterly destroy faith, Wesley thought he could still discern its destructive influence. In his *Journal*, Wesley writes of William Osgood: "He was a good man, and died in peace. Nevertheless, I believe his money was a great clog to him, and kept him in a poor, low state all his days, making no such advance as he might have done, either in holiness or happiness" (Dec. 13, 1767, III:309). But his more typical view is expressed in an earlier extract from his *Journal*: "I rode to S———, with one to whom a large estate is fallen, by her uncle's dying without a will. It is a miracle if it does not drown her soul in everlasting perdition" (April 30, 1754, II:312).

Whether in *Journal*, sermon, or correspondence, Wesley did not flinch from what he took to be the clear teaching of the New Testament, that the acquisition of possessions, the attainment of wealth in any form, must lead to the destruction of faith itself. Far from being the sign of divine favor, the increase of worldly prosperity destroys faith and love and so leads the unwary soul into perdition.

On this basis Wesley could give stern advice to parents, which flew in the face of convention, or as Wesley would say, "worldly prudence." To those who took thought to the career of their sons (daughters did not yet come into view here) Wesley wrote in his sermon "On Family Religion":

> "In what business will your son be most likely to love and serve God? In what employment will he have the greatest advantage for laying up treasure in heaven?" I have been shocked above measure in observing how little this is attended to, even by pious parents! Even these consider only how he may get most money; not how he may get most holiness! (VII:84)

By now there should be no need to indicate that for Wesley these were not simply different but incompatible aims. One cannot serve both God and mammon. Thus getting more money is incompatible with getting more holiness. The same principle is invoked with respect to marriage (and here both daughters and sons come into view): "Now you know what the world calls a *good match*,—one whereby much money is gained. . . . It is a melancholy thing to see how Christian parents rejoice in selling their son or their daughter to a wealthy Heathen!" (VII:85). And in the sermon on "The Difference Between Walking by Sight and Walking by Faith," Wesley asks:

> Which do you judge best,—that your son should be a pious cobbler, or a profane lord? Which appears to you most eligible,—that your daughter should be a child of God, and walk on foot, or a child of the devil, and ride in a coach-and-six? (VII:261; see also the sermon "On a Single Eye," VII:302)

Thus Wesley does not hesitate to enforce his view of the harmful influence of wealth even in the most concrete terms.

It is wealth, then, that is inimicable to faith. But why is this so? In part Wesley is simply carrying forward a number of biblical maxims: "You cannot serve both God and mammon" (Matt. 6:24); "But those who desire to be rich fall into temptation, into a snare, into many senseless and hurtful desires that plunge men into ruin and destruction. For the love of money is the root of all evils" (I Tim. 6:9-10 RSV); "But the cares of the world, and the delight in riches, and the desire for other things, enter in and choke the word, and it proves unfruitful" (Mark 4:19 RSV, see also Matt. 13:22). These are, indeed, among Wesley's favorite texts for preaching.[4]

But more is at stake here than a random selection of texts. Wesley provides a consistent rationale for his position as well. It is not, he maintains, that "money is an evil in itself" (VI:265) or that it is "more sinful to be rich than to be poor. But it is dangerous beyond expression" (VII:250). The ground of this danger is that "the possession of riches naturally breeds the love of them" (VI:265). And it is by means of this love for or attachment to riches that the love of the world enters to subvert a simple reliance on the gospel.

Wesley's pastoral concern for the souls of his hearers was by no means simply otherworldly. He saw that the life of faith was mortally wounded when it fell unawares into the snare of acquisition and consumption. The ethos of mammon in the form of the desire to seek possessions was seen to be every bit as great a destroyer of faith as naked unbelief. Indeed there is nothing that Wesley so emphasizes as being destructive of the life of faith as the acquisition and expenditure of wealth. Nor should we forget that he is thinking here not of millionaires, but of what for us is scarcely middle-class status. His experience in the "care of souls" (and what theologian has ever had more?) convinced him that the New Testament warnings about wealth were all too correct. His message may well have seemed radical in the heyday of mercantile capitalism. How much more is this true in the world of consumer capitalism!

THE CONSTANTINIAN TEMPTATION

The corrosive power of wealth applies not only to individuals but to the Church as well. Thus Wesley sought to safeguard Methodists from this destructive force. His vigilance in safeguarding the community from the temptations of wealth was grounded in his understanding of the early history of the church. The glorious foundation of the church as Wesley saw it dated from Pentecost. But the fall from its original perfection came with Ananias and Sapphira, who disrupted the primitive communism of original Christianity by keeping back for themselves some of their own possessions (Acts 5:1-11). Wesley notes: "Mark the first plague which infected the Christian Church; namely, the love of money!" ("The Mystery of Iniquity," VI:256; see also "The Wisdom of God's Counsels," VI:328) And when it comes to understanding the situation of the churches described in the Apocalypse of John, Wesley wonders why the corruption of the churches had not overwhelmed Smyrna and Philadelphia (Rev. 2:8-11; 3:7-13), and he concludes: "It seems, because they were less wealthy. . . . So that these, having less of this world's goods, retained more of the simplicity and purity of the gospel" ("The Mystery of Iniquity," VI:260).

It was Wesley's intention that Methodism regain a full measure of the "simplicity and purity of the gospel," and thus to undo the fall of the Church at the hands of those who desired riches, whether in the first or the eighteenth centuries. In this way he supposed it to be possible to launch a new era of genuine Christianity by means of the people called Methodists. In this light, it is not hard to understand Wesley's repeated warnings to his societies.

> I gave all our brethren a solemn warning not to love the world, or the things of the world. This is one way whereby Satan will surely endeavour to overthrow the present work of God. Riches swiftly increase on many Methodists, so called: What, but the mighty power of God, can hinder their setting their hearts upon them? And if so, the life of God vanishes away. (*Journal*, July 11, 1764, III:187; see also the *Journal* entries for Oct. 20, 1764, III:200; June 28, 1765, III:227; Dec. 5 and 9, 1779, IV:172; and passim)

In a later chapter we will have occasion to explore the way in which this theme brought Wesley into fateful conflict with Methodism itself (see chap. 8). Here it is enough to note that Wesley's admonition to the people called Methodists springs from deeply held conviction and rigorously applied principle. The observation common to sociologists since the time of Weber that protestantism produces upward socioeconomic mobility would cause Wesley no comfort. Unlike those who find the growing prosperity of their members to be a sign of divine favor, Wesley knew that what beckoned was a snare of Satan.

For those who suppose that the success of the gospel may be correlated with social, political, and economic advancement, the conversion of Constantine in the fourth century, with the consequent end of persecution and inauguration of the era of Christendom, must naturally seem to be the divine vindication of Christianity. This event cements the alliance of the Church with the most powerful and influential, and so establishes Christianity as the defender of the status quo. But is the conversion of Constantine an appropriate paradigm of the success of the Christian mission?

Wesley's views on this point are most instructive. Despite his strong political conservatism, which made him an ardent defender of the king and a vigorous opponent of the American Revolution, he was not at all mesmerized by the Constantinian paradigm. On several occasions he makes clear that the true fall of the Church (for which Ananias and Sapphira prepared the way) is to be located in the conversion of Constantine. In his sermon "On the Mystery of Iniquity" he writes:

> Persecution never did, never could, give any lasting wound to genuine Christianity. But the greatest it ever received, the grand blow which was struck at the very root of that humble, gentle patient love, which is the fulfilling of the Christian law, the whole essence of true religion, was struck in the fourth century by Constantine the Great, when he called himself a Christian, and poured in a flood of riches, honours, and power, upon the Christians; more especially upon the Clergy. . . . Then, not the golden but the iron age of the Church commenced. (VI:261-62)

Thus Wesley finds himself in opposition to the view of "Dr. Newton, the late Bishop of Bristol," who understandably, if somewhat incautiously, took the view "that the conversion of Constantine to Christianity, and the emoluments which he bestowed upon the Church with an unsparing hand, were the event which is signified in the Revelation by 'the New Jerusalem coming down from heaven!' " ("Of Former Times," VII:164). In contrast, Wesley emphasizes that this event has especially pernicious consequences for the clergy who were made so greedy by the reception of these favors that "it soon grew common for one man to take the whole charge of a congregation in order to engross the whole pay" thereby destroying the multiple ministries of the laity. ("The Ministerial Office," VII:276)

Wesley makes clear that his view does not depend on the particular features of Constantine's conversion but rather bears upon any alliance of the gospel with wealth and power.

> From the time that the Church and State, the kingdoms of Christ and of the world, were so strangely and unnaturally blended together, Christianity and Heathenism were so thoroughly incorporated with each other, that they will hardly ever be divided till Christ comes to reign upon earth. So that, instead of fancying that the glory of the New Jerusalem covered the earth at that period, we have terrible proof that it was then, and has ever since been, covered with the smoke of the bottomless pit. ("Of Former Times," VII:164)

It is important to note the vast difference that separates Wesley's thought at this point even from that of those who have no experience with a State Church, for Wesley sees that any alliance with the power of the State must ultimately destroy the integrity of faith. Thus the attempts to gain influence, so characteristic of right-wing Christianity today in the United States, is completely contrary to Wesley's view. Of course, in thus attempting to forge an alliance with the government of the most powerful nation on earth, the "conservatives" are only imitating the tactics of their mainline cousins.

Wesley is even led by the logic of his position to celebrate the total separation of Church and State, enshrined in the then brand-new United States Constitution. In what may be his only positive statement about the results of the rebellion of the American colonies, he notes that "the total indifference of the government there, whether there be any religion or none, leaves room for the propagation of true, scriptural religion, without the least let or hindrance" ("Of Former Times," VII:165). Ironically, what Wesley saw as a remarkable providence is attacked today by the religious right as secular humanism!

From Wesley's point of view, this could only be due to ignorance about the true character of the gospel. For Wesley, the loyal priest of the established Church, an alliance with wealth and power must ever corrupt the gospel. That is, there is an inherent contradiction between the gospel of love and peace, on the one hand, and the possession of privilege in the world on the other. Thus an alliance with wealth and power must result in the establishment of a pseudo-Christianity whose interests would lie in the maintenance of the system of wealth and power rather than in the propagation of true, scriptural Christianity. In this way Christianity would become allied to the satanic opposition to the gospel.

This is in fact what Wesley himself encountered in his own attempt to preach good news to the poor. The firestorm of persecution was unleashed by a combination of ecclesiastical authority, the wealthy, and the gentry. The alliance of wealth and power with ecclesiastical privilege is today often pitted against the church of the poor in many places of Latin America. It is a situation that Wesley would have recognized.

The possibility of recognizing the opposition between Christianity and the powers of this world depends on the appropriation of apocalyptic imagery. Wesley supposed that Satan had control of the powers of the world and that Satan would not readily yield his dominion to the gospel of peace and love. Whether at the level of the individual heart or that of the socioeconomic arena, the entrance of the gospel must provoke a fierce struggle in which Satan would attempt to destroy the gospel. By allying itself with the very forces of wealth and privilege most intimately in league with Satan, Christianity walked into a trap. This is why Wesley could celebrate the entire separation of Church and State in the American experiment while the adherents to the gospel of wealth seek to make the State into the guarantor of its privileged position.[5]

Wesley's view of the conversion of Constantine as a catastrophe for the Church owes not to some notion that the wealthy and powerful should not be converted but to the effects of that conversion. If Constantine had indeed been converted to a gospel that was good news for the poor, no damage need have resulted. But instead Constantine's conversion resulted in the subversion of this gospel. This occurs through the inundation of the church with "a flood of riches, honours, and power" (VI:261-62; VII:164, 178, 276; X:1). But of these three, by far the worst is riches.

The demystification of wealth, which Wesley carried out with such rigor in the analysis of the life of faith, provides him then with the possibility of breaking through the constraints of essentially conservative political views to a critique of the alliance of Christianity and the structures of the world. This does not bring Wesley to the point of a break with the established Church or the religiously sanctioned monarchy. But it is remarkable that Wesley goes as far as he does, for the Constantinian paradigm was decisive for the Church of England, to which Wesley strove to be loyal. By bringing this paradigm into question, Wesley lays the ground work for a definitive break from that unity of religious piety and political loyalty that otherwise seems to characterize his political ethic. Wesley does not himself draw this political conclusion from the critique of the Constantinian paradigm. But this critique does open the way to a fundamentally radical socioeconomic ethic. Once the attraction of Constantinianism is broken it is possible to become open to new ways of seeing the poor and their affliction.

THE WEALTH OF NATIONS

The demystification of wealth as carried through in relation to persons and to the Church also gives Wesley the possibility of understanding society generally from this point of view. His analysis of the causes of the American Revolution, in his essay-sermon "Some Account of the Late Work of God in North America" (1778), makes use of some of the same themes he used in his analysis of the destruction of the work of God in the heart and in the Church. After noting the early history of the revival

43

of religion, forwarded by Whitefield and the Methodists, Wesley remarks:

> But now it was that a bar appeared in the way, a grand hinderance to the progress of religion. The immense trade of America, greater in proportion than even that of the mother-country, brought in an immense flow of wealth, which was also continually increasing. (VII:412)

Following an outline familiar to the reader or hearer of sermons on "The Danger of Riches," Wesley then traces on the wider stage of society at large the rise of those vices he had noted earlier on the personal plane. The American colonists now increased in pride (VII:412) and in luxury "particularly in food" (VII:413), and this was accompanied by sloth:

> Does not sloth easily spring from luxury? It did so here, in an eminent degree; such sloth as is scarce named in England. Persons in the bloom of youth, and in perfect health, could hardly bear to put on their own clothes. The slave must be called to do this, and that, and everything (VII:413).

This destruction of national virtue is what Wesley supposes to lie at the root of the spirit of "independency" and the consequent madness of the American rebellion. But the rebellion produces a loss of trade, a diminution of wealth, and so "by the adorable providence of God, the main hinderances of his work are removed" (VII:417).

The point here is not to argue the merits of Wesley's understanding of the causes of the American Revolution but to notice that his view of the dangers of wealth is applied to nations as well as to persons and to churches. Presumably Wesley would make a similar case with respect to the egregious wealth of contemporary heirs of that revolution and the pride, luxury (consumerism), and contempt for the poor that too often issue from that wealth.

Just as wealth corrupts the life of the individual and subverts the life of the church, so also does it produce greed and violence in the life of nations. And as Wesley never tired of repeating, the resulting behavior of so-called Christian nations caused the name of Christian to "stink in the nostrils" of the wretched of the earth. A similar case is made today by those who argue that the traditional alliance between Christianity and the structures of wealth and power make it inevitable that the poor and oppressed will turn from their faith when they reach out for freedom and justice, unless the church itself is converted to become in truth the church of the poor. The transformation in pastoral action called for and practiced by many of the theologians of liberation today in Latin America[6] has parallels to Wesley's call for a Christianity not allied with the powerful, a Christianity converted from the satanic snare of wealth and privilege.

CONCLUSION

While Wesley does not fully integrate his own demystification of wealth with what he would have called the "analogy of faith,"[7] he does provide a clearly articulated and consistently applied debunking of the basic assumptions of the pseudo-gospel of wealth and success. Indeed the concentration upon the personal life of faith, which is often cited as one of Wesley's weaknesses as a resource for social ethics, may actually be a source of strength. Wesley does integrate the demystification of wealth and power with an evangelical concern for the life of faith, which provides an indispensable point of contact to a grassroots Methodism for which "spiritual" concerns have an undoubted primacy. Moreover his concentration on the life of faith helps to make clear the extent to which the assumptions of cultural materialism have penetrated to the very heart and marrow of our consciousness. Think, for example, of his admonitions concerning marriage or the choice of a career.[8]

And Wesley's very practical turn of mind serves also to alert the Church to the degree to which it collaborates in its own bondage to the structures of wealth and power, giving itself as hostage to them through, for example, the construction of expensive churches and in other ways making itself dependent on the patronage of the rich and powerful. Any serious critique of society on the part of the people called Methodists must not forget to turn a critical eye on the aspects of its own institutional life that reflect the cultural values of getting and spending.

Although Wesley concentrates his attention on the personal and ecclesial aspects of a demystification of wealth and power, he does not ignore the larger social implications of this critique, as his analysis of the American Revolution indicates. Indeed, the critique of wealth and power makes it possible for Wesley to overcome some of the limits to his social ethic, imposed by his high church and monarchist convictions. It is precisely his understanding of the Constantinian temptation that opens the way toward a radical social ethic. While it is possible to fault Wesley for not having seen all the implications of this insight, it is one that does permit him to develop an evangelical economics that can be an important contribution to contemporary Christian ethics, even in the context of the discussion of contemporary liberation theology.

CHAPTER THREE

A PREFERENTIAL OPTION
FOR THE POOR

Whenever wealth and power are uncritically celebrated as the gift of God, and so as the sign of the divine favor, then the presence of poverty and powerlessness is all too naturally seen as an indication of divine disapproval, as punishment for sins of sloth or unbelief. The remedy suggested by the proponents of the gospel of wealth and success is conversion; this will then lead to those material blessings that, it is presumed, follow from a life of faith. Such a position makes it possible to hold the poor in contempt and makes the wealthy and powerful the role models of faith. But where wealth and power are not understood as the prima facie evidence of divine approval, where these are in fact understood in a negative light, then the way is open for what is today called a preferential option for the poor.

We have seen that Wesley has accepted this demystification of wealth and thus opened the way for a different assessment of the poor than that which attends the gospel of wealth. Of course, the danger is present that this turn toward the poor will remain at the sentimental level of extolling the virtues of poverty. This romanticizing of poverty then cuts the nerve of any attempt to alter the conditions of the poor. While the poor are not held in contempt, they are left in the condition of poverty as mere objects of charity. This is a danger that is present also today, when those who wish to evade the challenges of a liberation theology nevertheless employ the slogan of a preferential option for the poor in a sentimental way that leaves the conditions of poverty unexamined and unchanged.[1]

In our analysis of Wesley's relation to the poor, we will have to first attend to the question of whether he forms merely a sentimental attachment to the poor or whether he moves to a concrete solidarity with them. We will then consider the way in which Wesley becomes an advocate for the poor, a voice raised on their behalf, articulating their affliction. This then leads to a consideration of praxis, in which concrete service to the poor becomes the test of Christian action. The presentation of Wesley's form of a preferential option for the poor will also have to take into account the question of the move from an ecclesial praxis to concrete proposals for public policy.

ATTACHMENT TO THE POOR

To some it seems scandalous that Christians should speak of a preferential option for the poor. After all, should our love not be evenhanded? Do the poor really have any particular claim on our concern? One can occasionally find in Wesley an attempt to be evenhanded in his assessment of the relative merits of the rich and the poor. In his 1735 sermon at Oxford, for example, Wesley finds the rich and the poor equidistant from salvation by applying one of his favorite texts to the situation:

> O faith, working by love, whither art thou fled? Surely the Son of man did once plant thee upon earth. Where art thou now? Among the wealthy? No. "The deceitfulness of riches" there "chokes the word, and it becometh unfruitful." Among the poor? No. "The cares of the world" are there, so that it bringeth forth no fruit to perfection. However, there is nothing to prevent its growth among those who have "neither poverty nor riches:"—Yes; "the desire of other things." ("The Trouble and Rest of Good Men," VII:368-69)

Already, here, Wesley has developed the view that economic considerations are the principal threat to the Christian life.

While a few other passages among his writings indicate that Wesley did not simply exclude the rich from the possibility of salvation (*Journal*, I:203; II:52; III:229), his attitude generally reflects the view that the gospel may more readily take root among the poor than among the rich. In a letter to Freeborn Garretson, Wesley writes this rather typical assessment: "Most of those in England who have riches love money, even the Methodists; at least those who are called so. The poor are the Christians. I am quite out of conceit with almost all those who have this world's goods" (Sept. 30, 1786, XIII:71).

Thus when Wesley finds the well-to-do in his audience, he reports: "So I spake on the first elements of the Gospel. But I was still out of their depth. O how hard it is to be shallow enough for a polite audience!" (*Journal*, Sept. 25, 1771, III:442). And when the wealthy appear attentive, he remarks, "Is it possible? Can the Gospel have place where Satan's throne is?" (*Journal*, Mar. 8, 1767, III:274). And when they do not return to hear his plain speaking, he remarks: "These dare not hear *me* above once: They find it is playing with edged tools" (*Journal*, May 4, 1767, III:279). And when the rich are not discouraged by Wesley's pointed proclamation, Wesley himself might decide that it is time for him to go: "Many of the rich and honourable were there; so that I found it was time for me to fly away" (*Journal*, Apr. 15, 1745, I:490).

All of this is consistent with Wesley's missional priorities. In later years he could point to this as one of "the signs of the times," which confirmed the place of the Methodist revival in the eschatological plan of salvation: "And surely never in any age or nation, since the Apostles, have those words been so eminently fulfilled, 'The poor have the gospel preached unto them,' as it is at this day" ("The Signs of the Times," VI:308). Wesley explains the importance of this strategy by saying, "Religion must not go from the greatest to the least, or the power would appear to be of men" (*Journal*, May 21, 1764, III:178). Thus Wesley could say to some of his establishment critics, "The rich, the honourable, the great, we are thoroughly willing (if it be the will of our Lord) to leave to you. Only let us alone with the poor, the vulgar, the base, the outcasts of men" (*A Farther Appeal to Men of Reason and Religion*, VIII:239).

As Wesley pointed out, this outreach to the poor was in part forced upon him when he was excluded from the churches of London. While this was sometimes then (and almost always now) attributed to his proclamation of justification by faith, Wesley himself provides a different explanation: "The far more common (and indeed more plausible) objection was, 'The people crowd so, that they block up the church, and leave no room for the best of the parish' " (*A Short History of the People Called Methodists*, XIII:307). These are not really incompatible explanations, since the call for simple faith found a ready hearing among those who had nothing else to give. A church committed to a preferential option for the wealthy and the influential ("the best of the parish") is a Constantinian Church. Such a Church will always find the responsiveness of the poor to the gospel somewhat discomfiting.

As we have seen, Wesley's convictions about the corruption of faith by worldly prosperity lead naturally to a wariness concerning the effect of the wealthy and powerful on the commitment to scriptural Christianity. Thus Wesley can address a peer of the Realm: "I can truly say, I neither fear nor desire anything from your Lordship. To speak a rough truth, I do not desire any intercourse with any persons of quality in England. I mean, for my own sake. They do me no good; and I fear, I can do none to them" (Letter to Lord ———, July 26, 1764, XII:243). Wesley has come to see more clearly than he did before he was thrust out among the poor that it is the wealthy who are virtually impervious to the gospel, while the poor are willing and eager to hear.

It is not surprising, then, that Wesley should find the poor to be his favorite audience. Thus Wesley could write: "I love the poor; in many of them I find pure, genuine grace, unmixed with paint, folly, and affectation" (Letter to Miss Furly, Sept. 25, 1757, XII:200). The danger here is that this turn to the poor will simply be a sentimental attachment that ignores the harsh reality of poverty. Occasionally, passages in Wesley's works seem to indicate such a sentimental attachment. Thus he writes toward the end of his life: "O what an advantage have the poor over the rich! These are not wise in their own eyes, but all receive with meekness the ingrafted word which is able to save their souls" (*Journal*, Sept. 19, 1788, IV:437). And again, "O how much better is it to go to the poor, than to the rich; and to the house of mourning, than to the house of feasting!" (*Journal*, Apr. 2, 1782, IV:224). Despite these rare passages, which are susceptible of a sentimentalist reading, far more than a romantic attachment to the poor is involved here.

Attachment to and association with the poor, whatever motives may have inaugurated this movement, bring anyone with eyes to see and ears to hear into an encounter with the dehumanizing degradations of grinding poverty. Wesley had eyes. He also had a voice to lift up on behalf of the poor. Scorning the words of a poet who claimed that ridicule was the worst part of poverty, Wesley wrote:

> Has poverty nothing worse in it than this, that it *makes men liable to be laughed at?* It is a sign that this idle poet talked by rote of the things which he knew not. Is not want of food something worse than this? God pronounced it as a curse upon man, that he should earn it "by the sweat of his brow." But how many are there in this Christian country, that toil, and labour, and sweat, and have it not at last, but struggle with weariness and hunger together? Is it not worse for one, after a hard day's labour, to come back to a poor, cold, dirty, uncomfortable lodging, and to find there not even the food which is needful to repair his wasted strength? You that live at ease in the earth, that want nothing but eyes to see, ears to hear, and hearts to understand how well God hath dealt with you,—is it not worse to seek bread day by day, and find none? perhaps to find the comfort also of five or six children crying for what he has not to give! Were it not that he is restrained by an unseen hand, would he not soon "curse God and die?" O want of bread! want of bread! Who can tell what this means, unless he hath felt it himself? ("Heaviness Through Manifold Temptations," VI:96)

Here speaks far more than sentiment. It is the voice of one who has entered into solidarity with the poor, of one who, unlike the poet, knows by long and intimate acquaintance the horrors of abject poverty.

Once compassion has been awakened, it opens the way to an identification with the poor and despised that protests on their

51

behalf the horror of their plight. For Wesley, this leads him to speak out not only on behalf of the poor but also on behalf of those whom society has incarcerated as criminals and lunatics.

In his *Forms of Prayer*, Wesley includes the petition: "Pity idiots and lunatics, and give life and salvation to all to whom thou hast given no understanding" (XI:225). And when, as an instrument of that compassion for which he has prayed, Wesley visits the infamous Bedlam, he writes:

> It must be owned, a confinement of such a sort is as fit to cause as to cure distraction; For what scene of distress is to be compared to it?—To be separated at once from all who are near and dear to you; to be cut off from all reasonable conversation; to be secluded from all business, from all reading, from every innocent entertainment of the mind, which is left to prey wholly upon itself, and day and night to pore over your misfortunes; to be shut up day by day in a gloomy cell, with only the walls to employ your heavy eyes, in the midst either of melancholy silence, or horrid cries, groans and laughter intermixed; to be forced by the main strength of those
>
> Who laugh at human nature and compassion,
>
> to take drenches of nauseous, perhaps torturing, medicines, which you know you have no need of now, but know not how soon you may, possibly by the operation of these very drugs on a weak and tender constitution: Here is distress! (*A Farther Appeal to Men of Reason and Religion,* VIII:133)

Scarcely a word of this description would have to be changed to make it applicable to the "mental health" hospitals of our time.

Wesley is equally passionate in his description of the horrifying conditions in which prisoners were kept:

> You may easily be convinced of this, by going into either Ludgate or Newgate. What a scene appears as soon as you enter! The very place strikes horror into your soul. How dark and dreary! How unhealthy and unclean! How void of all that might minister comfort! . . . I know not, if, to one of a thinking, sensible turn of mind, there could be any thing like it on this side hell. (Ibid., VIII:173; cf. *Journal,* Feb. 3, 1753, II:279)

Wesley protested not only the cruelty of this punishment but also its effect, that it merely served to make its victims "completely fitted for any kind or degree of villainy, perfectly brutal and devilish, thoroughly furnished for every evil word and work" (Ibid., VIII:173). Happily Wesley was, some years later, to find that these conditions could be improved (see *Journal*, Jan. 2, 1761, III:33).

AND YOU VISITED ME

How is an attachment to the poor transformed from sentiment to solidarity? This question is one that is no less important for us today. Perhaps it is even more urgent today than it was in former times. Except for flickering images brought to us in the comfort of our homes by the modern miracle of satellite television, most of us live in entire isolation from the scenes of distress of which Wesley so eloquently spoke. Thus talk of those who are impoverished or oppressed or imprisoned or in other ways marginalized becomes abstract. We have no direct experience to draw on to awaken passion or to provoke commitment.

Wesley was, if nothing else, the theologian of experience. This did not mean for him a concentration upon isolated moments of interior religious excitement, but rather the immersion in lived experience, in the texture and duration of sensory involvement. If you want to know what love is, you live the life of love and reflect on the vicissitudes of this journey through time. Similarly, if one is to know something of poverty one must spend the time and energy to be with the poor and to appropriate what is encountered there.

It is in this light that we can understand the importance for Wesley of "visiting" the sick, the poor, the imprisoned. Apart from this practice of visitation, no real experience of the plight of the poor is possible. Without it, the nerve of compassion is cut and the possibility of a pertinent and transforming praxis is lost.

The practice of visiting the destitute and marginalized of

English society was a feature of Wesley's own Methodist discipline from the early days at Oxford until the end of his long career. Wesley's early motivation may have been simply to obey what, on the basis of Matthew 25, he took to be a clear command of the gospel. In his view, this would seem to be adequate motivation for anyone. Thus he maintained that although he certainly had plenty of other work to occupy his time (lovely understatement) and dearly loved solitude, "Yet I find time to visit the sick and the poor; and I must do it, if I believe the Bible" (Letter to a Member of the Society, Dec. 10, 1777, XII:304). And he warned that the rich would learn that they should have "constantly" visited the poor "in that day when 'every man shall receive his own reward according to his own labor' " (*Journal*, Jan. 15, 1777, IV:92).

However, Wesley realized that there were additional, and no less weighty, reasons for this practice than the sheer force of dominical authority. Thus he could remark that it was far better "to *carry* relief to the poor, than to *send* it" not only for their sake but also because this was "far more apt to soften our heart, and to make us naturally care for each other" (*Journal*, Nov. 24, 1760, III:28). This last point is reinforced by Wesley when he adds that this visitation may also serve as a means of "increasing your sympathy with the afflicted, your benevolence, and all social affections" ("On Visiting the Sick," VII:119). Without this sort of personal engagement "you could not gain that increase in lowliness, in patience, in tenderness of spirit, in sympathy with the afflicted, which you might have gained, if you had assisted them in person" (Ibid., VII:120). Thus the practice of visitation was directly necessary for developing the sort of compassion that, for Wesley, was the heart of true religion.

Indeed Wesley could even maintain that visiting the poor and sick and imprisoned was a means of grace, to be ranked alongside private and public prayer or the sacraments themselves ("On Zeal," VII:60). Thus Wesley said of visiting those whom today we would call the marginalized: "The walking herein is essentially necessary, as to the continuance of that faith whereby we are already saved by grace, so to the attainment of everlasting salvation" ("On Visiting the Sick," VII:117).

Closely connected to this is what we might today call the

consciousness-raising function of visiting the poor. Thus in his sermon on this theme Wesley remarked: "One great reason why the rich, in general, have so little sympathy for the poor, is, because they so seldom visit them" (Ibid., VII:119). Of the importance of this, especially in dispelling false stereotypes by which an indifference to the poor is often justified, Wesley attests from his own experience:

> On *Friday* and *Saturday*, I visited as many more [of the poor] as I could. I found some in their cells underground; others in their garrets, half-starved both with cold and hunger, added to weakness and pain. But I found not one of them unemployed, who was able to crawl about the room. So wickedly, devilishly false is that common objection, "They are poor, only because they are idle." If you saw these things with your own eyes, could you lay out money in ornaments or superfluities? (*Journal*, Feb. 9-10, 1753, II:279-80)

And on the next page of his *Journal* he reenforces the point:

> I visited more of the poor sick. The industry of many of them surprised me. Several who were ill able to walk, were nevertheless at work; some without any fire, (bitterly cold as it was,) and some, I doubt, without any food. (*Journal*, Feb. 21, 1753, II:281)

The value, then, of visiting the poor is that both hearts and minds may be transformed, that experience may lead to understanding.

The stereotype that Wesley explodes here and throughout his *Journal* is that of the laziness of the poor. Then as now there were those who shrugged off the plight of the poor and even made the poor culpable of their poverty with the smug assertion that the poor are indigent because they are indolent. Neither then nor now could such a generalization survive any acquaintance with the poor themselves.[2] This blindness can only be cured by the sort of concrete experience with the poor that Wesley insisted on as part of Methodist discipline in his own day. Only in this way is it possible to experience the transformation of heart and mind that comes of visiting the poor.

With a change of heart and mind comes the possibility of

action. It is then possible to speak out on behalf of the marginalized, as Wesley does when he speaks of the horrors of poverty or attacks the "devilishly false" bromide that the poor are lazy. This leads to a call for the transformation of others in their attitudes and behavior. Again Wesley reflects on his experience:

> In the afternoon I visited many of the sick; but such scenes, who could see unmoved? There are none such to be found in a Pagan country. If any of the Indians in Georgia were sick, (which indeed exceedingly rarely happened, till they learned gluttony and drunkenness from the Christians,) those that were near him gave him whatever he wanted. O who will convert the English into honest Heathens! (*Journal*, Feb. 8, 1753, II:279)

We will return to develop this theme of protest on behalf of the poor in the next chapter. Here it is important to note that this protest grows out of the practice of visitation.

The result of this visiting, finally, is an appropriate action aimed at aiding the poor. Thus Wesley writes again, "On the following days, I visited many of our poor, to see with my own eyes what their wants were, and how they might be effectually relieved" (*Journal*, Feb. 13, 1785, IV:296; see also Feb. 8, 1787, IV:358). This is another theme that we will have to explore in more detail.

Before exploring those themes, however, it is important to be clear about what Wesley has in mind when he speaks, as he so often does, of visiting the sick or visiting the poor. Wesley defines the *scope* of visiting the sick as follows: "I would include all such as are in a state of affliction, whether of mind or body; and that, whether they are good or bad, whether they fear God or not" ("On Visiting the Sick," VII:118).

It is important to note this scope, since it makes clear that more is involved here than simply visiting one's friends or parishioners when they happen to be in the hospital. What recommends a person as a candidate for visitation is simply and solely her or his need. Wesley's practice, and that he urged upon all who thought of themselves as Methodists, was to find the afflicted and visit them. This is a deceptively innocuous looking bit of advice, until one asks, "But how do I find the poor, the oppressed, the afflicted?" Then it becomes clear that what is at stake here is a breaking down of the walls that make so much human affliction invisible to us. Whether these are the walls of a prison, behind which we hide the "criminal"; the walls of a hospital, behind which we hide the mentally ill; the stained-glass walls with which we hide ourselves from those who are of a different (or of no) faith. These must be penetrated if we are to visit the sick in Wesley's sense. Wesley was not unaware of the difficulty of this or of the radicalism it involved. To a gentlewoman who had become a member of one of his societies, Wesley writes a series of letters that pound relentlessly on this theme:

> Go and see the poor and sick in their own poor little hovels. Take up your cross, woman! Remember the faith! Jesus went before you, and will go with you. Put off the gentlewoman: You bear a higher character. (Letter to a Member of the Society, June 9, 1775, XII:300)

And in a subsequent letter: "I want you to converse more, abundantly more, with the poorest of the people. . . . Creep in among these, in spite of dirt, and a hundred disgusting circumstances; and thus put off the gentlewoman" (Letter to a Member of the Society, Feb. 7, 1776, XII:301). And so it continues, through several more letters (XII:301-5) in which Wesley never lets up in exploding every excuse for avoiding this truly "converting ordinance."

It has been necessary to examine closely Wesley's views about visiting the sick since it is so easy to miss its critical importance, not only for an understanding of Wesley's thought and practice, but also for any clear understanding of what can prevent a preferential option for the poor from degenerating into sentimental or abstract rhetoric. By seizing on something so apparently simple as visiting the sick, Wesley has provided the Methodists with a practical grounding for what can become a radical praxis. In visiting the marginalized, we invite them to transform us, to transform our hearts, to transform our understanding, to transform us into instruments of the divine mercy and justice.

THE WELFARE OF THE POOR

As we have seen, this transformation can be accomplished only on the supposition that one is already acquainted with the dimensions of this need and is mobilized into service. That is the immediate result of visiting the poor. In his *Forms of Prayer,* Wesley includes the petition: "Make me zealous to embrace all occasions that may administer to their happiness, by assisting the needy, protecting the oppressed, instructing the ignorant . . . " (XI:210). The manner in which this prayer was answered is the theme of this section.

What we may term a first level response is that of seeking to meet those needs oneself. This was the practice of Wesley's first group of Methodists at Oxford. Thus he reported in a letter to his father: "The poor at the Castle have still the gospel preached to them, and some of their temporal wants supplied, our little fund rather increasing than diminishing" (June 11, 1731, XII:7). As we shall see, Wesley eventually turns this practice into the basis of a radical practice of Christian stewardship (see chap. 5).

A second level of response is what Wesley called "begging for the poor." This sometimes took the form of making a collection for the poor among the crowds that came to hear Wesley speak. Thus when the rain forces a crowd indoors Wesley remarks, "I took the opportunity of making a collection for the poor; many of whom can very hardly support life in the present scarcity" (*Journal,* June 19, 1757, II:413; see also May 7, 1757, II:443; Jan. 7, 1759, II:467; and passim). Similarly Wesley might take a collection for the French prisoners of war, whose needs he knew because he visited them (*Journal,* Oct. 15, 1759, II:516; Oct. 24, 1760, III:23).

But more is involved here than the familiar church collection. Indeed, what is normally meant by this plays a relatively small role in Wesley's work. Wesley's practice, and that of early

Methodism in general, was to receive offerings or to make collections for the poor. Even in such an ordinary thing as "taking up a collection" a vast difference separates the Methodism of today from the Methodism of Wesley.[5] It is the difference between an influential institution and a community of and for the poor.

But more than this is involved in begging for the poor, as the following passage from the *Journal* makes clear:

> At this season [Christmas] we usually distribute coals and bread among the poor of the society [of London]. But I now considered, they wanted clothes, as well as food. So on this, and the four following days, I walked through the town, and begged two hundred pounds, in order to clothe them that needed it most. But it was hard work, as most of the streets were filled with melting snow, which often lay ankle deep; so that my feet were steeped in snow-water nearly from morning till evening. (*Journal*, Jan. 4, 1785, IV:295)

This was written in 1785, when Wesley was eighty-two years old! The same activity is reported in subsequent years (see *Journal*, IV:328, 358). But Wesley did not regard this as being in any way exceptional. In his sermon "On Visiting the Sick," he admonishes his hearers/readers: "You might properly say in your own case, 'To beg I am ashamed;' but never be ashamed to beg for the poor; yea, in this case, be an importunate beggar" ("On Visiting the Sick," VII:121). This is the same sermon in which he makes clear the fact that this is an activity to be undertaken for the poor, "whether they are good or bad, whether they fear God or not" (Ibid., VII:118). In later years, with the great numbers of poor in the large urban societies, the outreach to the poor who were not of the society became more difficult to keep focused. So Wesley instituted a new sort of society: "the Strangers' Society, instituted wholly for the relief, not of our society, but for poor, sick, friendless strangers" (*Journal*, Mar. 14, 1790, IV:481). When, after Wesley's death, the Methodists became so preoccupied with themselves that they turned their backs on the poor and homeless, a young Methodist named William Booth broke away to launch the Salvation Army in order to keep alive this dimension of Wesley's vision.

It is worth noting again the close connection between visiting the poor and begging for them. The following passage indicates the connection:

> Observing the deep poverty of many of our brethren, I determined to do what I could for their relief. I spoke severally to some that were in good circumstances, and received about forty pounds. Next I inquired who were in the most pressing want, and visited them in their houses. (*Journal*, Sept. 26, 1783, IV:261)

> All my leisure hours this week I employed in visiting the remaining poor, and in begging for them. Having collected about fifty pounds more, I was enabled to relieve most of those that were in pressing distress. (*Journal*, Sept. 28, 1783, IV:261)

The point is that Wesley does not countenance an anonymous charity that leaves in place the barriers that separate us from the poor we design to aid.

ORGANIZATION FOR THE POOR

The elimination of these barriers makes room for more imaginative responses to the plight of the marginalized. Thus Wesley and the early Methodists organized institutions for and of the poor in order to provide more lasting relief than begging for the poor could afford.

An illustration of this is the attempt to employ the poor so that they could meet their own needs. Wesley describes the design of this enterprise:

> Our aim was, with as little expense as possible, to keep them at once from want and from idleness; in order to which, we took twelve of the poorest, and a teacher, into the society-room, where they were employed for four months, till spring came on, in carding and spinning of cotton: And the design answered: They were employed and maintained with very little more than the produce of their own labour. (*Journal*, Nov. 25, 1740, I:292)

Although the development of sewing collectives to employ the poor was an important step, its benefits were limited to those who might be thus organized. Thus Wesley hit upon the idea of a "lending stock," which would enable the poor to acquire for themselves the tools and materials to develop their own businesses. Wesley provides the following account:

> I made a public collection towards a lending-stock for the poor. Our rule is, to lend only twenty-shillings at once, which is repaid weekly within three months. I began this about a year and a half ago [1746]: Thirty pounds sixteen shillings were then collected; and of this, no less than two hundred and fifty-five persons have been relieved in eighteen months. (*Journal,* Jan. 17, 1748, II:81; see also II:17-18, and *A Plain Account of the People Called Methodists,* VIII:267)

A further activity, and one very dear to Wesley's heart, was the attempt to provide free health care for the poor. Wesley was incensed at the iniquity of doctors who charged exorbitant fees for medicines that seldom worked (see the next chapter), and was himself fascinated with the study of folk and herbal remedies. He published several editions of his *Primitive Physick,* a book on inexpensive family medicine, which was his principal best-seller. But he also set up a clinic so that he could see the poor personally and prescribe appropriate remedies (often including "electrification," based on the experiments of the only American rebel of whom he thought well, Benjamin Franklin). Concerning the provision of this service, Wesley notes, "I did not regard whether they were of the society or not" (see *A Plain Account of the People Called Methodists,* VIII:263-65).[4] In his *Journal* he notes:

> I mentioned to the society my design of giving physic to the poor. About thirty came the next day, and in three weeks about three hundred. This we continued for several years, till, the number of patients still increasing, the expense was greater than we could bear. Meantime, through the blessing of God, many who had been ill for months or years, were restored to perfect health. (Dec. 4, 1746, II:39)[5]

The development of collectives, of a lendingstock, and of free health clinics represents activities of one sort that could be undertaken with the poor in mind. But an essential ingredient in all this was the maintenance of effective solidarity with the poor. Thus when Wesley started a "poor house for destitute widows and children," he had it set up so that he and the other Methodist preachers would also live with them, thereby maintaining solidarity.

> For I myself, as well as the other Preachers who are in town, diet with the poor, on the same food, at the same table; and we rejoice herein, as a comfortable earnest of our eating bread together in our Father's kingdom. (*A Plain Account of the People Called Methodists*, VIII:265)

Again, the breaking down of the barriers between the givers and the receivers of aid, between those who have and those who have not, is an essential expression of the solidarity that liberates the privileged from their blindness and the marginalized from their invisibility.

Many of these projects eventually foundered. They did so because Wesley could not bear the burden alone and could not find enough other Methodists who were either willing or able to carry them forward. He laments: "The whole weight lay on me. If I left it to others, it surely came to nothing. They wanted either understanding, or industry, or love, or patience, to bring anything to perfection" (Undated Letter to "Mr. ———," XIII:148). The history of Methodism is not one of triumph but of failure, of failure to carry through the vision of Christian solidarity with the poor.

THE CRITERION OF THE POOR

Wesley's development of programs for the poor was an important aspect of solidarity with the poor. But it was also important to keep the poor in mind when engaging in other activities, in order to orient even ecclesial activities toward the benefit of the poor. In this way social action would not become dissociated from the life of the community of faith. If ecclesial life went on alongside of, but uninformed by, the concern for the poor, then this "business as usual" approach to church life would leave the concern for the poor, like the poor themselves, marginalized. But for Wesley, concern for the poor could not be something peripheral. Thus it became a critical test for the appropriateness of other activities of the Christian community.

We have already seen that for Wesley the significance of the Methodist revival had to do with its concentration on the poor. Upon this emphasis depended the eschatological significance of Methodism: "Never in any age or nation, since the Apostles, have those words been so eminently fulfilled, 'The poor have the Gospel preached unto them,' as it is at this day" ("The Signs of the Times," VI:308). Even the work of evangelization must meet the test: How does it benefit the poor?[6]

In addition to being an indefatigable preacher, Wesley was also one of the most prolific writers and editor/publishers of his age. Here, too, the criterion of the benefit of the poor prevailed. Again Wesley railed against publishers who put out unnecessarily long and expensive volumes only, it would seem, to enrich themselves. Wesley remarks with satisfaction that one of his editorial labors resulted in "retrenching at least one-third of what was published in those five volumes, more to the satisfaction of the bookseller than of the judicious reader" (Preface to *The History of the Earl of Moreland*, XIV:295). Thus he sought to make available inexpensive versions of his own work, as well as that of others, so that the poor could afford to read. Concerning his *Dictionary*, Wesley writes:

> I must avow, that this Dictionary is not published to get money; but to assist persons of common sense, and no learning, to understand the best English authors; and that with as little expense of either time or money as the nature of the thing will allow. (Preface to *The Complete English Dictionary*, XIV:233)

Not even here have we left behind the significance of visiting, for, as Wesley notes:

> Those only who frequently and familiarly converse with men that are wholly uneducated can conceive how many expressions are mere Greek to them which are quite natural to those who have any share of learning. (Preface to *Explanatory Notes upon the Old Testament,* XIV:248)

Later, the societies were asked to subscribe to the *Christian Library* (Wesley's multivolume compendium of the writings of Christians through the centuries on the life of faith) so that those who could not afford to buy could borrow the books. It remained only to encourage those who already knew how to read to teach the poor who did not (see, for example, XIII:119). From this arose the germ of the Sunday school, aimed at teaching literacy to those who were employed during the week.[7] Again, the test of the needs of the poor was the criterion for the work and program of the community.

Although Wesley was a firm believer in the importance of education, and indeed founded a school for the children of poor preachers (and determined the curriculum, and where necessary wrote it—including the grammars), he was more concerned about the concrete needs of the poor than about education *per se.* Thus he wrote to George Whitefield, who was planning to transform an orphanage into a college: "Can anything on earth be a greater charity, than to bring up orphans? What is a College or an Academy compared to this?" After protesting his commitment to education, he continues, "But still, I cannot place the giving it to five hundred students, on a level with saving the bodies, if not the souls too, of five hundred orphans" (Letter of Feb. 21, 1770, XII:159).

When it became necessary to raise money for the building of preaching houses and the support of the preachers, even here the test of the poor was applied. Under great pressure to raise money for this purpose, still Wesley wrote to his preachers: "We must beware of distressing the poor. Our substantial brethren are well able to bear the burden" (Letter to Joseph Benson, July 31, 1776, XII:424). Can one imagine one of our modern television evangelists of the gospel of wealth asking that the poor *not* send money?

Thus Wesley was appalled by the construction of churches that appealed to the taste of the wealthy. After describing "Dr. Taylor's new meeting-house," the Crystal Cathedral of its day, "with sixteen sash-windows below, as many above, and eight skylights in the dome," Wesley wonders: "How can it be thought that the old, coarse Gospel should find admission here?" (*Journal,* Nov. 23, 1757, II:431). But the reason for the contradiction is made clearer when Wesley gives instructions for the building and financing of Methodist preaching houses:

> Let all preaching-houses be built plain and decent; but not more expensive than is absolutely unavoidable: Otherwise the necessity of raising money will make rich men necessary to us. But if so, we must be dependent upon them, yea, and governed by them. And then farewell to the Methodist discipline, if not doctrine too. ("The Large Minutes," VIII:332)

Despite the fact that these instructions were included in the document from which the United Methodist *Book of Discipline* derives, it must be admitted that the Methodists have been no more willing to be instructed by Wesley on the manner of building churches than they have in the essentials of Christian stewardship. The result, just as Wesley foresaw, has been the loss of both Methodist discipline and doctrine.

In a similar vein Wesley noted with horror the method of choosing elders in the Church of Scotland:

> And what are these [elders]? Men of great sense and deep experience? Neither one, nor the other. But they are the *richest* men in the parish. And are the *richest,* of course, the *best* and the *wisest* men? Does the Bible teach this? I fear not. What manner of Governors then will these be? Why, they are generally just as capable of governing a parish, as of commanding an army. (*Journal,* May 30, 1759, II:482)

Perhaps it was after reflection on this example that Wesley advised one of his preachers concerning the selection of leaders for the classes: "Put the most insignificant person in each class to be the Leader of it" (Letter to Mr. John Cricket, Feb. 10, 1783, XIV:361). Thus did Wesley seek to be consistent with the demystification of wealth and privilege even in the details of Methodist discipline. The natural consequence both of Wesley's distrust of the wealthy and of his turn toward the poor was an empowerment of the poor, a fostering of their own leadership abilities. Again the question was not who may be the most influential, not even who will be the most effective, but who is the least of these.

The turn toward the poor, then, which is made possible by a critique of wealth and is nourished by the practice of visiting the poor, leads not only to "works of mercy" whereby their concrete needs may be addressed, but also to the principle that the welfare of the poor should be the litmus test of *all* activity. From Wesley's practice, we may learn that solidarity with the poor is not one program among others, however important, but is the norm of all activity of the people called Methodists, of those who seek to embody scriptural Christianity.

POLICY FOR THE POOR

While Wesley's solidarity with the poor cannot be seriously brought into question if his own writings and actions are allowed to speak for themselves, he has often been faulted for not taking sufficiently into account the structural aspects of poverty and for proposing remedies for the plight of the poor that ignored these structural realities. Wesley's political vision was indeed truncated by royalist Anglican assumptions. It is also the case that Wesley lived and worked in the eighteenth century, when the powers and responsibilities of government were defined quite differently than they are now. Despite all of this, it simply is not the case that Wesley has nothing to say about the relation of poverty to government policy. Indeed it is precisely by way of his very solidarity with the poor and consequent awareness of their plight that the way is opened for Wesley to propose for government economic policy the same criterion he had found himself applying to the work of launching the Methodist movement.

The critical document is Wesley's *Thoughts on the Present*

Scarcity of Provisions (1773). His starting point is, revealingly, as follows: "First, Why are thousands of people starving, perishing for want, in every part of the nation? The fact I know; I have seen it with my eyes, in every corner of the land" (XI:53). Perhaps his readers have not the same experiential base as Wesley and so will either not believe the fact or will not be motivated to earnestly desire a solution. Wesley will then give the reader some of the harvest of his own experience:

> I have known those who could only afford to eat a little coarse food once every other day. I have known one in London (and one that a few years before had all the conveniences of life) picking up from a dunghill stinking sprats, and carrying them home for herself and her children. I have known another gathering the bones which the dogs had left in the streets, and making broth of them, to prolong a wretched life! I have heard a third artlessly declare, "Indeed I was very faint, and so weak I could hardly walk, until my dog, finding nothing at home, went out, and brought in a good sort of bone, which I took out of his mouth, and made a pure dinner!" Such is the case at this day of multitudes of people, in a land flowing, as it were, with milk and honey! abounding with all the necessaries, the conveniencies, the superfluities of life! (XI:53-54)

What must be found, then, is a response to this problem, the problem of the poor. All that follows has its origin and its aim here.

The immediate answer is that "they have no meat, because they have no work." As we have seen, Wesley will not accept the comfortable idea that the poor suffer because they are lazy. But why is unemployment so high?

> Because the persons that used to employ them cannot afford to do it any longer. . . . They cannot, as they have no vent for their goods; food being so dear, that the generality of people are hardly able to buy anything else. (XI:54)

Thus far it is clear that Wesley not only has some experiential base for his concern but also a fair grasp of economic principles.

Wesley proceeds to indicate why various commodities are expensive, so expensive that the majority of people can afford little besides food (if they can buy that), and so there is no demand for other goods, which leads to unemployment, which leads to starvation, and so on. He suggests that half of the annual corn crop is funneled into distilleries. To those who reply that this distilling should not be limited because it produces needed revenue for the king, he answers:

> Is this an equivalent for the lives of his subjects? Would His Majesty sell an hundred thousand of his subjects yearly to Algiers for four hundred thousand pounds? Surely no. Will he then sell them for that sum, to be butchered by their own countrymen? "But otherwise the swine for the Navy cannot be fed." Not unless they are fed with human flesh! Not unless they are fatted with human blood! O, tell it not in Constantinople, that the English raise the royal revenue by selling the flesh and blood of their countrymen! (XI:55)

Wesley's opposition to the distilling business is well known. What is often forgotten is that this opposition had little to do with individualistic moralism; it grew out of concern for the effects of this business upon the poor.[8] It is notable that Wesley the patriot gives way to Wesley the radical when the welfare of the poor is at stake.

In a similar vein, Wesley protests the emergence of big farm monopolies that throw tenant farmers (sharecroppers, campesinos) off the land (XI:56). This action is not only an evil in itself, he maintains, but it also means that the produce of these small farmers (poultry and pork) becomes rarer and thus costlier. What is the land used for? Why, to raise fancy horses, either for export or to draw the fashionable chariots of the rich (XI:55-56)—in a word, for luxury. But it does not stop there, for the wealthy consume and waste so much in other ways that they drive up prices while their neighbors starve.

The third cause for the scarcity of goods, as Wesley sees it, is the level of taxation used to support wasteful government spending (XI:57). His conclusion then is: "Thousands of people throughout the land are perishing for want of food. This is owing to various causes; but above all, to distilling, taxes, and luxury" (XI:57).

But what then? Having diagnosed the problem, does Wesley

then retire from the fray in the name of staying out of politics? He does not. He proposes concrete measures: prohibit distilling (not affecting beer and wine); tax exported horses and the gentry's carriages; reduce the size of farms so that small farmers will not be thrown off the land (a policy still at the heart of many movements for agrarian reform in Latin America today); and turn to "repressing luxury; whether by laws, by example, or by both." And, finally, pay off the national debt and terminate needless expenses which benefit only the gentry (see XI:58-59).

Although many profess to find in Wesley no precedent for such "meddling" in government policy, his own practice contradicts this. In addition to his essay on *The Present Scarcity of Provisions,* which deals with national policy, we find Wesley also commending the urban policy of the Mayor of Cork:

> —an upright, sensible man, who is diligently employed, from morning to night, in doing all the good he can. He has already prevailed upon the Corporation to make it a fixed rule, that the two hundred a year, which was spent in two entertainments, should for the future be employed in relieving indigent freemen, with their wives and children. He has carefully regulated the House of Industry, and has instituted a Humane Society for the relief of persons seemingly drowned; and he is unwearied in removing abuses of every kind. When will our English Mayors copy after the Mayor of Cork? (*Journal,* May 12, 1787, IV:374)

The criterion of Wesley's own work is the benefit of the poor. Through the sort of analysis he provides in his essay on *The Present Scarcity of Provisions,* he recommends this as the criterion of government policy as well. But what if the nation does not act in ways that bring relief and justice to the poor? Wesley himself has scant hope that it will: "It seems as if God must shortly arise and maintain his own cause. But, if so, let us fall into the hands of God, and not into the hands of men" (XI:59). Wesley expects that his country is so far gone in wickedness that it will not act to defend the poor, so that God must act. Act how? Wesley is thinking here like an Old Testament prophet. He means: God will have to overthrow the wicked in order to relieve the poor.

CHAPTER FOUR

PROTEST AGAINST INJUSTICE

We have seen that Wesley's demystification of wealth and power opens the way to a preferential option for the poor. While such an option may be merely sentimental or ideologically abstract, this is prevented in Wesley's case by the constant practice of visitation, which embeds this option in lived experience and gives it both concreteness and urgency. This then leads to actions based on concrete commitment. But Wesley's commitment to the poor is not simply one among other commitments. Instead it becomes normative for all action. Thus for Wesley the mission of proclamation, the work of writing, and the organization of the community are all tested against the norm of a commitment to the poor.

When such a commitment is pursued in such a thorough-going way, then the plight of the poor is or may be experienced as a product, not of blind fate, but of concrete forms of injustice. This is especially the case where the prophetic tradition plays a role in the formation of one who has experience with the suffering of the poor. Thus solidarity with the poor includes not only a positive concern for their welfare but a protest against concrete forms of injustice as well.

What is at stake here is the way in which a demystification of wealth and power engenders a prophetic protest against the oppression of the poor. Thus wealth and power are seen not only to be dangerous to faith but, on the basis of a normative commitment to the poor, also as forces arrayed against the welfare of the poor. Where there is no concrete commitment to the poor, injustice remains invisible. This is why those who are mesmerized by the pseudo-gospel of wealth simply cannot see the dynamics by which wealth and power operate at the expense of the poor. Although they have eyes to see, they cannot see. But solidarity with the poor opens the eyes and makes possible the protest against injustice.

In this chapter, we will explore the ways in which this protest against injustice was expressed in the thought and work of John Wesley. Although Wesley's opposition to slavery is well known, other aspects of this protest are also of importance in clarifying its scope. We will begin with a consideration of Wesley's protest against some of the concrete forms of injustice in his own society before considering his protest against the iniquities of war, imperialism, and slavery. We will then consider some of the ways this protest leads to what may be termed a politics of transformation.

AGAINST EXPLOITATION

Because of the concreteness of Wesley's thought and action, it is instructive to examine his attitude toward those groups or professions that he perceived to be particularly destructive in their relation to the poor. Here it will be clear that Wesley was not prepared to exempt even the most powerful and respected groups from his critique.

Merchants

In his long treatise on *The Doctrine of Original Sin* (1757), Wesley remarks:

I must acknowledge, I once believed the body of English merchants to be men of the strictest honesty and honour. But I have lately had more experience. Whoever wrongs the widow and fatherless, knows not what honour or honesty means. And how very few are there that would scruple this! I could relate many flagrant instances. (IX:228)

It is important to notice what it is that has changed Wesley's mind. He has "had more experience." That is, his orientation to the poor, his practice of visiting the poor, has enabled him to see with their eyes. And this produces outrage and protest.

This outrage does not stop short of bringing into question the otherwise normal practice of trade.

Is it not generally, though not always, "Cheat that cheat can: Sell as dear as you can, and buy as cheap?" And what are they who steer by this rule better than a company of *Newgate-birds?* Shake them all together; for there is not a grain of honesty among them. (IX:233)

What Wesley condemns here is the most general and obvious rule of the marketplace: Buy cheap; sell dear. This is, in his view, criminal behavior, nothing less than thievery. What produces his harsh and radical judgment? Experience with the effect of this practice on the poor.

Distillers

Wesley's opposition to the distilling industry is well known, if poorly understood. It was no part of Wesley's purpose, for example, to oppose the consumption of beer or wine, both of which he enjoyed and recommended in moderation.[1] Nor was his opposition to "hard liquor" based on narrow moralistic considerations. Rather, he was again motivated by his engagement with the poor. It is this that inflames his rhetoric against those who make themselves wealthy by making and selling "spirituous liquors" for other than medicinal purposes.

But all who sell them in the common way, to any that will buy, are poisoners general. They murder His Majesty's subjects by wholesale, neither does their eye pity or spare. They drive them to hell like sheep. And what is their gain? Is it not the blood of these men? Who then would envy their large estates and sumptuous palaces? A curse is in the midst of them: The curse of God cleaves to the stones, the timber, the furniture of them! The curse of God is in their gardens, their walks, their groves; a fire that burns to the nethermost hell! Blood, blood is there: The foundation, the floor, the walls, the roof, are stained with blood! And canst thou hope, O thou man of blood, though thou art "clothed in scarlet and fine linen, and farest sumptuously every day;" canst thou hope to deliver down thy *fields of blood* to the third generation? Not so; for there is a God in heaven: Therefore, thy name shall soon be rooted out. ("The Use of Money," VI:129)

Quite apart from being a splendid piece of rhetoric, this passage shows the way in which a suspicion of wealth here is mobilized into denunciation by a perception of it as gained through the exploitation of the poor. This perception expresses itself in the familiar cadences of prophetic rhetoric, which announces the curse of God on the unjust.

Doctors

In his sermon "On the Use of Money," Wesley warns Methodists against participating in the iniquitous trade in spirituous liquors, and immediately warns them in similar terms against making their living as "Surgeons, Apothecaries, or Physicians" (VI:129). Indeed, Wesley's denunciations of the practitioners of the medical profession are, if anything, more frequent, if less inflammatory, than his attacks on distillers. What motivates this protest? Wesley asks whether doctors are not guilty:

who play with the lives or health of men, to enlarge their own gain? who purposely lengthen the pain or disease, which they are able to remove speedily? who protract the cure of their patient's body, in order to plunder his substance? Can any man be clear before God, who does not shorten every disorder "as much as he can" and remove all sickness and pain "as soon as he can?" ("On the Use of Money," VI:129)

Wesley does not suppose this to be the case with only the occasional physician, but he believes it to be deeply ingrained in the profession as such, as he makes quite clear by his thumbnail sketch of the history of medicine in the preface to *Primitive Physic*, his own book of self-help medicine:

> Physicians now [in ancient times] began to be had in admiration, as persons who were something more than human. And profit attended their employ, as well as honour; so that they now had two weighty reasons for keeping the bulk of mankind at a distance, that they might not pry into the mysteries of the profession. (Preface to *Primitive Physic*, XIV:310)

> Those who understood only how to restore the sick to health they branded with the name of empirics. . . . And thus both their honour and gain were secured; a vast majority of mankind being utterly cut off from helping either themselves or their neighbours, or once daring to attempt it. (Ibid., XIV:311)

The root of abuses in the medical profession, then, is the profit motive (see also his letter to Mr. "John Smith," Mar. 25, 1747, XII:89). These abuses are compounded in Wesley's view by the collusion between physicians and pharmacists. So he opposes the practice of making compound medicines, which make people depend so heavily on pharmacies.

> Experience shows that one thing will cure most disorders, at least as well as twenty put together. Then why do you add the other nineteen? Only to swell the apothecary's bill; nay, possibly, on purpose to prolong the distemper, that the doctor and he may divide the spoils. (Preface to *Primitive Physic*, XIV:313)

Wesley credits this collusion between doctors and pharmacists with a conspiracy to discredit inexpensive remedies, including one of his own favorites, the use of electricity: "Who can wonder that many gentlemen of the Faculty [of medicine], as well as their good friends, the Apothecaries, decry a medicine so shockingly cheap and easy, as much as they do quicksilver and tar-water?" (*Journal,* Jan. 20, 1753, II:279). And Wesley supposes that there will be little chance of the transformation of the practice of medicine into a helping profession.

> Not till the gentlemen of the faculty have more regard to the interest of their neighbours than their own: at least, not until there are no Apothecaries in the land, or till Physicians are independent

of them. (Preface to *The Desideratum: Or, Electricity Made Plain and Useful*, XIV:243)

All this in a century when the practice of medicine and the pharmaceutical industry were not yet Big Business!

Lawyers

Wesley's most animated condemnation of the professions comes when he turns his attention to the practice of law. Concerning the English system of justice, he writes: "Such perjury, and such a method of law, we may defy the whole world to produce" (*A Farther Appeal to Men of Reason and Religion*, VIII:201). He notes, concerning the audience for one of his sermons: "I saw but one trifler among all, which, I understood, was an Attorney. Poor man! If men live what I preach, the hope of his gain is lost" (*Journal*, Mar. 26, 1764, III:163). Later he allows: "I breakfasted at the Devizes, with Mr. B———, a black swan, an honest Lawyer!" (*Journal*, Oct. 2, 1764, III:198). What is the basis for Wesley's dismissal of an entire profession?

In *A Farther Appeal to Men of Reason and Religion*, Wesley gives a long list of the sorts of standard legal practices of which he thoroughly disapproves. A portion of that list will indicate what he has in mind:

Of those who are called exceeding honest Attorneys, who is there that makes any scruple,—
   (1.) To promote and encourage needless suits, if not unjust ones too:
   (2.) To defend a bad cause, knowing it so to be,—
By making a demur, and then withdrawing it;
By pleading some false plea, to the plaintiff's declaration;
By putting in an evasive answer to his bill;
By protracting the suit, if possible, till the plaintiff is ruined:
   (3.) To carry a cause not amounting to ten shillings into Westminster-Hall, by laying it in his declaration as above forty:
   (4.) To delay his own client's suit knowingly and wilfully, in order to gain more thereby. . . .
   (12.) To fill up his bill with attendances, fees, and term-fees, though his client is no whit forwarder in his cause?

This is he that is called an *honest* Attorney! How much honester is a pickpocket! (VIII:165-66)

The full list makes clear that Wesley had an intimate acquaintance with the practices of the legal profession. There are other examples of this protest against these practices (see *Original Sin,* IX:221). As anyone acquainted with the law then or now knows, these are, as Wesley says, not extraordinary, but common practices.

Indeed, one wonders what all the fuss is about. Why this outrage about the disadvantages, if they are such, of Anglo-Saxon law? The answer is that Wesley is viewing the law from the standpoint of the poor and oppressed. It is this standpoint that transforms a list of professional peccadillos into a prophetic protest against oppression. Thus he asks in his treatise *The Doctrine of Original Sin*:

> Do they never knowingly defend a bad cause, and so make themselves accomplices in wrong and oppression? Do they never deliver the poor into the hand of his oppressor, and see that such as are in necessity have not right? Are they not often the means of withholding bread from the hungry, and raiment from the naked, even when it is their own, when they have a clear right thereto, by the law both of God and man? Is not this effectually done in many cases by protracting the suit from year to year? (IX:229)

In *A Farther Appeal,* the question is even sharper:

> Suppose a great man to oppress the needy; suppose the rich grinds the face of the poor; what remedy against such oppression can he find in this Christian country? If the one is rich and the other poor, doth not justice stand afar off? And is not the poor under the utmost improbability (if not impossibility) of obtaining it? Perhaps the hazard is greater among us, than either among Jews, Turks, or Heathens. (VIII:164-65)

And Wesley's conclusion is an indictment that still has the ring of truth: "Without money, you can have no more law; poverty alone utterly shuts out justice" (VIII:165).

Wesley's protest against the legal profession is, then, a protest in the name of the poor, a protest grounded in solidarity with the poor. Legal practices that seem quite normal, or at worst only somewhat shady, take on a rather different aspect when seen from the vantage point of those who are victimized by the system. Then the system of English law, upon which patriotic Englishmen (Wesley included) prided themselves, comes to be seen as the systematic oppression of the poor. Particular experiences with victims of such a system (such as the one that led Wesley to exclaim, "Where is the mercy of thus grinding the face of the poor? thus sucking the blood of a poor, beggared prisoner?" [*Journal,* July 3, 1761, III:66]), are magnified by the practice of regularly visiting the poor and the imprisoned. This, then, opens the eyes to the iniquity of the system, so that the very necessity of recourse to lawyers appears as unjust.

> A man has wronged me of a hundred pounds. I appeal to a Judge for the recovery of it. How astonishing is it that this Judge himself cannot give me what is my right, and what evidently appears so to be, unless I first give, perhaps, one half of the sum to men I never saw before in my life! (*A Farther Appeal,* VIII:167)

Wesley's experience with the poor and his commitment to them makes it possible for him to see things in a new light, a light that would have seemed strange to those who either remained mesmerized by wealth and privilege or who lacked the new vision provided by constant contact with the poor. When the commitment to the poor takes on the status of a normative claim, then what appears to others as the common and self-evident practice of merchants, doctors, and lawyers appears instead as the practice of injustice and oppression. It is then not enough to seek relief for the poor in the form of free health clinics, for example. It is necessary to cry out publicly against injustice.

AGAINST OPPRESSION

We have seen that Wesley's protest against injustice grows out of his firsthand experience with the poor. This experience produces solidarity and so makes it possible to see the world of wealth and privilege with new eyes, to see it as a structure of injustice that must be denounced. But this experience with and commitment to the poor also provides a kind of hermeneutic, a principle of interpretation, for understanding situations far removed from one's own personal experience. On this basis it is possible to develop a sensitivity to injustice, which reaches out beyond the borders of immediate acquaintance to take in a more global horizon. Thus a new dimension appears to Wesley's protest against injustice, which reaches well beyond the shores of the British Isles. We will consider here Wesley's protest against war, colonialism, and slavery.

War

In his discussion of the doctrine of original sin, Wesley provides a catalogue of the various self-inflicted calamities from which humanity suffers. These expressions of original sin infect all, he maintains, even the "Christian countries." After mentioning many of these (including the English system of law), he writes:

> There is a still more horrid reproach to the Christian name, yea, to the name of man, to all reason and humanity. There is war in the world! war between men! war between Christians! . . . Now, who can reconcile war, I will not say to religion, but to any degree of reason or common sense? (*The Doctrine of Original Sin,* IX:221)

Now we know that it is possible, especially if one is a patriot, as Wesley undoubtedly was, to see war not as something wholly contrary to religion or reason. What, then, produces in Wesley so negative an assessment? The clue may be found in his description of a typical battle:

> Let us calmly and impartially consider the thing itself. Here are forty thousand men gathered together on this plain. What are they going to do? See, there are thirty or forty thousand more at a little distance. And these are going to shoot them through the head or body, to stab them, or split their skulls, and send most of their souls

into everlasting fire, as fast as they possibly can. Why so? What harm have they done to them? O none at all! They do not so much as know them. But a man, who is King of France, has a quarrel with another man, who is King of England. So these Frenchmen are going to kill as many of these Englishmen as they can, to prove the King of France is in the right. (*The Doctrine of Original Sin,* IX:222)

Instead of seeing war from the elevated point of view of national pride or patriotic duty or even national self-interest, Wesley sees it from "below," from the vantage point of those who do the dying and the killing, from the vantage point of the poor.

Although Wesley did protest the use of press gangs to seize men for the Navy as a violation of all law and liberty (*Journal,* July 21, 1739, I:212; see also the second letter to Bishop Lavington, IX:40), he did not by any means launch a pacifist movement. There is some evidence that Wesley felt uneasy about this half-way position. He could find no reply to the argument that no follower of Jesus could possibly agree to participate in a war (see A Letter to . . . Quakers, X:187). But his clear perception that war was inglorious was never effectively mobilized into any sort of anti-war movement. That may have meant too final a break with his beloved Anglican heritage. But he did see the absurdity of war and did not offer for it the sort of rationalizations and justifications so often invoked by those who are mesmerized by the spell of power and privilege.[2]

Colonialism

Certainly, the numbers of those who were to be mesmerized by dreams of empire and glory were destined to grow in England in the course of the next century, as the people who had heard Wesley shouldered what some would later call "the white man's burden." But Wesley knew too well what things looked like from another perspective to be thus taken in. Far from filling him with pride, the reports of British conquest provoked outrage.

The Great Mogul, Emperor of Hindostan, one of the mightiest Potentates on earth, is become a poor, little, impotent slave to a

Company of Merchants! His large, flourishing empire is broken in pieces and covered with fraud, oppression, and misery! And we may call the myriads that have been murdered happy, in comparison of those that still groan under the iron yoke. Wilt thou not visit for these things, O Lord? Shall the fool still say in his heart, "There is no God?" (*Journal,* Feb. 23, 1776, IV:68)

Far from feeling pride, Wesley anticipates the wrath of a just God to come upon his own nation for the evils of colonialism![3]

The capacity for compassion, nurtured by the practice of solidarity with the poor, makes it possible for Wesley to bemoan the plight of the people of India: "How many hundred thousands of the poor, quiet people, have been destroyed, and their carcases left as the dung of the earth," he laments in his sermon on "The Imperfection of Human Knowledge" (VI:345). And in his *Journal* he indicts his countrymen:

What consummate villains, what devils incarnate, were the managers there! What utter strangers to justice, mercy, and truth; to every sentiment of humanity! I believe no heathen history contains a parallel. I remember none in all the annals of antiquity: Not even the divine Cato, or the virtuous Brutus, plundered the provinces committed to their charge with such merciless cruelty as the English have plundered the desolated provinces of Indostan. (*Journal,* Nov. 13, 1776, IV:89)

So strongly does Wesley feel the monstrousness of these crimes that he can compare Christians and Heathens and find, not for the first time, that Christianity (so-called) comes out wanting.

Look into that large country, Indostan. There are Christians and Heathens too. Which have more justice, mercy, and truth? the Christians or the Heathens? Which are most corrupt, infernal, devilish, in their tempers and practice? the English or the Indians? Which have desolated whole countries, and clogged the rivers with dead bodies? . . . O earth, earth, earth! how dost thou groan under the villanies of thy *Christian* inhabitants! ("The Mystery of Iniquity," VI:265)

Wesley needs no atheist to tell him of the monstrosities of Christendom, even in its supposedly more enlightened form of

Protestantism. He sees all too clearly the collapse of Christianity before the Constantinian temptation of wealth, power, and influence. He sees all too clearly the result of all this on the marginalized, the very people to whom the gospel should have been good news. How far is all this from the modern-day apostles of wealth, who shut their eyes to the evils of contemporary colonialism and capitalism in the name of a Christian crusade against "godless communism"?

Slavery

It is no fluke, then, but the result of a very precise process of praxis and reflection that Wesley comes to his position on the evils of slavery. Wesley's first contact with slavery appears to be his trip to Charleston, South Carolina, in July of 1736. In his *Journal,* Wesley does not seem to have been driven by this experience to reflect explicitly on the institution of slavery. But he is sensitive to the plight of the "Negroes": "O God, where are thy tender mercies? Are they not over all thy works? When shall the Sun of Righteousness arise on these outcasts of men" (*Journal,* July 31, 1736, I:40). Interestingly, Wesley does not refer to the black people, as "slaves" at all, but rather simply as "Negroes"—that is, as persons not essentially determined by their situation of slavery. For Wesley, the issue appears to be the development of a means for their evangelization (see *Journal,* April 27, 1737, I:49). This does not seem to be a particularly radical step until we recall that it was vehemently opposed by many slaveholders as bringing into question the very foundation of chattel slavery.

Wesley first mentions the *institution* of slavery in one of the many small book reviews with which he frequently edified the reader of his *Journal*:

> In returning, I read a very different book, published by an honest Quaker, on that execrable sum of all villanies, commonly called the Slave Trade. I read of nothing like it in the heathen world, whether ancient or modern: And it infinitely exceeds, in every instance of barbarity, whatever Christian slaves suffer in Mahometan countries. (Feb. 12, 1772, III:453)[4]

Just two years later he published his own pamphlet on the subject, *Thoughts Upon Slavery* (XI:59-79). This small book,[5] which Wesley caused to be published in several editions, contains a history of the slave trade and a description of the conditions of slaves in the slave ships and on the plantations, as well as a passionate denunciation of slavery and an appeal for its abolition. While this text deserves a close reading, we will only note some of its salient features.

After a definition of slavery and a sketch of its history from ancient times to its reintroduction by Portugal in the sixteenth century, Wesley turns to give a description of Africa. Here he draws upon his wide reading of what today would be called cultural anthropology to provide a picture of strong civilizations with peaceable, prosperous, and decent populations. But this happy picture is soon marred by the arrival of—Christians! "The Christians, landing upon their coasts, seized as many as they found, men, women, and children, and transported them to America" (XI:65). But soon a way was found to increase the number of captured slaves "by prevailing upon them to make war upon each other, and to sell their prisoners" (XI:65). This, as Wesley notes, only compounded the villainy, since "till then they seldom had any wars; but were in general quiet and peaceable" (XI:65). Nor does the villainy end here, for Wesley reports that of perhaps one hundred thousand slaves captured every year, a third die en route to America: "O Earth, O Sea, cover not their blood!" (XI:67).

Wesley then provides wrenching accounts of conditions on slave ships, of the humiliations of the auction block, and of the dehumanizing realities of life on the plantation—all from the slaves' point of view. He asks: "Did the Creator intend that the noblest creatures in the visible world should live such a life as this?" (XI:68).

He then surveys the "laws" that apply to slaves and that, so far from affording them any protection or redress, utterly deprive them of any hope of either. But the main objection is made in the name of justice.

> Where is the justice of inflicting the severest evils on those that have done us no wrong? of depriving those that never injured us in

word or deed, of every comfort of life? of tearing them from their native country, and depriving them of liberty itself, to which an Angolan has the same natural right as an Englishman, and on which he sets as high a value? Yea, where is the justice of taking away the lives of innocent, inoffensive men; murdering thousands of them in their own land, by the hands of their own countrymen; many thousands, year after year, on shipboard, and then casting them like dung into the sea; and tens of thousands in that cruel slavery to which they are so unjustly reduced? (XI:70)

Here Wesley has applied his understanding of human rights to demonstrate the injustice of slavery. Whatever other faults his political theory may have had, it was not without its virtues, especially as regards this principle.

But Wesley goes even further, in response to the objection that slavery is legal:

The grand plea is, "They are authorized by law." But can law, human law, change the nature of things? Can it turn darkness into light, or evil into good? By no means. Notwithstanding ten thousand laws, right is right, and wrong is wrong still. There must still remain an essential difference between justice and injustice, cruelty and mercy. (XI:70)

Here Wesley, who on so many occasions must appeal to the appropriateness of obeying the law, breaks out into a clear statement of the relativity of all laws, the necessity of obeying the dictates of mercy and justice before any law. He is compelled to this view, first, by the Bible and, second, by the hermeneutic of solidarity, which enables him to see injustice where others see only economic and imperial benefit.

But if slavery is unjust and its legality not worth considering, there are still those who argue that it is an economic necessity. Otherwise it would be impossible to settle and cultivate the islands of the Caribbean.

I answer, First it were far better that all those islands should remain uncultivated for ever; yea, it were more desirable that they were altogether sunk in the depth of the sea, than that they should be cultivated at so high a price as the violation of justice, mercy, and truth. (XI:73)

But slavery is necessary for trade and so for the wealth and power of the nation.

> Wealth is not necessary to the glory of any nation; but wisdom, virtue, justice, mercy, generosity, public spirit, love of our country. These are necessary to the real glory of a nation; but abundance of wealth is not. (XI:73)

> Better is honest poverty, than all the riches bought by the tears, and sweat, and blood, of our fellow-creatures. (XI:74)

Thus Wesley's demystification of wealth stands him in good stead when it comes to resisting the appeals of those who believe riches to be, because the principal gift of God, the legitimation of personal, ecclesial, or national policy. Those who remain mesmerized by wealth and power would find Wesley's response here to be mere Greek. They are defenseless before the Constantinian temptation. When, during the American Revolution, the slave trade ceased, Wesley contemplated the idle ships of Liverpool and rejoiced: "So the men of Africa, as well as Europe, may enjoy their native liberty" (*Journal,* April 11, 1777, IV:96). And when people attacked the policy of the king for having destroyed English trade and cited the loss of the slave trade, Wesley responded:

> I would to God it may never be found more! that we may never more steal and sell our brethren like beasts; never murder them by thousands and tens of thousands! . . . Never was anything such a reproach to England since it was a nation, as the having any hand in this execrable traffic. (*A Serious Address to the People of England,* XI:145)

Thus when Wesley turns to call for the abolition of slavery, he emphasizes the role that the acquisition of wealth has in the system in order to assess blame. To the merchants, he writes:

> It is you that induce the African villain to sell his countrymen; and in order thereto, to steal, rob, murder men, women, and children without number, by enabling the English villain to pay him for so doing, whom you overpay for his execrable labour. It is your money that is the spring of all, that empowers him to go on: So that

whatever he or the African does in this matter is all your act and deed. (*Thoughts Upon Slavery*, XI:77)

And to the plantation owners, he says:

Now, it is your money that pays the merchant, and through him the captain and the African butchers. You therefore are guilty, yea, principally guilty, of all these frauds, robberies, and murders. You are the spring that puts all the rest in motion; they would not stir a step without you; therefore, the blood of all these wretches who die before their time, whether in their country or elsewhere, lies upon your head. (*Thoughts Upon Slavery*, XI:78)

Wesley's earlier demystification of wealth and power enables him to expose the profit motive as the foundation of the slave trade and thus to follow the money trail in the assigning of responsibility.

Wesley's condemnation of the slave trade, then, grows naturally out of his understanding of human rights, his demystification of wealth, and his solidarity with the poor and oppressed. In combination, these produce his protest against this form of injustice.

It is important to see how Wesley's view of human rights works out in a situation made concrete by the demystification of wealth and solidarity with the poor. It is all too easy for talk of rights to be used as a cover for injustice; the "rights" of the powerful may be so stressed as to vitiate any call for change. If the protection of "life, liberty, and property" is understood abstractly, then the "rights" of slaveholders are on a par with those of slaves. Indeed, they who have greater "property" may have correspondingly more rights, unless the privilege of wealth and power is demystified. More is at stake here than the question of slavery, as the ongoing debate about the justice of a redistribution of wealth or the selective view of human rights exemplified by presumably freedom loving apostles of wealth and power make clear. As we know only too well, talk of liberty all too easily becomes a cloak for reactionary policies and regimes. Thus the mere presence of an interest in human rights means little unless this is freed from the tendency to stabilize the status quo through a critique of wealth and power, and made concrete through a preferential option for the poor.[6] Since these two conditions are present in Wesley's thought, his application of human rights principles to the question of slavery results in an appeal for abolition.

We have already encountered Wesley's view that enslavement is unjust because it is a deprivation of liberty, "to which an Angolan has the same natural right as an Englishman" (*Thoughts Upon Slavery*, XI:70). This principle is subsequently applied by Wesley to those who protest that they own slaves through no fault of their own, having merely inherited them, and that these slaves had been born into this condition, which, therefore, should be regarded as natural to them: "Liberty is the right of every human creature, as soon as he breathes the vital air; and no human law can deprive him of that right which he derives from the law of nature" (XI:79). No matter what the legal situation of the slaveholder may be, no person has "a right to use another as a slave" (XI:79). Here, then, the conflict between justice and law becomes concrete, depriving the slaveholder of the legal, but fictional, right to his "property."

There is, then, nothing left but that the slaveholder must relinquish his unjust claim to the slave:

> If, therefore, you have any regard to justice, (to say nothing of mercy, nor of the revealed law of God), render unto all their due. Give liberty to whom liberty is due, that is, to every child of man, to every partaker of human nature. (XI:79)

What should not escape attention here is the fact that Wesley's allusion to Romans 13 ("render unto all their due") is freed of the reactionary sense given to it by those who employ it only to maintain the status quo. Such a reactionary usage is not impossible for Wesley, when he is thinking abstractly (see "Thoughts Concerning the Origin of Power," XI:47-48). But where his thought becomes concrete through the mediation of a lively solidarity with the oppressed, as in the case of slavery, then Romans 13 becomes a call for the transformation of that status quo.

On the basis of the foregoing analysis of the injustice of the slave trade, Wesley found it appropriate to preach against slavery, and he even organized a vigil for the liberation of the slaves.

> We set *Friday* apart as a day of fasting and prayer, that God would remember those poor outcasts of men; and (what seems impossible with men, considering the wealth and power of their oppressors) make a way for them to escape, and break their chains in sunder. (*Journal*, Mar. 3, 1788, IV:408)

When we recall Wesley's principle that usually God is pleased to work good to humanity through the actions of their neighbors, this prayer that God would help the slaves escape and break their chains is far from a harmless proposition.

FROM PROTEST TO TRANSFORMATION

Wesley's call for the transformation of the status quo does not limit itself to personal appeals to slaveholders or to sermons and prayers. He was prepared to move into the sphere of political transformation as well. The result is a multi-layered approach to the question of the realization of justice.

Coalition

In other contexts he was prepared to form alliances with causes whose aims he regarded as worthy, as in his preaching sermons to raise money for the support of a hospital (*Journal*, Feb. 5, 1784, IV:266) or for the Humane Society—an organization for the promotion of techniques of artificial respiration to save victims of drowning (*Journal*, Nov. 23, 1777, IV:112). Here, too, in the case of slavery, Wesley joined himself with the abolitionist movement. Thus Wesley writes to Mr. Thomas Funnell in 1787 in these terms:

> Whatever assistance I can give those generous men who join to oppose that execrable trade, I certainly shall give. I have printed a large edition of the "Thoughts on Slavery," and dispersed them to every part of England. But there will be vehement opposition

made, both by slave-merchants and slave-holders; and they are mighty men: But our comfort is, He that dwelleth on high is mightier. (Nov. 24, 1787, XII:507)

The minutes of the Abolition Committee record the receipt of encouragement from Wesley (see Jackson's note, XIII:153-54).

Legislation

Wesley was not optimistic that Parliament could be persuaded to give the question of abolition the attention it deserved. In his *Thoughts Upon Slavery*, he remarked: "So many things, which seem of greater importance, lie before them, that they are not likely to attend to this" (XI:75). This was in 1774, when incipient rebellion was abroad in the colonies, and England was coping with the severe economic crisis that had occasioned Wesley's *Thoughts on the Present Scarcity of Provisions*. But when, several years later, Parliament was induced to consider this question at the insistence of Lord Wilberforce, Wesley wrote to Wilberforce in what was to prove to be his last letter.

Unless God has raised you up for this very thing, you will be worn out by the opposition of men and devils. But, "if God be for you, who can be against you?" Are all of them together stronger than God? O "be not weary in well doing!" Go on, in the name of God and in the power of his might, till even American slavery (the vilest that ever saw the sun) shall vanish away before it. (Feb. 26, 1791, XIII:153)

Three quarters of a century were to pass before that "vilest" form of slavery was to pass away, and still we are trying to overcome its legacy of injustice.

Wesley was not one of those who supposed that government cannot legislate against moral evil. Whatever we may think of some of the legislative causes he favored, such as the laws against sabbath-breaking or public use of profane language, the wastefulness of the rich (what he called luxury), or, finally, the abolition of slavery, it is clear that those who would limit the power of the State so as to absolve government of the responsibility for the enforcement of justice and right can find scant comfort in the thought and practice of Wesley. He believed that government must do this if it is to avoid the calamity of divine judgment upon the nation. That such a divine judgment was in Wesley's view more than a rhetorical flourish is clear from his comments on "The Late Earthquake at Lisbon."

> And what shall we say of the late accounts from Portugal? That some thousand houses, and many thousand persons, are no more! that a fair city is now in ruinous heaps! Is there indeed a God that judges the world? And is he now making inquisition for blood? If so, it is not surprising, he should begin there, where so much blood has been poured on the ground like water! where so many brave men have been murdered, in the most base and cowardly as well as barbarous manner, almost every day, as well as every night, while none regarded or laid it to heart. "Let them hunt and destroy the precious life, so we may secure our stores of gold and precious stones." [There follows Wesley's own explanatory note] . . . Merchants who have lived in Portugal inform us, that the King had a large building filled with diamonds; and more gold stored up, coined and uncoined, than all the other princes of Europe together. (XI:1-2)

Whatever we may think of Wesley's theodicy, it is clear that for him there was ample justification for an attempt to make one's own society more just, if only to avoid the fate of Lisbon. To be sure, his own priority was to change the lives of persons. But this was no excuse for being shy with respect to the plain duty of the leaders of a nation to correct the most blatant forms of injustice, lest God "visit" the nation with destruction. In supporting the work of Wilberforce to enact a legislative prohibition of the slave trade, Wesley was merely carrying forward the same instinct that had earlier led him to propose legislative remedies for the "present scarcity of provisions." Where justice is concerned, Wesley has no hesitation to include in his response a call for governmental intervention. Such an intervention is, after all, in the "national self-interest," if one supposes that there is indeed a God in the world. Thus in the face of the rebellion in the American colonies, Wesley could write (in 1776):

As we are punished with the sword, it is not improbable but one principal sin of our nation is, the blood that we have shed in Asia, Africa, and America. Here I would beg your serious attention, while I observe, that however extensively pursued, and of long continuance, the African slave trade may be, it is nevertheless iniquitous from first to last. It is the price of blood! It is a trade of blood, and has stained our land with blood! (*A Seasonable Address to the Inhabitants of Great Britain*, XI:125)

And Wesley sees that this slave trade does not stand alone, but is closely tied to the policy of colonialism in India.

And is the East-India trader a jot better? I fear not. They seem very nearly allied. For though here is no leading into captivity, as in the former; yet the refined iniquity practised there, of fomenting war amongst the natives, and seizing the chief of the plunder, has been as conspicuous to the serious and attentive. What millions have fallen by these means, as well as by artificial famine! O earth, cover not thou their blood! It will speak to heaven and to the inhabitants of the earth to the latest posterity. (Ibid., XI:125-26)

Here Wesley is by no means dealing with isolated phenomena. The slave trade monopoly acquired from Portugal in 1703 was the basis of British power as a trading nation in the eighteenth century. The occupation of India was launched to destroy the textile industry of India in order to obtain a similar monopoly. This monopoly was the basis of the ascendancy of the British Empire. Therefore, in linking these Wesley was attacking the very heart of mercantile capitalism and the institutions that were to serve as the basis of the subsequent industrial capitalism in Britain.[7] Wesley denounces this trade in blood, and he does not stop short of calling his government to account.

O ye Governors of this great nation, would to God that ye had seen this, and timely done your utmost to separate those tares from the wheat of fair and honest trade! What peace therefore can we expect, while these evils continue? "There can be no peace, saith the Lord." While "the voice of thy brother's blood crieth unto me from the ground." (*A Seasonable Address*, XI:126)

That God is a God of justice entails that those who seek the true welfare of their nation will root out injustice whatever the cost.

Only in this way can they hope to avoid the divine punishment of civil war. Clearly, for Wesley, an atheistic or deistic politics (one that imagines that there is no God of justice) is as unacceptable as personal unbelief.

Liberation

We have seen that Wesley's solidarity with the poor results in a protest against social evil. But does this protest go far enough? In our own day the question of the right of the oppressed to shake off their bonds has occasionally taken the form of the question of their right to rise up in rebellion against unjust structures. This question is sometimes raised in the form of a "theology of revolution." Indeed, liberation theology is sometimes made to be the equivalent of a rationalization for armed struggle. But this identification is generally the tactic of the enemies of liberation theology. In truth, most of the proponents of liberation theology favor nonviolence, and this not as a matter of expediency but as a matter of principle.[8]

If their criticism of revolutionary violence is sometimes muted, this is usually due to their refusal to be lured into the trap of supposing that only those who demand change are violent. They are far too keenly aware of the institutional violence employed against the poor to be seduced into an abstract evenhandedness that makes it seem that there is nothing to choose between those who take up the cause of the poor and those who systematically deprive the poor of their most basic rights. The question of a right to rebel against injustice is not the same as that of the rationalization of revolutionary violence. With this distinction in mind, let us see how Wesley, given the conditions of his time and his forms of thought, approached this question.

Of course, a *prima facie* case is often made that Wesley simply could not be sympathetic to any rebellion against injustice. After all, was he not an unrepentant monarchist? Did he not oppose the American Revolution? Did he not, at least occasionally, employ the reactionary rhetoric that encouraged the poor to be content with their situation? Thus both those who espouse and those who oppose the right to rebel against unjust structures find in Wesley an example of a pietism uncongenial to any possibility of radical change in the structures of injustice. But is Wesley's position as unidimensional as all this? Is there, in fact, no evidence that he could side with those who rebelled against injustice?

It is instructive to take the case of slavery as an opening to this question. Indeed, it is little noted that Wesley's opposition to the American Revolution was, in part at least, governed by his awareness of the plight of slaves there. This made him abundantly suspicious of the claims of the colonists that theirs was the cause of liberty. Therefore, when the apologists for the rebellion claimed that they were seeking to liberate themselves from conditions of slavery in relation to the government in England, Wesley replied with massive sarcasm: "You and I, and the English in general, go where we will, and enjoy the fruit of our labours: This is liberty. The Negro does not: This is slavery" (A Calm Address to Our American Colonies, XI:81). The fact that those who were most vocal in defense of the American cause of "liberty" were themselves slaveholders made their rhetoric mere empty cant as far as Wesley was concerned. A rebellion of the rich and powerful could not be expected to gain the sympathy of one whose commitments were to the poor (see the discussion of Wesley and politics in the Appendix, pages 199-222).

However, if the poor and oppressed assert their right to rebel, that is a different matter. Wesley recites the description by "Sir Hans Sloan" of the punishments inflicted on slaves. One of these is especially severe: "They fasten them down to the ground with crooked sticks on every limb, and then applying fire, by degrees, to the feet and hands, they burn them gradually upward to the head" (Thoughts Upon Slavery, XI:68). But for what crime? For rebellion. Does Wesley believe this to be a crime for which one could only protest the severity of the punishment? He does not. His own comment on this "crime of rebellion" is: "That is, asserting their native liberty, which they have as much right to as to the air they breathe" (ibid., XI:68). Thus the difference between the rebellion of the colonist and the rebellion of the slave is the difference between an unjust and a just cause, between an illusory and a real claim to liberty from slavery.

Nor does this instance stand alone in Wesley's writings. As we have seen, he protested the unjust treatment the poor received at the hands of merchants and landlords. Occasionally, this protest provoked more than groans on the part of the poor. What was Wesley's reaction when this occurred? Did he warn them against defying the wealthy? Did he tell them to resign themselves to their lot in life? He did not. In his *Journal*, he refers to one such incident in the town of Sligo.

> The mob had been in motion all the day. But their business was only with the forestallers of the market, who had bought up all the corn far and near, to starve the poor, and load a Dutch ship, which lay at the quay; but the mob brought it all out into the market, and sold it for the owners at the common price. And this they did with all the calmness and composure imaginable, and without striking or hurting anyone. (May 27, 1758, II:446)

Wesley had ample reason to fear the mob, since one was so often incited against the Methodists.[9] This occasioned many of Wesley's appeals to authority against mob rule. But here there is no such condemnation. Rather, Wesley seems to admire their action. The key phrase to explain this unexpected reaction is his description of the action of those who bore the brunt of the mob's gentle, but determined, ire: "to starve the poor." That is, Wesley's approbation of the mob is stimulated by their just response to injustice, directed against the poor. Does Wesley complain about the trampling of the rights of the merchants to make a profit? He does not!

Many years later (in 1773) Wesley has occasion to investigate an insurrection in Ireland. Here things had not been as nonviolent as in Sligo. Having heard about this insurrection (probably in the London press), Wesley's indefatigable curiosity leads him to investigate the situation when he is in the neighborhood. In consequence, we get the following report and commentary.

> When I came to Belfast, I learned the real cause of the late insurrections in this neighbourhood. Lord Donegal, the proprietor of almost the whole country, came hither to give his tenants new leases. But when they came, they found two merchants of the

town had taken their farms over their heads; so that multitudes of them, with their wives and children, were turned out to the wide world. It is no wonder that, as their lives were now bitter to them, they should fly out as they did. It is rather a wonder that they did not go much farther. And if they had, who would have been most at fault? Those who were without home, without money, without food for themselves and families? Or those who drove them to this extremity? (*Journal*, June 15, 1773, III:499)

Here the economic oppression of the poor by wealthy merchants and landlords produces in Wesley what can only be termed a sympathy for insurrection. He does not here rebuke the poor for rising up against their oppressors, nor does he take refuge in an abstract denunciation of violence, as much as he abhorred violence in any form. Rather he makes clear that those who are guilty of the violence of an insurrection are those who, by oppressing the poor, drive them to this extreme. Whatever may be the case with Marxist theory, the protagonists of liberation theology contend for no more than this.[10]

Conclusion

We have seen that Wesley's demystification of wealth and his resulting solidarity with the poor enable him to see practices that to others appear innocuous as forces that oppress the poor and must, therefore, be denounced as unjust. This denunciation of injustice takes the form of an attack on the powerful who exploit the poor in Wesley's own society as well as an exposure of the oppressive structures of colonialism and slavery. Wesley has also shown a willingness to join in coalition with those who, on other than strictly Methodist principles, also oppose injustice. Indeed, his experience with the poor leads him to apply his view of human rights in such a way as to open the door to a solidarity with the oppressed that accepts their right to rebel against their oppression.

To be sure, Wesley does not anticipate all the work that would be necessary to develop a theology of liberation applicable to the altered circumstances in which we, and the world's poor, now live. A reading of Wesley does not absolve us from the theological and ethical tasks that confront any attempt at faithful witness today. But Wesley does provide us with a provocation to take up this task in our own day with something of the same energy and urgency that he exhibited in his. As he was always prepared to admit, Wesley made many errors of judgment in his own work. So will we. His thought is not perfect, but it is a serviceable instrument in the struggle to witness to the inbreaking of the divine reign of justice. That is all we can ask, either of him or of ourselves.

CHAPTER FIVE

STEWARDSHIP: THE REDISTRIBUTION OF WEALTH

In the nature of the case, the protest against injustice is a negative enterprise. In this chapter we turn to Wesley's positive understanding of economic and, therefore, social responsibility. The question here is whether Wesley envisions a manner of establishing economic justice that goes beyond the work of assisting the poor in their affliction or denouncing those groups and structures that occasion, and benefit from, that affliction.

To put the matter a bit differently, if the life of faith entails a critique of existing economic arrangements so as both to prevent faith from falling into the traps of prosperity and to enable the faithful to commit themselves to the welfare of the poor, then what are the positive values inherent in faith that may produce a different—indeed fundamentally different—set of economic relationships and values? Does faith itself entail a counter economics that provides a real alternative to the given structure so productive of human affliction and spiritual jeopardy? Is there an evangelical economics? Can economics be made the theme of a specifically theological discourse?

What we are looking for is not Wesley's advice about capitalism and socialism as opposing secular systems of economic life, but for Wesley's attempt as a practical theologian to develop an understanding and practice of economics based on the same theological principles that govern his reflection on the Christian life generally.

Certainly Wesley was no believer in the sort of separation between the religious and the secular that would leave the latter free of the transforming effects of grace. He supposed that a revival of scriptural Christianity would indeed transform the life of the nation, and ultimately of the earth. But it could have such a result only if conversion and holiness really did necessarily transform "secular" relations and institutions as well. Thus he writes in one of his sermons:

> If a man pursues his business, that he may raise himself to a state of figure and riches in the world, he is no longer serving God in his employment. . . . For vain and earthly designs are no more allowable in our employments, than in our alms and devotions. ("Sermon on the Mount, Discourse VIII," V:361)

That is, a Christian cannot engage in economic activity on the basis of economic motives![1] The God-centeredness of faith must invade this sphere and lay claim to it just as it does the sphere of our religious life. Wesley is clearly no advocate of a two kingdoms theory.

What is at stake in Wesley's view of stewardship is nothing less than the theological critique of one of the most basic presuppositions of modern Western society, that of "private" property. As developed and applied by Wesley, the idea of stewardship puts property in a theological context and so challenges some of the most fundamental presuppositions of consumer capitalism. This position may come as something of a surprise to those who suppose that Protestantism is the bulwark of capitalism or that evangelical Christianity, even in its specifically Wesleyan form, can somehow be made the apologist for "economic democracy." Accordingly, it will be necessary to explain Wesley's view with some care.

STEWARDSHIP VERSUS OWNERSHIP

In his *Journal,* Wesley reports an encounter with one who was apparently a precursor of the "gospel" of wealth:

I had a conversation with an ingenious man who proved to a demonstration, that it was the duty of every man that could, to be "clothed in purple and fine linen," and to "fare sumptuously every day;" and that he would do abundantly more good hereby than he could do by "feeding the hungry and clothing the naked." O the depth of human understanding! What may not a man believe *if he will?* (Jan. 21, 1767, III:271)

We could easily enough supply the man's arguments, since they are the staple of contemporary political propaganda: It is good for the economy. It employs people. It gives them something to strive for, and so on. Yet, Wesley finds it frankly incredible that persons of sense could persuade themselves of this sort of superstition. (But then, as Wesley was fond of saying, a person who will not believe the Bible will believe anything.)

From Wesley's point of view the fallacies in this position are numerous, but the chief among them has to do with the way it leaves God out of the picture. It begins by imagining that we could approach economics as if there were no God. Wesley would be just as ready to leave economics to the free interchange of the marketplace as he would be to turn over the care of souls to psychologists.

From Wesley's point of view, God is the Creator of heaven and earth and is, moreover, the source of that bounty of the earth that is the basis of human prosperity. Since economics deals with the relationships governing the acquisition and use of that same bounty, it is indeed the fool who in economic theory or practice says that there is no God. This practical atheism pretends to own what it in fact receives from the hand of a merciful creator. But there is only one Owner, just as there is only one Creator. In his sermon "On Worldly Folly," Wesley responds to the rich man who has "much goods" and wonders what he is to do with *his* possessions:

Thou no longer talkest of *thy* goods, or *thy* fruits, knowing they are not thine, but God's. The earth is the Lord's, and the fulness thereof: He is the Proprietor of heaven and earth. He cannot divest himself of his glory; he must be the Lord, the possessor, of all that is. Only he hath left a portion of his goods in thy hands, for such uses as he has specified. ("On Worldly Folly," VII:308-9)

What, then, becomes of the claim to property? Wesley finds the very idea astonishing. To the same figure of the parable, when he objects that he can do as he pleases with his own property, his own fruits, Wesley replies: "*My* fruits! They are as much thine as the clouds that fly over thy head! As much as the winds that blow around thee" (Ibid., VII:306). Again, he says in a different sermon: "Nay, may I not do what I will with *my own*? Here lies the ground of your mistake. It is not your *own*. It cannot be, unless you are Lord of heaven and earth" ("The Danger of Increasing Riches," VII:362).

Nor is Wesley at all averse to using this same polemic against a real, as opposed to a fictional, rich man. Therefore, Wesley writes to one of his many correspondents:

> As to yourself, you are not the proprietor of any thing; no, not of one shilling in the world. You are only a steward of what another entrusts you with, to be laid out, not according to your will, but his. (*Journal,* Oct. 28, 1754, II:319)

That God is the Creator and Lord means that God alone can truly be said to be the owner or proprietor of created things. To render unto God what belongs to God, as Wesley at least briefly saw, means rendering to God "all we are, and all we have" ("The Danger of Increasing Riches," VII:361).[2]

Taking the view that God alone can properly be said to own anything means that our own relationship to the things of the world is an indirect one. We have them only as we receive them from God. It is commonly said that this is true for ourselves as well, that we owe our lives to God, or that our souls belong to God. But it quickly becomes obvious that this is not taken seriously when, having claimed that we belong to God, we nevertheless insist on our property rights to something less important, but more palpable, like our money or our house. Wesley wants to maintain both the one and the other. We belong to God and so does our "property."

On this basis, Wesley could either say that we are "debtors" to God in the sense that we ought to be thankful, or he could use the image that is more common in the Gospels, that of stewards.

He chooses the second since it makes clear that God has given us instructions about how to use what we have received.

This is a crucial choice, for saying that we are debtors very easily results in setting up a relationship of exchange, in which God gives us gifts (houses, land, a bank account, and so on) and we give God—thanks! This is a pretty good exchange, since the thanks cost us nothing (except, perhaps, attending church service as the appropriate occasion to give thanks). We are then free to do as we please with what is now ours—all the more so if we pay the "guilt tax" of a tithe to the church. But, of course, such a view pretends that God has given no particular instructions about the use of these goods. It amounts to a sort of economic Deism. God gives us the gifts and then quietly retires from the scene. Wesley was not a Deist. Whatever may be the case with a debtor, Wesley writes:

> It is not so with a steward; he is not at liberty to use what is lodged in his hands as *he* pleases, but as his Master pleases. He has no right to dispose of anything which is in his hands, but according to the will of his Lord. For he is not the proprietor of any of these things, but barely entrusted with them by another; and entrusted on express condition,—that he shall dispose of all as his Master orders. Now, this is exactly the case of every man, with relation to God. We are not at liberty to use what he has lodged in our hands as *we* please, but as he pleases who alone is the possessor of heaven and earth, and the Lord of every creature. We have no right to dispose of anything we have, but according to his will, seeing we are not proprietors of any of these things. . . . And he entrusts us with them on this express condition,—that we use them only as our Master's goods, and according to the particular directions which he has given us in his word. ("The Good Steward," VI:137)

Wesley's view with respect to goods is entirely congruent with the basic structure of his theology as a whole. Just as he was not a Deist, so also he was not a Lutheran—that is, he did not suppose that grace was given in such a way that there were no expectations with respect to the behavior of the recipient. Not "faith alone," but "faith working by love," was his slogan. God's gift of grace comes with God's demand of obedience, that we use that grace in such a way as to grow more and more into the likeness of God. It is just so with the gifts of the earth's bounty. We receive them with the expectation, nay, the command that we employ them in a particular way. Wesley was well aware of the dangers of a cheap grace. He was also on guard against a cheap providence.

The image of the steward is not, then, a harmless homiletical device. It is a critical blow to the economic atheism and economic deism that legitimate the existing economic arrangements and protect them against the demands of the gospel.

THE CLAIM OF THE POOR

What, then, is the demand of the gospel with respect to worldly goods? What are the Proprietor's instructions? Here we must distinguish between Wesley's basic view and his somewhat accomodationist attempt to promote this view among his societies. One finds the latter in the sermon "On the Use of Money," with its threefold rule to "gain all you can, save all you can, and give all you can." We will return to this sermon later, when we consider why Wesley failed to persuade Methodists to undertake the evangelical economics he called for.

Again, what are the Proprietor's intentions or instructions? In reply to the objection that one can afford to use his or her money for some extravagance, Wesley writes:

Perhaps you say you can now *afford* the expense. This is the quintessence of nonsense. Who gave you this addition to your fortune; or (to speak properly) *lent* it to you? To speak more properly still, who lodged it for a time in your hands as his stewards; informing you at the same time for what purposes he entrusted you with it? And can you *afford* to waste your Lord's goods? . . . Away with this vile, diabolical cant! . . . This *affording* to rob God is the very cant of hell. Do not you know that God entrusted you with that money (all above what buys necessaries for your families) to feed the hungry, to clothe the naked, to help the stranger, the widow, the fatherless; and, indeed, as far as it will go, to relieve the wants of all mankind? ("The Danger of Increasing Riches," VII:360)

The very basis of a consumer ethos, the basic structure of our societies, Wesley describes as "the very cant of hell."

But beyond this we have here the indication of the positive command of the Proprietor: "Feed the hungry, clothe the naked, help the stranger, the widow, the fatherless . . . relieve the wants of all mankind." This is a tall order, but it is, in Wesley's view, the only justification for having goods in the first place. In this way, Wesley is able to give limited place to the notion that material prosperity is the gift of divine providence, while at the same time pointing out the way to escape the snare of riches, so destructive of the life and the community of faith (see chap. 2).

Wesley is aware that the importance of escaping the snare of riches, the temptation to "lay up treasures on earth," is not widely recognized. Indeed, the community of faith seems entirely oblivious to this teaching. He writes:

> They have read or heard these words an hundred times, and yet never suspect that they are themselves condemned thereby, any more than by those which forbid parents to offer up their sons or daughters to Moloch. O that God would speak to those miserable self-deceivers with his own voice, his mighty voice; that they may at last awake out of the snare of the devil, and the scales may fall from their eyes! ("Sermon on the Mount, Discourse VIII," V:366)

But far more is at stake here than a means of escaping the snare of riches. The demystification of wealth and power opens the way to a solidarity with the poor, which takes their welfare to be the litmus test of ecclesial and even governmental activity. Thus it should not be surprising that Wesley applies his principle of solidarity with the poor as the general test of all economic activity.

> You may consider yourself as one in whose hands the Proprietor of heaven and earth, and all things therein, has lodged a part of his goods, to be disposed of according to his direction. And his direction is, that you should look upon yourself as one of a certain number of indigent persons, who are to be provided for out of that portion of his goods wherewith you are entrusted." ("The More Excellent Way," VII:36)

The very basis, then, of our economic relations is this community of the poor. It is as one of these that we are to conduct ourselves, distributing to each according to need. Of course, this solidarity presupposes the practice of that visitation whereby we become concretely aware of the needs of the poor and have our hearts and minds transformed thereby. It is then that we may, in other than the sentimental terms of Marie Antoinette, consider ourselves "as one of a certain number of indigent persons."

It is on the basis of this solidarity that it becomes clear what we are to do.

> What shalt thou do? Why, are not those at the door whom God hath appointed to receive what thou canst spare? What shalt thou do? Why, *disperse* abroad, and give to the poor. Feed the hungry. Clothe the naked. Be a father to the fatherless, and a husband to the widow. ("On Worldly Folly," VII:306)

Again, he writes:

> What shall I do? . . . Do good. Do all the good thou canst. Let thy plenty supply thy neighbour's wants; and thou wilt never want something to do. Canst thou find none that need the necessaries of life, that are pinched with cold or hunger; none that have not raiment to put on, or a place where to lay their head; none that are wasted with pining sickness; none that are languishing in prison? If you duly considered our Lord's words, "The poor have you always with you," you would no more ask, "What shall I do?" (Ibid., VII:307)

The questions "Are there not those at the door?" and "Canst thou find none. . . ?" make clear the important connection between effective stewardship and the practice of concrete solidarity through visitation. It is not likely that we will even be aware of these needs so long as we wrap ourselves in the protective cocoon of studied ignorance of the plight of the poor.

But the existence of the marginalized, whether as hungry, sick, or imprisoned, provides us with the concrete norm of our action. Thus Wesley understands the saying "the poor you have with you always" in its true, evangelical sense. The norm of our fidelity to Christ is the attitude and action we take toward the poor. Thus Wesley represents the interrogation of final judgment as follows:

> In what manner didst thou employ that comprehensive talent, money? . . . not squandering it away in vain expenses,—the same as throwing it into the sea? not hoarding it up to leave behind thee,—the same as burying it in the earth? but first supplying thy own reasonable wants, together with those of thy family; then restoring the remainder to me, through the poor, whom I had appointed to receive it; looking upon thyself as only one of that number of poor, whose wants were to be supplied out of that part of my substance which I had placed in thy hands for this purpose. . . ? Wast thou accordingly a general benefactor to mankind? feeding the hungry, clothing the naked, comforting the sick, assisting the stranger, relieving the afflicted? ("The Good Steward," VI:146; see also "The Great Assize," V:171-85)

Wesley then takes with full seriousness the judgment of the parable of Matthew 25:31-46, which gives orientation to his determination of the character of true stewardship.

We may now see how utterly different from common understandings of stewardship is Wesley's development of this idea, for in our day the term is used almost exclusively to raise money for the church. When our churches have stewardship campaigns, they focus on the importance of subscribing to the ecclesial budget. If it is said in the taking of a collection or an offering that this is returning to God a portion of what we have received, then the meaning of the offering is that we give to God by giving to the church. And this is precisely what Wesley does not mean by stewardship. For Wesley, stewardship means giving to the poor—period. *We give to God not by giving to the church, but by giving to the poor.* Stewardship is not a prolongation of the Temple tax; it is the practice of solidarity with the poor.[3]

So accustomed have we become to the distortion of the notion of stewardship that it may help to hear Wesley on this topic again. In the last quotation above, he had God saying, "Restoring to me, through the poor. . . . " In other sermons, he makes a similar point:

Give to the poor with a single eye, with an upright heart, and write, "So much given to God. . . .

. . . Be a steward, a faithful and wise steward, of God and of the poor. ("Sermon on the Mount, Discourse VIII," V:376, 377)

THE MEANING OF WEALTH

It is the view of Wesley that what we have is due to the poor, that the proprietor of all gives instruction to "feed the hungry." In order to see even more clearly what is at stake here, it is important to understand what we may call Wesley's theory of "surplus value." We have already encountered phrases like "whatever you can spare" and "give all you can." But what precise meaning does Wesley attribute to these limitations?

We should note that two things are at stake here: the surplus that brings us into the situation of spiritual danger represented by "riches," and the surplus that we are instructed to disperse abroad to the poor. As it happens, these coincide in Wesley's thought, as is already tolerably clear from Wesley's references to what we can or cannot afford to squander. Wesley is careful to define wealth on several occasions because he is aware of the attempted dodge, "but I'm not wealthy like so-and-so is wealthy." In his 1790 sermon "On the Danger of Increasing Riches," Wesley writes:

A person of note, hearing a sermon preached upon this subject several years since, between surprise and indignation broke out aloud, "Why does he talk about riches here? There is no rich man at Whitehaven, but Sir James L——r." And it is true, there was none but he that had forty thousand pounds a year, and some millions in ready money. But a man may be rich that has not a hundred a year, nor even one thousand pounds in cash. Whosoever has food to eat, and raiment to put on, with something over, is rich. *Whoever has the necessaries and conveniences of life for himself and his family, and a little to spare for them that have not, is properly a rich man.* (VII:355-56, italics added)

Wesley is consistent in using this definition:

By riches I mean, not thousands of pounds, but any more than will procure the conveniences of life. Thus I account him a rich man who has food and raiment for himself and his family, without running into debt, and something over. ("The Wisdom of God's Counsels," VI:331)

And he says in the earlier sermon, to which the first quote in this paragraph may have been a reference, that "whoever has sufficient food to eat, and raiment to put on, and a place where to lay his head, and something over, is *rich*" ("The Danger of Riches," VII:3). Riches, wealth, or surplus, then, amounts to whatever we have beyond what is necessary to live on (see also "Sermon on the Mount, Discourse VIII," V:367-68).

Now to a society awash in the values of mercantile capitalism, let alone consumer capitalism, this definition of wealth or surplus seems extreme. But it can only seem extreme if we are not acquainted with, or are blinded to the point of view of, the poor. As we have already seen, this point of view is normative for Wesley. From the point of view of the poor, anything more than adequate food, decent clothes, and shelter is wealth. If we consider ourselves "as one of a certain number of indigent persons," as Wesley said, then we will have a truer view of what is excess or surplus. Thus Wesley's advice depends for its intelligibility on the practice of solidarity:

Be a steward . . . of God and the poor; differing from them in these two circumstances only,—that your wants are first supplied, out of the portion of your Lord's goods which remains in your hands; and, that you have the blessedness of giving. ("Sermon on the Mount, Discourse VIII," V:377)

Only on the basis of a practice of solidarity is it possible to give concrete meaning to this instruction.

But on the basis of such a practice it becomes clear what it is that we owe to the poor. And what we owe is not some portion of this surplus, say a tithe, but *all*.[4] Thus Wesley, in commenting on the saying of Jesus, "except your righteousness exceed that of the scribes and Pharisees," inquires which of his hearers gives a fifth of their income (the Pharasaic proportion) to "God and the poor" ("Sermon on the Mount, Discourse V," V:324). And in his sermon on "The Danger of Increasing Riches," he commended the example of Zaccheus to the rich in that he gave half to the poor and vowed to restore fourfold to any he had wronged (VII:358). But in general the view was that by distributing all the surplus over what was necessary for health and holiness the Christian would effectually give all. Thus Wesley could inquire of the rich: "Are you not increasing in goods, laying up treasures on earth; instead of restoring to God in the poor, not so much, or so much, but all that you can spare?" ("On God's Vineyard," VII:212; see also "The Danger of Increasing Riches," VII:361).

PROPERTY AS THEFT

On the basis of his view of surplus wealth, Wesley completely undermines the conventional notion of private property. Indeed, for Wesley, the accumulation of property must be viewed concretely as theft! This comes to the fore when Wesley talks about any sort of needless expense, especially for clothes. This example of needless expense seems to have been suggested to him by the strictures of the Anglican Homily "Against Excess of Apparel,"[5] which notes:

> . . . that in abundance and plentie of all things, we yet complaine of want and penurie, while one man spendeth that which might serve a multitude, and no man distributeth of the abundance which [he] hath received, all men excessively waste that which should serve to supply the necessities of others. (p. 105)

> He that in abundance and plenty of apparel hideth his face from him that is naked, despitheth his owne flesh. (p. 106)

It particularly warns against the tendency of wealthy women "to devise new fashions to feede thy pride with, to spend so much upon thy carkasse, that thou and thy husband are compelled to robbe the poore" (p. 108). In Wesley's own time this teaching was especially emphasized by the Quakers and Moravians, whose example he frequently commended. Wesley instructs the Quakers, who seemed to have forgotten the meaning of their own policy regarding plainness of dress:

Surely you cannot be ignorant, that the sinfulness of fine apparel lies chiefly in the expensiveness: *In that it is robbing God and the poor;* it is defrauding the fatherless and widow; it is wasting the food of the hungry, and withholding his raiment from the naked to consume it on our own lusts. (*A Farther Appeal to Men of Reason and Religion,* VIII:186, italics added)

And he addresses his own societies in a similar manner:

Many of your brethren, beloved of God, have not food to eat; they have not raiment to put on; they have not a place where to lay their head. And why are they thus distressed? Because *you* impiously, unjustly, and cruelly detain from them what your Master and theirs lodges in *your* hands on purpose to supply *their* wants. ("The Causes of the Inefficacy of Christianity," VII:286)

Wesley does not hesitate to use strong language here. In his sermon "On Dress," for example, he is especially severe.

The more you lay out on your own apparel, the less you have left to clothe the naked, to feed the hungry, to lodge the strangers, to relieve those that are sick and in prison, and to lessen the numberless afflictions to which we are exposed in this vale of tears. . . . Every shilling which you save from your own apparel, you may expend in clothing the naked, and relieving the various necessities of the poor, whom ye "have always with you." Therefore, every shilling which you needlessly spend on your apparel is, in effect, *stolen from God and the poor!* . . .
. . . When you are laying out that money in costly apparel which you could have otherwise spared for the poor, you thereby deprive them of what God, the proprietor of all, had lodged in your hands for their use. If so, what you put upon yourself, you are, in effect tearing from the back of the naked; as the costly and delicate food which you eat, you are snatching from the mouth of the hungry. (VII:20, italics added; see also "Advice to Methodists on Dress," XI:470-71; and *A Farther Appeal,* VII:190)

The conclusion that needless expense, that the accumulation or expenditure of wealth, is theft has syllogistic force, given Wesley's view of stewardship. Unfortunately, we may be put off by the emphasis here on dress, thinking that it is a mere legalistic conceit. But it is not that at all. Wesley is not here propounding yet another in a set of detailed instructions concerning Methodist discipline. He is, rather, illustrating one of the basic principles of an evangelical economics that takes solidarity with the poor as its criterion. Of whatever sort of "consumerism," it follows that *"everything about thee which cost more than Christian duty required thee to lay out is the blood of the poor"* ("On Dress," VII:21, italics added).

From all of this it follows that when we engage in what are presumably "normal" economic practices, we make ourselves responsible for the suffering that we might otherwise have alleviated.[6] This, then, supplies Wesley with another reason for supposing that one who is rich (remember what that means according to Wesley's definition) is in such imminent danger of hell.

> May not this be another reason why rich men shall so hardly enter into the kingdom of heaven? A vast majority of them are under a curse, under the peculiar curse of God; inasmuch as, in the general tenor of their lives, *they are not only robbing God,* continually embezzling and wasting their Lord's goods, and, by that very means, corrupting their own souls, but *also robbing the poor, the hungry, the naked;* wronging the widow and the fatherless; and making themselves accountable for all the want, affliction, and distress which they may but do not remove. Yea, doth not the blood of all those who perish for want of what they either lay up, or lay out needlessly, cry out against them from the earth? ("Sermon on the Mount, Discourse VIII," V:375, italics added)

The blood of the poor, then, is on the heads of any who treat material things as if they were private property! The habits of accumulation and expenditure, which go hand in hand with the system of private property and our ethos of consumer capitalism, make us directly culpable of the deaths of those who perish for want of that which we hoard and waste.

Wesley's view is clearly a radical departure from the common sense of our churches. When do we ever hear that accommodation to the mores of a consumer society makes of us nothing less than thieves and murderers? We imagine that a Christian economics entails little more than being careful not to break the law. But to take seriously the prohibition of "laying up treasure on earth"? That is quite different! Wesley's complaint of two hundred years ago still rings true:

> There are many who neither rob nor steal; and some who will not defraud their neighbour; nay, who will not gain either by his ignorance or necessity. But this is quite another point. Even these do not scruple the thing, but the manner of it. They do not scruple the "laying up treasures upon earth;" but the laying them up by dishonesty. They do not start at disobeying Christ, but at a branch of heathen morality. So that even these honest men do no more obey this command than a highwayman or a house-breaker. Nay, they never designed to obey it. From their youth up, it never entered into their thoughts. They were bred up by their Christian parents, masters, and friends, without any instruction at all concerning it; unless it were this,—to break it as soon and as much as they could, and to continue breaking it to their lives' end. ("Sermon on the Mount, Discourse VIII," V:366)

It was, as we shall see, Wesley's hope that Methodism might alter this. But that hope remains unrealized.

The understanding of property as theft and of consumption as culpability for the blood of the poor follows with logical rigor from Wesley's view of stewardship. It cannot be dismissed as trifling legalism without also dismissing his basic theological commitments (see chap. 7). Although it is often said that Wesley was not a systematic thinker, it should be clear that the essential ingredients of his evangelical economics have a tight logical form, that here at least he does have a system.

THE PENTECOSTAL COMMUNITY

On the basis of this coherent view, Wesley was able to recognize the importance of the description of the early Christian community in Acts 2:41-47 and 4:32-37. In the following citation from Wesley's sermon on "The Mystery of Iniquity," we may both refresh our memories about that description and see what Wesley makes of it.

111

9. In order clearly to see how they [the Christians at Pentecost] were already saved, we need only observe the short account of them which is recorded in the latter part of the second and in fourth chapter. "They continued steadfastly in the Apostles' doctrine, and in the fellowship, and in the breaking of bread, and in the prayers:" That is, they were daily taught by the Apostles, and had all things common, and daily received the Lord's supper, and attended all the public service. (ii. 42) "And all that believed were together, and had all things common; and sold their possessions, and parted them to all men, as every man had need." (ii. 44, 45) And again: "The multitude of them that believed," now greatly increased, "were of one heart and of one soul: Neither said any of them that aught of the things which he possessed was his own; but they had all things common." (iv. 32) And yet again: "Great grace was upon them all. Neither was there among them that lacked: For as many as were possessors of lands or houses sold them, and brought the prices of the things that were sold, and laid them at the Apostles' feet: And distribution was made unto every man according as he had need." (Verses 33–35)

10. But here a question will naturally occur: "How came they to act thus, to have all things in common, seeing we do not read of any positive command to do this?" I answer, there needed no outward command: The command was written upon their hearts. It naturally and necessarily resulted from the degree of love which they enjoyed. Observe! "They were of one heart, and of one soul:" And not so much as one (so the words run) said, (they could not, while their hearts so overflowed with love,) "that any of the things which he possessed was his own." And wheresoever the same cause shall prevail, the same effect will naturally follow. ("The Mystery of Iniquity," VI:255-56)

It was, of course, Wesley's intent to foment the "cause" that would have this effect.

This vision of Christian communalism had a strange history in Wesley's thought. In an explanation of his reasons for going to Georgia, Wesley speaks first, as was his wont in those early days, of the ways in which this would benefit his own soul. Among the benefits he expected to derive was the possibility of actualizing this vision by living among the Indians.

The same faithfulness I hope to show, through His grace, in dispensing the rest of my Master's goods, if it please him to send me to those [Native Americans] who, like his first followers, have all things common. What a guard is here against that root of evil, the love of money, and all the vile attractions that spring from it! One in this glorious state, and perhaps none but he, may see the height and depth of the privilege of the first Christians, "as poor, yet making many rich; as having nothing, yet possessing all things." (Letter to a Friend, Oct. 10, 1735, XII:39.)[7]

Despite the attraction this vision held for Wesley, it plays almost no role in his first series of sermons. It does come into play as the culmination of the description of "personal holiness" in the very important sermon "Scriptural Christianity" (V:41-42). It appears again for the first time in his *Explanatory Notes Upon the New Testament* and subsequently plays an important role in the later sermons. It may be that in the time in which he was launching the Methodist revival he was cautious about unnecessarily raising the charge of enthusiasm and so muted the radical vision of a Christian community of property.[8] In any case, Wesley does come again to give this vision a place of importance in his social ethic as a natural consequence of the view of stewardship that he has developed.

Wesley supposes that the Methodist movement will not only produce a spread of the gospel throughout the earth but also, and therefore, bring in the kind of primitive commun(al)ist[9] society described in Acts 2 and 4. Therefore, speaking of the spread of the gospel by Methodism, he writes:

The natural, necessary consequence of this will be the same as it was in the beginning of the Christian Church: "None of them will say, that aught of the things which he possesses is his own; but they will have all things common. Neither will there be any among them that want: For as many as are possessed of lands or houses will sell them; and distribution will be made to every man, according as he has need." ("The General Spread of the Gospel," VI:284)

From this actualization of Christian identity would come the conversion of persons of other faiths to Christianity, for they would no longer have the excuse of Christian misconduct to prevent the reception of the gospel (see "The General Spread of the Gospel," VI:285-87). It is noteworthy that Wesley believed that the adherents of other faiths would be converted by the Christian practice of a pentecostal community of property and redistribution of wealth. This is a mission strategy that may have been overlooked by denominational mission boards! It seems scarcely more likely to be adopted by so-called evangelical groups that are little more than apologists for the ethos of pious capitalism. For Wesley, in any case, scriptural holiness entails the immitation of the pentecostal community.

While there are other texts that are relevant here, the *Explanatory Notes Upon the New Testament* provide important additional evidence of the importance of this view to Wesley.[10] He certainly does not share, for example, the view so dear to some of his commentators, that the example of the pentecostal community was either a failed experiment or one that was limited in applicability to the early Church.[11]

Wesley was prepared to allow the fact that some of the extraordinary gifts of the Spirit (like speaking in tongues) characterized the experience of only the first-century community. But this could not apply to the example of the economic practices of the pentecostal community, since those practices were not an expression of the extraordinary, but the ordinary working of the Spirit. He writes:

> And if the whole church had continued in this spirit, this usage must have continued through all the ages. To affirm, therefore, that Christ did not design it should continue, is neither more nor less than to affirm that Christ did not design this measure of love should continue. (*Explanatory Notes*, Note to Acts 2:45)

Indeed the affirmation that Christ did not intend a full measure of love to continue in his church would be to reject Wesleyan doctrine root and branch.

Wesley repeats this insistence on the continuing pertinence of the pentecostal example in his note to Acts 4:32: "So long as that truly Christian love continued, they could not but *have all things in common.*" And again, noting the connection between the presence of grace and the abolition of want through the practice of community of property and redistribution of wealth, Wesley insists:

And it [the abolition of want through the practice of commun(al)ism] was the immediate, necessary consequence of it [grace]; yea, and must be, to the end of the world. In all ages and nations, the same cause, the same degree of grace, could not but, in like circumstances, produce the same effect.

"In all ages and nations"—thus does Wesley dismiss the idea of the limited relevance of the example of the pentecostal community.

If any doubt remained that Wesley understood that what is at stake here is something utterly opposed to the idea of private property, this is dispelled by his comment on the story of Ananias and Sapphira. We have already seen that for Wesley this story functions in relation to the church in the same way as the story of Adam and Eve functions in relation to humanity in general: It is the story of the Fall. Here in his *Notes* Wesley shows that this has to do precisely with the introduction of private property: "This was the first attempt to bring propriety of goods into the Christian church" (Acts 5:3). Wesley goes so far as to defend this hypothesis by insisting that Ananias and Sapphira were, at the time, only candidates for church membership. Accordingly, Peter's remark that they were free not to sell or not to donate all the proceeds of the sale (Acts 5:4) was the same as saying that they were still free not to be Christians. Contradiction only arises when they profess to be Christians while refusing to participate fully in the pentecostal community of goods. Thus Wesley comments on Acts 5:1: *"But a certain man named Ananias.*—It is certain, not a believer; for all that believed 'were of one heart and of one soul.' Probably not baptized; but intending now to offer himself for baptism." And on Acts 5:4 he comments:

It is true, "whosoever" among the Christians, not one excepted, "had houses or lands sold them, and laid the price at the feet of the apostles:" but it was in his own choice to be a Christian or not, and consequently, either to sell his land or keep it. *And when it was sold*

115

was it not in thy power. . . . . For it does not appear that he [professed himself a Christian when he sold it."

And finally, in his note to Acts 5:12-3, he writes: *"None of the rest*—No formalists or hypocrites. *Durst join themselves*—In outward show only, like Ananias and Sapphira." Wesley was clearly already aware of the evasion of the example of the pentecostal community made possible by a different reading of Acts, and he took steps to counter it. The attempt on the part of some interpreters to suppress Wesley's radicalism at this point can only be described as disingenuous.[12]

CONCLUSION

We have seen that Wesley's understanding of stewardship is a frontal assault on the principles of capitalism and the ethos of accumulation and consumption of wealth. He believed that the gospel entailed such a radical change of behavior that its spread would result in the actualization of a new society in which injustice was abolished. If we take seriously the primitive communist, or communalist, ideal as one way of characterizing the aim of the spread of scriptural holiness, then we can also see that Wesley had a rather sophisticated strategy to accomplish that end. He realized that the rich were not promising candidates for such a message. They felt they had too much to lose, were too caught in the snare of riches. Therefore, the message must be directed to the poor, the dispossessed, the marginalized. And these would be organized as disciplined cadres, steeped in the point of view (ideology) that entailed these values and held together by strict discipline. The privileged classes, meanwhile, would be confronted with a relentless call to repentance of their complicity in the snares of wealth and the practice of injustice, in the hope that some of these at least would respond. In this way would be launched an international movement whose aim would be the realization within a relatively short period of time of a transformed social, economic, and world order.

Wesley's view of stewardship is a blow at the root of the

economics of greed, which continues to dominate our planet. For Wesley, the only legitimate claim to the earth's resources is based not on industry or capital or enterprise or labor, but on the needs of our neighbor. This is the heart of evangelical economics.

CHAPTER SIX

ACTUALIZATION AND CONTROVERSY

I n the previous chapter we saw that Wesley's view of stewardship leads him to a radical reversal of the values of private property and of the accumulation and consumption of wealth. This leads to a pentecostal "communism" or "communalism," which he believed to be the necessary result of scriptural holiness. But for Wesley it would not be appropriate to permit this to remain in the sphere of the abstract or visionary. It must be practiced. Indeed Wesley develops no theory at all except in the crucible of reflected practice. We must accordingly turn to examine some of the ways in which Wesley and (some of) his followers sought to practice this stewardship before considering the polemic of Wesley against those who failed to practice what he both preached and practiced.

PERSONAL EXAMPLE

One of the staples of Methodist hagiographic legend concerns the occasion when, in infancy, Wesley was rescued from the burning parsonage. While the legend dwells on the "brand plucked from burning" theme, Wesley himself offers another and more revealing clue to the meaning of this event. It is that the next day his father found in the smoldering rubble a leaf of a Bible with the legible line: "Go, sell all that thou hast; and take up thy cross, and follow me" ("Remarkable Providence," 1778,

XIII:518). Whatever we may think of this anecdote's historical objectivity, it is clear that Wesley did think that these words had particular relevance for his own life. Although we shall see that he sometimes failed to recognize the general applicability of the command to "sell all," it is clear that his own life-style was governed by the attempt to live without the snare of possessions, to give all to the poor, and so to follow the precepts of the gospel as he understood them.

The development at Oxford of a group determined to actualize the essentials of Christian life was always regarded by Wesley as the founding event of Methodism.[1] This attempt brought upon Wesley and his friends the charge of "singularity," especially with respect to their practice of solidarity with the poor and the style of stewardship that was concomitant thereto. Thus Wesley argued that by letting his hair grow unfashionably long he was able to save money to give to the poor (Letter to Brother Samuel, Nov. 17, 1731, XII:21)! And in reply to university critics, Wesley and his friends developed a rebuttal in the form of a set of questions, which included the following points:

> Whether we can be happy at all hereafter, unless we have, according to our power, "fed the hungry, clothed the naked, visited those that are sick, and in prison;" and made all these actions subservient to a higher purpose, even the saving of souls from death?
>
> . . . Whether, upon the considerations above-mentioned, we may not try to do good to those that are hungry, naked, or sick? In particular, whether, if we know any necessitous family, we may not give them a little food, clothes, or physic, as they want?
>
> . . . Whether we may not contribute, what little we are able, toward having their children clothed and taught to read?
>
> . . . Whether, upon the considerations above-mentioned, we may not try to do good to those that are in prison? In particular, Whether we may not release such well-disposed persons as remain in prison for small sums?
>
> Whether we may not lend smaller sums to those that are of any trade, that they may procure themselves tools and materials to work with? (Letter to Richard Morgan, 1732, used as the "Introductory Letter" to the first Abstract of the *Journal*, 1:9-10)

As we can see, much of the agenda that subsequently was elaborated in Wesley's more mature thought and practice is already embryonically present at this stage. We have already noted that Wesley was drawn to America, at least in part, because of the prospect of practicing the primitive communalism of the Native Americans.[2]

Wesley was especially scrupulous in his use of money when the Methodists became a popular movement, following his return from Georgia. He had to respond, in the early days, to critics who charged that this was somehow a scheme for the enrichment of Wesley himself. In one such response he wrote: "I love money no more than I love the mire in the streets; that I seek it not. And I have it not, any more than suffices for food and raiment, for the plain conveniences of life" (Letter to the Rev. Mr. Downes, IX:108). And Wesley made clear that this was his attempt to live out the plain requirements of his own teaching regarding stewardship:

> All that is contributed or collected in every place is both received and expended by others; nor have I so much as the "beholding thereof with my eyes." And so it will be, till I turn Turk or Pagan. For I look upon all this revenue, be it what it may, as sacred to God and the poor; out of which, if I want anything, I am relieved, even as another poor man. (*A Plain Account of the People Called Methodists*, VIII:268)

Thus Wesley attempts to demonstrate in his own life the meaning of solidarity ("even as another poor man") and of his view of property ("sacred to God and the poor").

A particularly striking instance of Wesley's attempt to employ personal example as a way of inculcating the precepts of his economic ethic is his attempt to encourage abstinence from the drinking of tea.[3] Wesley launched this ill-fated campaign on the presupposition that tea was injurious to the health of some people and with the knowledge that its consumption was injurious to the budgets of the poor.

> If they used English herbs in its stead, (which would cost either nothing, or what is next to nothing,) with the same bread, butter, and milk, they would save just the price of the tea. And hereby they

might not only lessen their pain, but in some degree their poverty too. (Letter to a Friend Concerning Tea, Dec. 10, 1748, XI:505)

Rather than immediately launch a campaign to induce the poor to do what was good for them, Wesley and his friends tried giving up tea themselves, as an example. When, on the basis of this experiment, the plan seemed workable, Wesley turned his attention to those who could "afford" to drink tea. He tells them that whether or not it is prejudicial to their own health they may still gain by leaving off its use, since then "you may have the more wherewith to give bread to the hungry, and raiment to the naked" (Ibid., XI:508) He is able in this case as well to cite his own example:

> I have been enabled hereby to assist, in one year, above fifty poor with food or raiment, whom I must otherwise have left (for I had before begged for them all I could) as hungry and naked as I found them. You may see the good effects in above thirty poor people just now before you, who have been restored to health, through the medicines bought by that money which a single person has saved in this article. (Ibid., XI:513)

He then encourages the Methodists to follow him in this, resolving:

> I will compute this day what I have expended in tea, weekly or yearly. I will immediately enter on cheaper food: And whatever is saved hereby, I will put into the poor-box weekly, to feed the hungry, and to clothe the naked. (Ibid., XI:506)

This is a particularly instructive example, since it helps to give concreteness to the social dimension of Wesley's piety. Wesley's interest in abstinence from tea was motivated by a concern for bodily health and for the welfare of the poor. It is linked to Christian duty by way of the evangelical theme of the good of the neighbor and solidarity with the poor. Unfortunately the distinguishing feature of later, non-Wesleyan piety is the disappearance of the principle of the welfare of the poor as the norm for the evaluation of personal practice.[4]

The idea that Wesley actualized his conceptions of solidarity with the poor and of stewardship as stewardship for God and the poor should not require extensive proof. His own example is too well known. And it was precisely this lived experience with the implementation of these notions that persuaded Wesley, at least, that he was not asking anything impossible of those who joined themselves to him as Methodists. He did not suppose that Scripture placed before us a set of unattainable ideals or impracticable visions, but that it proposed a practical method of living that was suited to those beings who had been created by the same God who gave them instruction concerning how to live and, through grace, the power to live in that way. It was, of course, possible to misunderstand these instructions, so it was necessary to test them (or rather, our understanding of them) by experience. This is what Wesley intended to do with his economic practice. And it was for this reason that personal example could be viewed as a cogent argument.

Into this category falls not only Wesley's own example, but also that of others whom he commended to the attention of his readers. For example, in his *Journal* Wesley commends the example of persons like Mary Cheesebrook (Nov. 22, 1747, II:74) and Sarah Peters (Nov. 13, 1748, II:120) and an unnamed former persecutor of Methodists (Sept. 6, 1757, II:423). Wesley was a tireless gatherer and reporter of the testimonies of Methodists. Many of these had to do with peculiar experiences or with edifying deaths. But the actualization of Wesley's economic principles is not without its testimonies as well. For example, Wesley prints in his *Journal* a long letter from an earnest Methodist. This excerpt will give the idea:

To be short, the expense for myself,—meat, drink, clothes, and washing, is not twenty-eight pounds per annum; so that I have near twenty pounds to return to God in the poor. Now, if every Christian family, while in health, would thus far deny themselves, would twice a week dine on the cheapest food, drink in general herb-tea, faithfully calculate the money saved thereby, and give it to the poor over and above their usual donations, we should then hear no complaining in our streets, but the poor would eat and be satisfied. He that gathered much would have nothing over, and he that gathered little would have no lack. . . . I mentioned this some time ago in a meeting at London, when a brother said, "These are but little things," As I went home, I thought of his words: "Little things!" Is the want of fire, in frost and snow, a little thing? Or the want of food, in a distressed, helpless family? (Nov. 20, 1767, III:306-7)

It is clear that at least one person had understood Wesley and found his advice to be practicable. The reaction of the other Methodist shows quite well the difference in mentality. One thinks in terms of the addition of regulations concerning food and drink. But the Wesleyan thinks of the poor. From the first point of view, these are little things, *adiaphora*. But for the other they are a means of addressing concrete human affliction, both personally and socially. Both are speaking of the same thing, but they are not on the same planet. In Methodism the main arguments have been about the "little things," while the determining question of the poor has faded from center stage.[5]

Wesley sought to demonstrate by both his own example and that of others that the economic ethic he propounded was not an unworkable dream but the plain and practical consequence of "faith working by love." While some could see here nothing but a compulsive legalism, preoccupied with "little things," others clearly caught a truer vision and joined in the practice of solidarity.

COMMUNAL EXAMPLE

But Wesley did not imagine that Christianity was something that could be practiced by isolated individuals. It required community. That is why Wesley found it necessary to found societies in which Christians could "watch over one another in love." And the importance of communal example applied to the principles of Wesley's economic ethic as well. We have already seen that Wesley tried to organize his societies in such a way as to always take into account the priority of the poor.

In some cases this takes the form of joining with Wesley in his attempts to relieve the poor (see *Journal*, 1:309, 451, 458, and passim). More systematically, it takes the form of organizing the societies themselves so that they may be agents for the relief of the poor. Thus Wesley gives this account of the role of stewards:

> They met together at six every Thursday morning; consulted on the business which came before them; sent relief to the sick, as every one had need; and gave the remainder of what had been contributed each week to those who appeared to be in the most pressing want. So that all was concluded within the week; what was brought on Tuesday being constantly expended on Thursday. (*A Plain Account of the People Called Methodists,* VIII:262)

One can scarcely imagine that the principle business of church stewards, trustees, or treasurers would be the sending of relief to the poor, let alone their reaction to being told that nothing was to be saved, but all was to be sent out the same week it came in! Yet, the example was important for Wesley. For himself, for his hearers, and for his societies his rule was: "As it comes, daily or yearly, so let it go: Otherwise you 'lay up treasures upon earth.' And this our Lord as flatly forbids as murder and adultery" ("The More Excellent Way," VII:37). Neither individuals nor communities were to "lay up for themselves treasures on earth" but give it all away to the poor and so (and only so) "lay up treasure in heaven." It is the task of the community of faith to demonstrate by its visible life that the gospel is not an idle dream but a truthful prescription for the transformation of reality.

Accordingly, Wesley was greatly encouraged by the existence of societies in which all the members together practiced the economic ethic he found to be mandated by the gospel. Of one such he writes: "I rode with Mr. Hodges to Neath. Here I found twelve young men, whom I could almost envy. They lived together in one house, and continually gave away whatever they earned above the necessaries of life" (*Journal,* Aug. 18, 1746, II:21).

But Wesley's favorite example was the society of Tetney. An account of this society appears not only appears in his *Journal,* but also in the history of Methodism that he later prepared as a summary of the salient events recorded in the *Journal* proper. Although the famous events of the night at Aldersgate do not make the cut for inclusion in Wesley's *Short History of the People Called Methodists*, the society at Tetney does:

> On Tuesday I examined the little society at Tetney. I have not seen such another in England, no, not to this day [1781, referring to the events of 1747]. In the class-paper (which gives an account of the contribution for the poor), I observed one gave eightpence, often tenpence, a week; another, thirteen, fifteen, or eighteen pence; another, sometimes one, sometimes two shillings. I asked Micah Ekmoor, the Leader, (an Israelite indeed, who now rests from his labour), "How is this? Are you the richest society in England?" He answered, "I suppose not; but as we are all single persons, we have agreed together to give ourselves, and all we have, to God. And we do it gladly, whereby we are able to entertain all the strangers that from time to time come to Tetney, who have often no food to eat, or any friend to give them a lodging. (*A Short History of the People Called Methodists*, XIII:324-25; see also *Journal*, Feb. 24, 1747, II:45-46)

Here at least was an indication that the views of stewardship that Wesley propounded were practicable. But the more melancholy truth is that thirty-four years after encountering this society Wesley could still let stand the observation that he had not encountered another like it. Clearly there were quite impressive testimonies, both individual and communal, to the practice of a countereconomics of the gospel, an evangelical economics. But equally clearly this actualization was an uphill battle, one that Wesley finally lost—though not without a struggle.

COUNTERARGUMENTS

Despite the example of Wesley and some of the other Methodists, the practice of an evangelical economics was by no means widespread in the movement that Wesley led. It seems that many put forward what they thought of as arguments as to the impracticability of this project. Wesley attempted to answer these. Since some of these objections are still heard today, it may be well to rehearse briefly some of them, together with Wesley's responses.

We have already seen the way in which some responded to Wesley's strictures against becoming rich; they compared themselves to the wealthiest persons they knew or had heard of in order to conclude that they were not rich, and so were excused from the requirement to give to the poor or from the dangers that Wesley associated with the accumulation of wealth. Wesley exploded this objection with his definition of wealth, which took the point of view, not of relative degrees of affluence, but of poverty itself. "Think of yourself as one among a certain number of indigent persons," he said ("The More Excellent Way," VII:36). Other subterfuges of like kind were confronted by Wesley.

> But many have found out a way never to be rich, though their substance increase ever so much. It is this: As fast as ever money comes in, they lay it out, either in land, or enlarging their business. By this means, each of these, keeping himself bare of money, can still say, "I am not rich;" yea, though he has ten, twenty, a hundred times more substance than he had some years ago. ("The Danger of Increasing Riches," VII:357)

But Wesley will have none of it. One whose "substance" increases, whether he or she has money or not, is convicted of laying up treasure on earth.

Others maintain that they will do more when they have more. It seems that his fellows at Oxford had tried to persuade Wesley that he should improve his own financial condition before attempting to aid the poor. Wesley was not impressed then (see his letter to his father, June 13, 1733, XII:8), and his later experience with people showed him that it was vain to expect that one who was better off would do better.

> How many have less will when they have more power! Now they have more money, they love it more; when they had little, they did their "diligence gladly to give of that little;" but since they have had much, they are so far from giving plenteously, that they can hardly afford to give at all. (*Address to the Clergy* [1756], X:496)

127

To be sure, the dominical counsel to take no thought for the morrow—even as modified by Wesley in the rule "as it comes in so let it go out"—has always seemed to many the counsel of folly. But not to Wesley:

> "How then must we live? Must we not take care of ourselves and our families?" And this they imagine to be a sufficient reason for continuing in known, wilful sin. They say, and perhaps think, they would serve God now, were it not that they should, by and by, lose their bread. They would prepare for eternity; but they are afraid of wanting the necessaries of life. So they serve the devil for a morsel of bread; they rush into hell for fear of want; they throw away their poor souls, lest they should, some time or other, fall short of what is needful for their bodies! ("Sermon on the Mount, Discourse IX," V:390)

Whatever one may think of this sort of "hell fire and brimstone" as a persuasive device, it is clear that for Wesley the practice of evangelical economics was a matter of ultimate concern.

He was no more gentle to the suggestion that if people didn't consume, then the economy would falter. When this sort of objection was raised to his strictures against costly clothes, Wesley replied:

> I answer, God certainly considered this before ever he gave these commands, And he would never have given them, had he not seen, that, if they were universally observed, men in general would live better than they otherwise could; better in this world, as well as that to come. . . .
>
> If those who do observe them [give to the poor] then a part of what before only served to fat a few rich tradesmen for hell, will suffice to feed and clothe and employ many poor that seek the kingdom of heaven. ("Advice to Methodists, With Regard to Dress," XI:473)

This is certainly a double-edged response. It reminds us that prosperity, as it is normally understood, is not an unmixed blessing. It is indeed the high road to hell. But true prosperity, that which assures that all have the "necessaries" of life, is precisely the aim of a polity that places the welfare of the poor in the place of test, norm, or criterion. Of course, the apologists for consumer capitalism today make much the same argument, only with the difference that they sometimes have the temerity to argue that capitalism is the way to generate so much prosperity that the hungry are fed. Perhaps it is regarded by them as testimony to the efficacy of this approach that only fifteen million children died of poverty last year.

There are inevitably those who will seek to find in the faults of the poor a reason for avoiding their own responsibility. Wesley did not imagine that the poor were perfect (although it was his mission to call them to perfection). But he had too much experience with the poor to believe that they were miserable by their own choice. We have already noted his response to those who claimed that the poor are only so because they are lazy. He well knew the back-breaking industry by which so many of them desperately, and often vainly, sought to keep starvation at bay. Yet, he also encountered those who affirmed that it really did no good to the poor to try to alleviate their misery; it might only confirm them in their "vices," and in any case did not treat the true spiritual problem. He replied: "Whether they will finally be lost or saved, you are expressly commanded to feed the hungry, and clothe the naked. If you can, and do not, whatever becomes of them, you shall go away into everlasting fire" ("Sermon on the Mount, Discourse IV," V:307).

But then as now, a pretended piety is adept at finding some way of wrapping its rebellion against God in the mantle of spirituality. So to those who maintained that the only thing that matters is conversion, that only God can do that, and that if the poor are converted God will supply them with abundant material blessings, Wesley replies:

> Though it is God only changes hearts, yet he generally doeth it by man. It is our part to do all that in us lies, as diligently as if we could change them ourselves, and then to leave the event up to him. God, in answer to their prayers, builds up his children by each other. (Ibid., V:307)

Thus Wesley's synergism served to guard against the sort of pretended piety that, in the name of praising the omnipotence of God, sat on its hands.

These examples of Wesley's attempt to answer objections to his evangelical economics show that he was vitally concerned to persuade his fellow Methodists their relationship to God depended on their practice of these principles. For Wesley, a matter of such ultimate concern was generally expressed in terms of ultimate judgment, of "hell fire and brimstone" as we now say. By this he sought to make clear that our final relation to God depends on our relation to the poor. In this he knew that he had the witness of the Bible on his side. Thus the question of solidarity with the poor was ultimately a question of the authenticity of the Christian's confession of faith.

But these responses to objections do more than provide insight into how seriously Wesley took these questions. They also exhibit specimens of objections that anyone may encounter today. It is true that much has changed in the two centuries that separate us from the time of Wesley, and our theological responses must take this into account. But it is also true that the demands of the gospel retain recognizable shape and that the desire on the part of Christians to say "Lord, Lord," but escape the doing of what is required, persists.

Whatever we may think of Wesley's use of fire and brimstone or his particular way of asserting the authority of Scripture or his emphasis on the law, in one respect his responses are exemplary: They are theological responses. That is, they see and say that the question of what I have been calling an evangelical economics is a theological question, demanding a theological response. It is not *adiaphora*. We can no more leave God out of our economics than we can leave God out of our liturgy.

WESLEY AGAINST THE METHODISTS

In a sense we can say that Wesley was writing essays on the history of Methodism almost before there was such a thing. In the early decades, these were written with the aim of countering the charges of critics "so that the good that is in you not be evil spoken of," as he liked to say (misapplying Rom. 14:16). But in the later years Wesley wrote such sketches as much for the benefit of the Methodists themselves as for the benefit of history. After all, in the later years of his ministry the majority of Methodists had not even been born when he began to preach in the fields and gather people into societies. These reflections on Methodist history are found in his later sermons and essays and provide insight into Wesley's own view of both the promise and the failure of Methodism.

Occasionally these sermonic histories have a slightly triumphalist ring, as in the sermon we have already cited on "The General Spread of the Gospel." In this sermon, Wesley supposed that the renewal of Christianity, launched in England some half century before, must spread throughout Christendom and that the effect of this renewal would be the return to the practice of a pentecostal community of goods and redistribution of wealth, which would prove an irresistible argument for the truth of the gospel to the adherents of other faiths. This would then lead to an end to the dispute among nations, leading to the universal reign not only of justice but also of peace. Such was the scope of Wesley's vision of the inevitable transformation of the social and world order by the grace of God through the instrumentality of the movement of Methodists.[6]

Although this was the vision that Wesley hoped would be realized and committed his considerable energies to realizing, he was aware that this vision was threatened. The threat came not from declining membership or dwindling Sunday school enrollments, nor from diminished influence in the halls of power or groves of academe, nor from a falling off of church extension or shrinking budgets or any of the other things that spread existential *angst* amongst us. It was, rather, that Methodism was suffering from a fatal illness for which no church-growth nostrums could avail. Methodists were entering the middle class and leaving the poor behind.

While this theme is a constant feature of Wesley's warnings concerning individual Methodists, from about 1760 on Wesley increasingly addresses himself to the problem among Methodists as such. Thus we find in 1760 this warning in the *Journal*:

131

On the three following days I spoke severally to the members of the society. As many of them increase in worldly goods, the great danger I apprehend now is, their relapsing into the spirit of the world: And then their religion is but a dream. (*Journal,* Oct. 12-21, 1760, III:23)

These warnings come with increasing frequency and urgency. In 1764 we find, for example:

I gave all our brethren a solemn warning not to love the world, or the things of the world. This is one way whereby Satan will surely endeavour to overthrow the present work of God. Riches swiftly increase on many Methodists, so called: What, but the mighty power of God, can hinder their setting their hearts upon them? And if so, the life of God vanishes away. (*Journal,* July 11, 1764, III:187; see also Oct. 20, 1764, III:200; June 28, 1765, III:227; and so on)

There still remained a faithful remnant whose views Wesley cited with approval to drive home this warning. Thus we find in the *Journal* for 1767 Wesley's quotation of a letter he had received from one of these, together with his response to it:

" . . . I find one chief part of my striving must be, to feed the hungry, to clothe the naked, to instruct the ignorant, to visit the sick and such as are in prison, bound in misery and iron.

"But if you purge out all who scorn such practices, or at least are not found in them, how many will remain in your society? I fear scarce enough to carry your body to the grave! Alas, how many, even among those who are called believers, have plenty of all the necessaries of life, and yet complain of poverty! . . . How many have linen in plenty, with three or four suits of clothes, and can see the poor go naked! . . . Pray, Sir, tell these, you cannot believe they are Christians, unless they imitate Christ in doing good to all men, and hate covetousness, which is idolatry."

[Wesley answers] I do tell them so: And I tell them it will be more tolerable in the day of judgment for Sodom and Gomorrah than for them. I tell them, the Methodists that do not fulfil all righteousness will have the hottest place in the lake of fire! (*Journal,* Nov. 20, 1767, III:305)

But it appears that Wesley took to heart the necessity of insisting more strenuously on this theme in his sermons. In his sermon "On the Wisdom of God's Counsels," Wesley has shown that Christianity first fell with Ananias and Sapphira and that this fall had been ratified on that catastrophic day "when Constantine first called himself a Christian." But with the reform of the sixteenth century, doctrine and worship began to be purged, and with the beginning of Methodism Christian life and discipline too began to be purified. So far we are on ground familiar from "The General Spread of the Gospel." But the old enemy that first struck through Ananias and Sapphira now menaces:

> They *gain all they can,* honestly and conscientiously. They *save all they can,* by cutting off needless expense. . . . But they do not *give all they can;* without which they must needs grow more and more earthly-minded. Their affections will cleave to the dust more and more; and they will have less and less communion with God. Is not this *your* case? Do you not seek the praise of men more than the praise of God? Do not *you* lay up, or at least desire and endeavour to "lay up, treasures on earth?" Are you not then (deal faithfully with your soul!) more and more alive to the world, and, consequently, more and more dead to God? It cannot be otherwise. That *must* follow, unless you give all you can, as well as gain and save all you can. ("The Wisdom of God's Counsels," VI:332)

And in even more severe terms, he writes: "Do you give all you can? else your money will eat your flesh as fire, and will sink you to the nethermost hell! O beware of 'laying up treasures on earth!' Is it not treasuring up wrath against the day of wrath?" (Ibid., VI:334). He concludes with one of his increasingly frequent appeals to God:

> Lord I have warned them! but they will not be warned, what can I do more? I can only "give them up unto their own heart's lusts, and let them follow their own imaginations!"
> 19. By not taking this warning, it is certain many of the Methodists are already fallen; many are falling at this very time; and there is great reason to apprehend, that many more will fall, most of whom will rise no more! (Ibid., VI:334)

This diagnosis, this warning, and this complaint to God about the Methodists all become regular features of Wesley's writings in the last two decades of his leadership.

In his sermon "On Obedience to Pastors," Wesley complains that the Methodists do not obey his instructions regarding dress, which, as we have seen, serve as the focal point for Wesley's attack on the ethos of consumption (VII:115-16). And to those who complain that he is insisting on trifles, he exclaims: "There can be no little sin, till we can find a little God!" (VII:116)

One of Wesley's most vigorous attacks on the Methodists comes in his sermon "On God's Vineyard." Here he recounts all the benefits the Methodists have received with regard to both doctrine and discipline. They have, he complains, brought forth "sour grapes." After briefly instancing enthusiasm and judgmentalism (things that have not entirely disappeared from our ranks), he turns to his main complaint: The Methodists have increased in goods, have sought happiness in prosperity, and have failed to restore "to God in the poor" all that they can spare (see VII:211-13).

The same theme is enforced in the sermon "On the Causes of the Inefficacy of Christianity" (1789). Here he cites his ill-fated rule concerning the gaining, saving, and giving "all you can," and complains:

> But how many have you found that observe the Third rule, "Give all you can"? Have you reason to believe, that five hundred of these are to be found among fifty thousand Methodists? And yet nothing can be more plain, than that all who observe the two first rules without the third, will be twofold more the children of hell than ever they were before. (VII:285-86)

It is plainly becoming increasingly clear to Wesley that his movement is faltering. Fully 99 percent of Methodists have failed to heed his warnings, his reproaches, his calling God to witness on his behalf and against the Methodists. One of his last sermons, "On the Danger of Increasing Riches" (Sept. 1790), seeks for a final time to sound the warning: "After having served you between sixty and seventy years; with dim eyes, shaking hands, and tottering feet, I give you one more advice before I sink into the dust" (VII:361). A careful reading of Wesley's last sermons would put an end to the smug complacency of the endless books, articles, and especially speeches at Annual and General Conferences, about the glorious heritage of Methodism. Wesley, it is clear, had a more somber view.

But Wesley did more than warn and plead and exhort and threaten. He also tried to understand. The thesis that Protestantism results in middle-class prosperity has been one of the "discoveries" of modern social history.[7] Writing more than a century before this idea gained currency, Wesley proposed his own view of the theory:

> Does it not seem (and yet this cannot be) that Christianity, true scriptural Christianity, has a tendency, in process of time, to undermine and destroy itself? For wherever true Christianity spreads, it must cause diligence and frugality, which, in the natural course of things, must beget riches! and riches naturally beget pride, love of the world, and every temper that is destructive of Christianity. Now, if there be no way to prevent this, Christianity is inconsistent with itself, and, of consequence, cannot stand, cannot continue long among any people; since, wherever it generally prevails, it saps its own foundation. ("The Causes of the Inefficacy of Christianity," VII:290)

For Wesley there was only one way to show that Christianity was not inconsistent with itself: "If you have any desire to escape the damnation of hell, *give* all you can; otherwise I can have no more hope of your salvation, than of that of Judas Iscariot" (VII:290).

Wesley's diagnosis of the problem is clear: The renewal of Christianity, whether in the reform of the sixteenth century or the revival of the eighteenth century, seems to beget riches by encouraging the virtues that result in the accumulation of wealth. But he could not regard this as a simple fact to be noted; it was a betrayal of the gospel. Thus the practice and theory of evangelical economics is the only way of rescuing Christianity from its own tendency to self-destruct. It is easy to see that we are not dealing here with something peripheral to Wesley's concern, but with the central question of the possibility of Christianity as such.

CONCLUSION

Wesley developed a clear and forceful view of evangelical economics and sought to actualize this view in his own life and in the corporate life of his societies. By citing personal and communal examples, by showing its relation to the history of the church, by answering objections and ferreting out evasions, he sought to persuade the Methodists to practice this economics. With warnings and pleas, he increasingly exhorted them to flee what he regarded as the tempter's snare. Yet, more and more he sensed that the revival of scriptural Christianity was floundering and would fail. This failure owed not to declining enrollments or to loss of influence. On all these fronts Methodism was the success story so beloved of triumphalist Methodist self-congra-tulation. For Wesley what mattered was not the creation of another more or less successful institution, but the renewal of scriptural holiness. And with increasing urgency he warned that this was what would and must be lost the more Methodists succeeded in other respects.

In 1786, Wesley wrote the last of his retrospective essays on the history of Methodism, which was then, by his calculation, fifty-five years old. The essay begins with one of Wesley's most-quoted lines:

> I am not afraid that the people called Methodists should ever cease to exist either in Europe or America. But I am afraid, lest they should only exist as a dead sect, having the form of religion without the power. (*Thoughts Upon Methodism*, XIII:258)

Many quote this line to introduce their own diagnosis of the malaise of Methodism, usually having to do with the loss of a certain "evangelical fervor." But what is Wesley worried about here? What is the absence of power that threatens to leave Methodism as only a dead sect?

Wesley begins with a review of the rise of Methodism (as usual this means its origin in 1729 at Oxford, with no mention of the "Aldersgate experience"). He warns that "if ever the essential parts should evaporate, what remains will be dung and dross" (XIII:260). Then he comes to the point:

It nearly concerns us to understand how the case stands with us at present. I fear, wherever riches have increased, (exceeding few are the exceptions,) the essence of religion, the mind that was in Christ, has decreased in the same proportion. (Ibid.)

What threatens the "essence" of Methodism, the "power" of religion, is not a loss of membership, not a lack of emphasis on personal conversion, but prosperity. The people called Methodists are rising into the middle class:

For the Methodists in every place grow diligent and frugal; consequently, they increase in goods. Hence they proportionably increase in pride, in anger, in the desire of the flesh, the desire of the eyes, and the pride of life. So, although the form of religion remains, the spirit is swiftly vanishing away. (Ibid.)

It is precisely this rise in worldly success that imperils the Methodist movement. What others regard as the sign of God's favor, Wesley sees as the destruction of "true religion." And the only remedy is that Methodists must rid themselves of this prosperity:

What way, then, (I ask again,) can we take, that our money may not sink us to the nethermost hell? There is one way, and there is no other under heaven. If those who "gain all they can," and "save all they can," will likewise "give all they can;" then, the more they gain, the more they will grow in grace, and the more treasure they will lay up in heaven. (Ibid., XIII:260-61)

In this and the preceding chapter, we have seen that Wesley means by "give all you can" not the practice of prudential philanthropy, but a commitment to the evangelical economics that places the welfare of the poor at the center of all economic activity. It is the failure to do this that is already, in Wesley's view, destroying the Methodist movement. Methodism was growing, but at the cost of its commitment to scriptural holiness.[8]

We are the inheritors of this debacle. We can take small comfort in our relationship to Wesley, for this relationship is, in large part, one of forgetfulness if not of outright betrayal. The very measures of our "success" are the yardstick of our decline. Wesley is not simply the founder of Methodism. He is also its most severe judge. In a note he added to the text of *A Farther Appeal* in 1746, Wesley pronounces what we may call a curse upon the Methodists. It comes at the point of his discussion of the Quakers' attempt to promote simplicity of life in order to be able to relieve the poor of their own number. But when there ceased to be poor Quakers, instead of continuing to insist on the practice of an evangelical economics in order to commit themselves to the poor generally, they relaxed their adherence to these precepts and so forgot the poor. Here stands Wesley's curse, which falls, I fear, on us:

> Lay this deeply to heart, ye who are now a poor, despised, afflicted people [the Methodists]. Hitherto ye are not able to relieve your own poor. But if ever your substance increase, see that ye be not straitened in your own bowels, that ye fall not into the same snare of the devil. Before any of you either lay up treasures on earth, or indulge needless expense of any kind, I pray the Lord God to scatter you to the corners of the earth, and blot out your name from under heaven! (*A Farther Appeal to Men of Reason and Religion,* VIII:187, Wesley's note of 1746)

CHAPTER SEVEN

THE THEOLOGICAL BASIS OF WESLEY'S ETHIC

We have already seen that for Wesley the practice of a new economics was a matter of ultimate concern, that salvation itself was at stake. But in order to understand how this was so for him, it is necessary for us to see the connection between evangelical economics and the soteriological themes of justification and sanctification, of grace and faith, of love and holiness, which are generally recognized to be at the heart of Wesley's thought and practice. Is this evangelical economics really central and necessary from the perspective of these themes, or is it, in spite of Wesley's rhetoric, only *adiaphora* after all?

Our task in this chapter, then, is to review the dominant themes of Wesley's proclamation in order to see how they do or do not entail the transformation of economic relations, which we have discussed in previous chapters. In order to do this it will be necessary to sketch these themes in such a way as to see their relevance to the economic question. Obviously, we cannot provide here a detailed study of Wesley's soteriology. That would be the task of another book! But we can attempt to show how some of the major themes combine in such a way as to make plausible Wesley's sense of the centrality of a transformed economics as being essential to the practice of faith. Perhaps also in this way we may see some of these themes in a new light, as we view them not as an abstract dogmatics but as a reflection on transformed and transforming praxis.

THE HOLINESS PROJECT

From at least 1725 until the end of his days, Wesley was committed to the realization of holiness of life. Despite all vicissitudes of formulation and expression, this was the aim of his life, the organizing center of his thought, the spring of all action, his one abiding project. This meant becoming a creature worthy of the Creator, a finite representative and image of the divine subject.

Such a correspondence to the divine life meant a rupture with the world, a transformation of life that separated the new from the old, the spirit from the flesh, the life of faith from the world. The possibility of such a project was based on the divine self-revelation that provided a paradigm and clear instructions for the actualization of this holiness.

The first Methodists (Wesley, his brother Charles, and a few of their friends at Oxford) sought to realize this project. From the very first it entailed a new economic practice, a dedication of all resources to the poor on the basis of the instructions of the Gospels. Some of the other aspects of the practice of the first Methodists were later modified. The adherence to the rubrics of the Church, for example, was later relaxed. But the practice of a new economics, consciously opposed to the economics of "the world," remained despite all changes in interpretation and explanation.

This holiness project itself remains constant. But on the basis of detailed discussion with the Moravians, and especially Peter Böhler, Wesley comes to be persuaded that the foundation of this project must be reconceived. It must be understood as flowing from grace. Thus, as José Míguez Bonino has correctly affirmed, Wesley comes to proclaim sanctification through grace by faith.[1] This change affects neither the content nor the aim of Wesley's project, but it does alter its basis. Holiness is no longer merely an outward correspondence to an external law. It is a glad and peaceful (not alienated) correspondence to the same "law" now internalized.[2]

Grace does not, then, provide a dispensation *from* holiness but serves as the capacitation *for* holiness. In one sense nothing has changed. The insistence upon holiness and the necessity of following the divine instructions to the letter do not vary a hair. In another sense everything is changed in that the basis of this correspondence to the divine is an inward appropriation made possible by grace.[3]

But if grace is the basis of this transformation, then consequences for the *manner* of realizing holiness follow. It is no longer necessary to retire from the world to be holy. Grace is available not just to an elite but to all. Therefore, even those who had before been utterly given over to sin could be utterly renewed by grace. The cloister of Oxford could be exchanged for the fields, the streets, the marketplace, even the gallows. Anyone could become holy in life through the operation of grace.[4]

Thus the holiness project is unleashed upon the world. All people everywhere, and not only contemplative scholars or mystics, were called to correspond to the divine nature, and the grace that would make such a correspondence actual was freely offered to all.

But note that *this* grace is the grace that makes us really and effectively holy. The good news is that we can become holy, not that we have been made exempt from holiness. But holiness is transformed from an elitist to a populist project by the power of grace.

THE EFFICACY OF GRACE

The introduction of grace into the project of holiness entails a critical reconstruction of the understanding of grace. Since the sixteenth-century Protestant Reformation, grace has often been understood in such a way as to menace its reality. The insistence on "grace alone" has bid fair to empty grace of its efficacy. Whether we think here of what Bonhoeffer called "cheap grace" or of a residue of nominalism or of a justification that is merely juridical, the result is a grace that changes nothing, or at least nothing visible.

This was not the sort of grace in which Wesley was interested.[5] For Wesley, grace really works. It really changes things, people, relationships, and the world. God is not in the business of changing names while leaving the things themselves untouched. God is not a nominalist. God really does transform, change, do.

When it is said that God justifies the ungodly, this does not mean that the ungodly remain, to all intents and purposes, ungodly. It means that they become just. Sanctification produces holiness. Justification makes us just. We are not merely declared to be so, but are made to be so. *Simul justus et peccator*, as normally understood, is fancy Latin for open defiance of God. To say that justification leaves sinners still in the grasp of sin as before is like saying that resurrection leaves the dead in their graves. If God's declaration of us as justified does not result in our really being just, then God is a liar and faith is illusion. Wesley will not accept an illusory faith, a phantom grace, or a deceptive or impotent God.

Wesley's rejection of phantom grace is the leading edge of his rejection of all forms of Deism, which excludes God from real agency in the world. He is even prepared to defend ghost stories so as not to yield an inch to the Deists! His talk of particular providence that sees the hand of God in the stilling of the wind when Wesley is about to preach, or the failure of rocks hurled by a mob to find their target, is all of a piece. Wesley will not surrender the competence of God. Whatever we may think of some of Wesley's ways of defending divine agency, we cannot ignore the fact that this is a unifying theme of his thought. And this theme finds its most cogent expression in the insistence upon the real efficacy of grace.

If grace is to be real, then it must have real effects. And these effects must be palpable, visible. No Barthian geometry will persuade Wesley of the reality of the ineffable. When the divine enters the world, it produces changes everyone can see, not invisible craters, but manifest "monuments of mercy."

Here we may see why it is that experience plays such an important, if frequently misunderstood, role in Wesley's thought. The effects of the divine action must be palpable. Just as the Creator produces a visible creation, so also the Redeemer produces a manifest redemption, a visible salvation. Despite Wesley's hope for a salvation beyond this world, his emphasis always lies in present salvation. Without the latter, the former is a pipe dream. Present salvation is the evidentiary basis of the hope for a future salvation. And evidence must be perceptible, experimental. The "evidence of things not seen" must itself be visible, seen, or it is no evidence at all.

Wesley often focuses on the "internal witness of the Spirit" because this evidence is indisputable to the experiencing subject. The subject immediately senses a change in "feeling." Where before there was fear, now there is peace and joy. Where before there was animosity and resentment, there is now love. One can't have peace and joy and love without knowing that one has them. It is empirical evidence. One has only to compare this to some interpretations of the Protestant tradition, which state that one cannot even know if one has faith, that faith is invisible even to the believing subject, to see what a difference is here.

But the indisputable self-evidence of immediate self-awareness is by no means the only sort of experience involved here. Faith that is manifest to the subject in the transformation of "tempers" is manifest to all in the transformation of behavior. Grace produces this visible transformation immediately and not indirectly. Otherwise the divine grace evaporates into meaningless abstraction. If there is no permanent and radical and visible transformation of behavior, then grace has vanished.

Unacceptable anthropological conclusions would also follow from a restriction of the efficacy of grace to the inward sphere. This would divide the subject into an inward and an outward self, producing a disembodied "soul" and an inert matter incapable of redemption. This is, of course, the tendency of Luther's "two kingdoms" theory as well as the well-known Cartesian dualism. Wesley firmly and explicitly rejects both. He rejects them because all forms of gnosticism are repugnant to him. The Creator created the whole creature. The Redeemer thus redeems the whole subject.

The transformation of inwardness is immediately expressed as the transformation of behavior. A conversion that left unchanged my manner of relating to my neighbor would be an imaginary conversion, an exercise in irreality. Grace produces real effects, visible, publicly testable effects, or it is not the grace of God the Creator.

If Wesley emphasizes the inward it is not because this is somehow more real or important than the outward. It is because an inward transformation must produce an outward one. It is one thing to hang a few apples on a pecan tree. It is quite another to grow apples on an apple tree. The latter is a more reliable source of apples.[6] Thus the regeneration of the apple tree, which then produces apples of itself and of natural necessity, is the best, indeed the only way to get apples. But those who claim to be apple trees without producing apples are kidding themselves. Wesley emphasizes inward transformation because he is so earnestly interested in outward behavior. We may contest this strategy, but we should not suppose that Wesley emphasizes inwardness because he is relatively disinterested in outward transformation.[7] Such a view would be possible only on the basis of invincible ignorance of Wesley's writings.

In this light, we can understand Wesley's struggle to come to terms with the problem of "sin in believers." This is a problem because it constitutes counterevidence to the real efficacy of grace. Once Wesley had identified grace as the basis of holiness, he maintained that conversion (justification/regeneration) produced sinlessness.[8] This was subsequently modified to allow for *inward,* but not *outward,* sin.[9] Finally it was necessary to separate perfection (as the "great salvation") from regeneration while still maintaining that perfection was available in this life and by faith alone—that is, as a gift. Then Wesley had to wrestle with the apparent (visible) loss of perfection, and so on. All of these "epicycles" on the view of holiness as produced by grace through faith are attempts to insist on the real efficacy of grace within the sphere of concrete experience. Efficacy and experienced (visible) transformation entail each other.

The idea of a progressive growth in grace is an attempt to simplify the system. But Wesley did not abandon the apparently contradictory notion of a sudden transformation with respect both to "justification" and to "entire sanctification," despite the way this tended to produce "epicycles," or odd complications in his view of the Christian life. He was aware of the danger that an unmodified "gradualism" of grace threatened to abolish the gracious character of grace and so vitiate this as the foundation of holiness.

When Wesley speaks of the importance of experience he normally means it in the way that we might say a farmer is experienced in the growing of apples or wheat. Religious experience is the lived and reflected history of those who engage in the project of holiness. It is not a question of extraordinary and essentially private moments, but of a clear and visible pattern and progression of behavior. Thus the experience of regeneration is the evidence of lives that demonstrate holiness. Wesley knows by experience that grace is efficacious because he sees that it produces altered patterns of life. He knows by experience that some of the tenets of the Moravians are false because they do not produce the requisite changes, the appropriate alteration of patterns of behavior. The reality of grace entails visible empirical alterations in the life-form of the believer. This empirical and experimental reality is then thematized as experience. Of course, where the real efficacy of grace is not understood in this way, then religious experience becomes the opposite of empirical. That is the way we all too often carelessly employ this concept. Wesley knew better.

Wesley then seeks to accept the Reformation view that grace—from the side of God—and faith—from our side—constitute the foundation of Christian life. Unlike many of the classic Protestant formulations of this idea, Wesley's view insisted on a real grace, an efficacious grace, a grace that produced real evidence and visible effects.

The proper meaning of experience, then, is something that one can see and touch. The experience that counted was the lived faith that produced visible holiness. Wesley put little stock in what we often call religious experience today. He was interested in something far more "empirical." Therefore, a life that was unchanged in behavior was a life without faith, a life in which whatever measure of grace had at one time been received was squandered, frittered away, lost. The experiential evidence of faith is a fundamentally transformed life.

THE NEW SUBJECT

The real efficacy of grace entails the transformation of the believing subject. And this transformation entails that the

145

subject becomes a partner in the saving work of grace. Grace energizes the subject, makes the subject one who is a participant in salvation. This participatory salvation is a consequence of taking grace seriously!

All of this runs against the grain of those who are schooled in classical Protestantism, for there we are led to suppose that the "sovereignty of God" or of "grace alone" entails the abrogation of the subject's responsibility. It is as though agency were a scarce good. The more one side has, the less the other can claim. But the result of this manner of thinking is that what begins by magnifying the divine agency must end in making it nugatory, without any real effect. Now one can simply throw up one's hands and claim paradox, or one can rethink one's view. Perhaps agency produces agency instead of destroying it. Perhaps we should think of it like love. It is not the case that the more I love my wife, the less she can be permitted to love me. Love provokes love. Divine agency provokes human agency. The more I am a recipient of a real and not imaginary grace, the more I become a responsible agent, a participant in working out my own salvation. In this way my action becomes the visible proof of God's action, not a denial of it.

Wesley does not work out his position in exactly the terms I have employed. I am not repeating Wesley, but am attempting to disclose the logic of his position. The more one insists on the reality of grace, the more one must insist on the agency of the believing subject. That is the ground of Wesley's "Arminianism." That is why Wesley so vigorously opposed Calvinism and quietism. Both rendered the human subject inert and so made grace null and void.

The participation of the believing subject in the project of salvation takes the form of appropriating the grace that is proffered and investing this grace in the transformation of life. The latter is only possible on the basis of the former. Life can be transformed only on the basis of grace. But grace is efficacious in that it does enable me to live a transformed life. This occurs through cooperation with grace. Thus Wesley can even think in terms of a quantification of grace. The more I use, the more I get. The less I use, the less I get, and the little that I have, I lose. If I am really converted, but do not work at being a new person, then the grace I received will be withdrawn. I am, then, "not saved" any more than I was prior to my conversion. Indeed, I am worse off, for now I have betrayed grace itself. When the converted do not exhibit transformation, Wesley does not need to contest the assertion that they were justified. He can simply say that they have failed to "improve" the grace that was then given.

God then will neither save nor condemn without the participation of the subject. I can't be damned for what I didn't do. I can't be saved without doing something.

Is this salvation by works? Wesley believes that it is not, since salvation is not something my works can merit, nor am I capable of any "good works" apart from grace. Wesley struggled with the question of good works before regeneration. Early on he denies it as being incompatible with the sole efficacy of grace, but later, with the aid of the idea of prevenient grace, he was able to reincorporate works as based on grace even outside the "Christian dispensation." If we don't get lost in slogans, we can see that Wesley does want to emphasize the fact that no one can be saved who is not holy, but that the basis of this holiness is grace. This grace is not imaginary, but real, producing a new subject who is then able to participate in the divine project of salvation by exemplifying holiness.

The new subject produced by grace is the "restored subject" of the creation. The subject created by God is the whole human being. The subject constituted by grace is, likewise, the whole human being, the image and likeness of God. This means that grace does not constitute an epiphenomenal subject, a religious one, but a whole subject. The newness of life is a newness in every dimension of that life. To countenance a division between the religious effects of grace and the rest of life (say, economic life) is to deny the Creator, to render the work of grace as impotent as the work of the Deist's god.

Thus the grace that makes one holy is the grace that is the basis of all of life, of every dimension of the created subject. This is why Wesley will not accept practical atheism in politics or economics any more than he would accept it in worship. The new subject becomes a participant in the divine project of salvation. This means that the new subject is holy. That which corresponds to God is by definition holy.

The participation in the divine project of salvation is not limited to working out our own salvation. Rather it includes becoming an agent in the salvation of others. Thus God helps through the instrumentality of renewed human subjects. While this divine aid certainly includes the proclamation of the gospel, it entails as well help in every form of distress and affliction. Salvation is holistic because the Savior is also the Creator. The subject energized, set in motion, by grace is the agent of the one who announces good news to the poor, who heals the broken, who releases the captives.

A subject who is not set in motion is a subject in which grace has no effect, no efficacy, no reality. But a subject who does in this visible and concrete way become a participant in the divine project is a "monument of mercy."

AGAINST THE WORLD

Holiness does not only mean corresponding to God, but it also means standing over against that which is opposed to God. Whether this be called sin, flesh and blood, the world, worldliness, or Satan, the basic structure is the same. The choice of the metaphor of holiness serves to emphasize this distinction between the new and the old.

Holiness is not, then, grace perfecting nature. It is grace overpowering sin. Such a view may, but does not necessarily, produce an ontological dualism. Everything depends on how certain propositions are co-ordinated. Wesley believes strongly in creation. But the created world is also the fallen world. It is because it is fallen that it needs salvation, it is because it is created that it can be saved. The same is true of persons as it is of creation as a whole.

Wesley's emphasis on the Fall—which is the theme of his longest book, *The Doctrine of Original Sin, According to Scripture, Reason, and Experience* (IX:191-464)—serves to make clear the necessity of salvation while at the same time providing a kind of negative description, or description by contrast, of the scope of that same salvation. If the fallen world is characterized by war, oppression, and injustice, then the world that God created and will renew is characterized by peace and love and justice. The fallen world is the negative index of the magnitude of the divine project.

We must not forget the proper function of a doctrine of original sin. It does not provide an alibi for continued sin in believers. It shows the necessity, not the impossibility, of redemption. To say that holiness cannot be realized because we are sinners is to say that there is no remedy for sin. The use of "original sin" to claim an exemption from the demands of the gospel is theologically incompetent. Wesley had his full share of faults, but he was not an incompetent theologian.

The theme of holiness is well adapted to express this relationship, since holiness suggests both correspondence to God and opposition to the world, within the world. Phenomenologically, holy things (shamans, mountains, chalices) are always things of the world, separated from the world, still remaining in the world, pointing beyond the world.

To speak of holiness, as Wesley constantly does, is to emphasize that the reality that corresponds to God is different from the simply given reality of the world. There is much peril here, for this can lead, and in Wesley does sometimes lead, to a kind of separatism from the world. But this is normally prevented by the principle of the efficacy of a grace whose source is the Creator.

To be holy is to be different. Wesley vigorously insisted that to be a Christian is to be singular. The efficacy of grace produces a real, indeed a vast, difference from the sort of life that is characterized by unbelief. Thus Wesley can oppose "worldliness" or "worldly prudence" as the way in which we render grace nugatory, of no effect. The efficacy of grace is measured by the difference between the old life and the new.

This difference must be manifest in all spheres of life if it is not to be reduced or limited and so denied. Holiness means difference, striking difference, from the form and structure of the old. Holiness is not just touching up the details of a pretty good portrait. It is a radical restoration.

THE LIFE OF LOVE

The singularity of Christian life is not only capable of a negative description by way of contrast with the world, but it may also be described positively as love. The divine love made manifest in Christ does not remain without effect. It is "shed abroad" so as to become the basis of a new life. The efficacy of the divine love is such that it awakens love in the one who receives it. This subject then becomes not only the loved subject but also the loving subject. Wesley regards this pure disinterested love for every human being as rational religion—rational because it corresponds to the true character of the created subject, rational because it corresponds, as that subject must, to the divine subject.

This love is, then, in one sense the most natural possible activity for the created subject. But it is startlingly different behavior for the fallen and distorted non-subject, the one who despite all activity can never be an agent of life but only of destruction for itself and others. Love is the opposite, then, of worldliness. It is the abolition of the captivity to self-preoccupation (pride) and self-aggrandizement (avarice). It sets itself apart from the world, which operates on a very different principle. But it does not abandon the world, for it is love. Thus it invades the world, summoning the world to a new identity.

The temptation inherent in the holiness project to withdraw from the world is overcome by the identification of that project as love. As the religion of love, scriptural religion is necessarily social. In this way Wesley is delivered from the mystics, and from Oxford, too. As a student he tried to avoid the parish, saying it was impossible to be holy if one had to deal with sinners![10] But the theme of grace made clear that the holiness of God consisted precisely in caring for sinners.

Wesley still managed to escape the parish, but not the world. To be holy as God is holy is to enter the world, to contest the rule of sin and pride and greed. The holiness project cannot consist in retiring from the world but rather in an assault upon the world. It is for all that the assault of love. It is the relentless calling of the world to a life commensurate with love.

The disciplines of holiness, then, are the disciplines of love.

The societies are constituted so that Christians can watch over one another in love, rooting out all forms of lovelessness in their behavior and in their "tempers." But this love cannot be simply encapsulated in the internal life of the community any more than it can be closed up in the interiority of the individual. Like the divine love, it reaches out, and does so concretely and visibly.

Just as grace must produce concretely visible effects, so also must love. Love seeks the benefit of the other. Of course, the other's benefit must mean that the other as well comes to live the life of love made possible by grace. But the love of the neighbor cannot restrict itself to some specifically religious sphere any more than the divine love does. To say that we should care only for our neighbor's soul would be an imitation of some other God than the one Wesley knows. This is, for Wesley, the importance of his notion of "particular providence." Whatever the defects of this notion, it makes clear the fact that God is not the prisoner of the "spiritual" sphere but is active in all of life, healing, feeding, and responding to all sorts of human distress. An imitation of this love will also direct itself to the relief of every form of human distress.

If love is the imitation of God, then a purely "spiritual" love would be an imitation of the Deist's god, the god who abandons the world. But if God is the one who hears the distress of the afflicted, then the imitation of God will likewise respond concretely to human affliction in whatever form.

Wesley was aware that the failure of Christians to behave in this way constituted evidence for atheism. This is why he was so vigorous in his attack on the forms of injustice, practiced by those who called themselves Christians. And this is why he could also suppose that if Christian love were to take the form of a pentecostal community of goods and redistribution of wealth, all the unbelievers (and other believers) would be converted. The visible and dramatic realization of love in the everyday world is the only proof that there is a God who is love.

THE HORIZON OF HOLINESS

While Wesley emphasizes the transformation of life in the present, this project must be viewed in terms of the wider horizon of creation and new creation. From the very beginning of his reflection on holiness, Wesley employed elements of eschatology and protology (creation) in the clarification of the meaning of holiness. Thus his most frequent characterization of holiness is the "renewal of the whole image of God." This was always seen in terms of an apocalyptic struggle against the forces of Satan, the world and sin. Thus this wider horizon is a constant feature of Wesley's reflection.

It could scarcely be otherwise for one who was as committed as Wesley was to the vindication of the creator and preserver of the world. His struggle against Deism in every form is a struggle for this wider horizon, a refusal of the diminishment of God, the restriction of divine efficacy. This wider horizon of faith is what makes it possible for the travelling evangelist to write a long textbook on natural science.

Even though this horizon is present—necessarily—from the very beginning of Wesley's reflection on the holiness project, it is increasingly clarified and made the subject of explicit reflection. Thus the second and third series of sermons engage in a much more explicit discussion of both protological and eschatological themes than we find in the so-called "Standard Sermons."

Indeed Wesley's theological imagination is such that he wrestles with such questions as the place of comets in the created order, the sort of weather the renewed earth will have (rather like Camelot, it seems), and the eschatological future of dogs and cats. Whatever we may think of the quaintness of some of these speculations, they show that the horizon of holiness was the whole world, created and recreated.

This theological realism (one is tempted to say, theological materialism) prevents the holiness project from evaporating into an invisible "spiritual" mist, not to say mysticism. Holiness is firmly embedded in the material world of visible relations and patterns of conduct. The restoration of the person launches the restoration of the earth. Thus the transformation of the human heart is the turning point in the transformation of the face of the earth, the beginning of cosmic transformation. It is because of this immediate relation between the transformation of the individual and the transformation of the cosmos that the former can serve as evidence for the latter.[11] When this connection is severed, as it is in some of Wesley's followers, then holiness is abandoned for pseudo-holiness, the sort of "outward" religiosity that Wesley opposed as being pseudo-Christianity.

Thus Wesley can see the Methodist project of "spreading scriptural holiness" as entailing the transformation of the economic and political order, the establishment of pentecostal commun(al)ism, and the abolition of war. The sort of holiness in which Wesley was interested was a holiness that stood within the horizon of creation and new creation and so was embedded in the concrete reality of the world. In this way it could be thought that the realization of this project must entail the transformation of all of life, of the nations, of the very earth itself.

THE ECONOMICS OF THE GOSPEL

This brief sketch of Wesley's soteriological theology shows that for all that he was a practical theologian, he had a system. The various themes have a tight logical relationship to one another such that one could develop a summary of Wesley's theology from any of these themes. They entail one another. I have not sought to trace the development of any one of these themes (that would be a different book), but to suggest their interrelation, the logical structure of their relations.

It remains, then, to show how all of this is brought to bear in such a way as to make evangelical economics an integral part, an essential element, of Wesley's project of scriptural holiness. In order to see this, it is only necessary to see how Wesley could suppose that the failure to instantiate evangelical economics could menace the whole holiness project, whose superstructure I have just sketched.

Wesley most often tackles this question in terms of worldliness. Economics is the point at which worldliness most evidently threatens holiness. This is not the way worldliness is most often deployed in "evangelical" rhetoric. There, worldliness is often associated with the failure to comply with strictly religious duties. But this was impossible for Wesley, since he was contesting a pseudo-Christianity that engaged in the outward observation of religious duties, but produced no true or evident holiness. Thus his conception of the holiness project was far closer to the prophetic denunciation of the religiosity of Israel, or to Jesus' denunciation of the Pharisees. (To be sure, Wesley sometimes seems to lose sight of this, but that is another story.)

That Wesley could not identify holiness with outward religion meant that he was free to see that worldliness was precisely where the Bible located it, in the sphere of unregenerate economics. Themes like not laying up treasure on earth, the impossibility of serving God and mammon, the choking of the seed of faith by "the cares of the world," the notion that the love of money was the root of all evil, that the desire for material security is a snare of the devil—all could be appropriated in a way as to give concreteness to the idea of worldliness and so to the notion of holiness.

Therefore, holiness cannot consist in religious observances. These can only be means of grace, not the aim or goal of grace. They are helps to holiness, not the marks of it or the content of it. Holiness must consist in a reversal of the worldliness of economics. It must, then, be the practice of an evangelical economics.

Any attempt to withdraw faith from this sphere is a surrender to worldliness, a repudiation of the divine claim to be the true lord of the earth. Thus Wesley enforces his view of stewardship by reference to the rights of the Creator. It is the task of holiness to render to God that which is God's. This must mean the whole of life, and especially the economic sphere, which is where we interact with the material creation. Mammon is this economic sphere in rebellion against God. It is the expropriation of creation from the Creator. Stewardship is the practice of the agents of the new creation. It is giving creation back to the Creator.

The holiness project depends on the efficacy of grace. Apart from grace, I am hopelessly entangled in worldliness. But if grace is real, it produces a visible transformation of my relationship to worldliness. This means that a transformed economics is testimony to the efficacy of grace, and an untransformed economics is counterevidence to the gospel. Since transformation must be visible to be real, must be publicly certifiable to be convincing, then my behavior in the sphere of visible interaction with the world must be changed. It is in the sphere of economics that avarice becomes quantifiable, that pride takes on the tactile properties of silk, that self-centeredness is blatantly obvious. It is also here that generosity of spirit, that humility, that benevolent love of every creature of God becomes visible, countable, empirical. If grace is to be said to produce effects, it is here that we may look for evidence.

It is here, too, that we see that a spiritualizing of grace, a false emphasis on the sovereignty of grace, leads to a denial of the efficacy of grace. A grace that allegedly saves my soul while leaving the concrete and visible relations of my life unaffected is merely illusory, whatever metaphysical compliments we may pay it.

Similarly, we may say that economics is the sphere of human agency *par excellence.* It is precisely here that we are most active in working, gaining, spending, and giving. Thus it is here that we are most driven by the forces of necessity. But it is also here that the new subject as agent, and not merely object, must come to expression. A transformation of the subject, which left untouched the very sphere of constant activity, would be an illusory transformation.

Finally it is here that the question of a real imitation of the divine love comes most concretely into question. This love is the opposite of a selfish self-regard; it is freely self-giving. It is the opposite of an economic exchange of robbery, or even an economics of strict accounting; it is gracious, generous. It seeks the good of the other without seeking to preserve itself. It chooses the least rather than the greatest. It sides with the poor and becomes as one of the poor. The life of love that imitates the divine love is, then, a reversal of worldly economic values. A love that does not reverse these values is a lie and illusion.

This rapid sketch should at least indicate the plausibility of Wesley's view that a failure to actualize evangelical economics would mean the collapse of the Methodist holiness project. This is the test case of the visible efficacy of grace, the demonstration of love, the victory of the creator, the agency of the new subject. It is not fortuitous that Wesley hits upon economic reality as the norm of holiness; it grows naturally out of his principal theological commitments. More precisely, Wesley's evangelical economics and his soteriology grow together, mutually implicating, reinforcing, and clarifying each other.[12]

CHAPTER EIGHT

WHY DID WESLEY FAIL?

That Wesley failed—on his own terms—is indisputable. The movement he launched in the hopes of spreading scriptural holiness throughout the land did not escape the snare of material prosperity. Indeed, it abounded in it. The practice of an evangelical economics had already nearly disappeared in Wesley's last years, and after his death it was expunged from the collective memory of Methodists. Wesley saw it happening and knew all too well what it implied for his own movement and for the project of scriptural Christianity as such. Why then this failure, which Wesley himself seemed incapable of reversing? Wesley puts the question in all sharpness:

> I am distressed. I know not what to do. I see what I might have done once. I might have said peremptorily and expressly, "Here I am: I and my Bible. I will not, I dare not, vary from this book, either in great things or small. I have no power to dispense with one jot or tittle of what is contained therein. I am determined to be a Bible Christian, not almost, but altogether. Who will meet me on this ground? Join me on this, or not at all. . . ." But, alas! the time is now past; and what I can do now, I cannot tell. ("Causes of the Inefficacy of Christianity," VII:287-88)

The question of the failure of Wesley's project is thus not one that comes from outside. It is indelibly inscribed in the thought

157

of Wesley himself. No study of Wesley's social ethic, and especially of what I have called his evangelical economics, can dispense with an attempt to take this question seriously.

But it is important to get clear just what is involved in this question. We are not concerned here to dispute the very possibility of this project. Undoubtedly there are many who would argue on theological or exegetical grounds that the attempt to actualize what Wesley called scriptural Christianity is doomed to failure because the gospel makes no such demand or claim. While I believe that contemporary liberation theology provides a strong case to answer this charge—especially as it concerns the central elements of solidarity with the poor, the demystification of wealth and power, the protest against injustice, and the practice of an alternative economics—a discussion of this would take us far from the immediate question of Wesley's own thought and practice.[1]

Still less can the critique of Wesley begin with the point of view that however well-based Wesley's view of evangelical economics may be in the New Testament, it is nevertheless a fool's dream that cannot be taken seriously. Such a view would no doubt be expressed by many of the secular proponents of various forms of "communism" and capitalism who suppose that faith has nothing important to say regarding what they are pleased to call "the real world" of political economy. While this point of view would have to be answered by a contemporary reformulation of evangelical economics, it would be entirely too facile to use this as the basis of an evaluation of Wesley.

Other questions might be raised from the point of view of contemporary advances in the science of biblical hermeneutics or theological anthropology, or the analysis of the contemporary character of human oppression and exploitation. These are essential for the constructive task of generating an adequate social or economic ethic for our time, and they are being ably pursued by theologians on all continents—especially in Latin America. Still it does not seem altogether fair to begin a critique of Wesley by employing perspectives and theories, analyses and experiences, that are new for us and to which Wesley can hardly be held accountable.[2]

What we must content ourselves with here is an internal

critique that takes Wesley's project seriously, indeed as seriously as he seemed to do, and on that basis seeks to understand how it could have happened that his social ethic appeared to fall on deaf ears.

To raise the question in this way should not lead us to suppose that a critique of Wesley somehow will let the Methodists off the hook. Undoubtedly Wesley's failure was not his alone, but that of the Methodists in general. Indeed, it would be an interesting and illuminating historical study to inquire just how it was that the Methodists justified to themselves their non-compliance with Wesley, how they managed even to forget that there ever was such a thing as a demystification of wealth, a solidarity with the poor that made their welfare the litmus test of action, a stewardship that aimed at the redistribution of wealth and the abstinence from consumerism, and so on.

It is, perhaps, time that someone wrote this history of decline, of failure, of subversion and betrayal, if only to expose the triumphalist self-deceit of so many histories of Methodism.[3] But this would be a question about Methodism and not about Wesley, the Wesley whose relationship with Methodism became increasingly polemical in the last years of his leadership.

What I instead propose to do here is to look for clues to the failure of his project in the evidence that Wesley himself provides. This is an exercise in the sort of "plain speaking" that Wesley himself so often called for. It is the essentially friendly attempt to observe and to expose the mistakes that lead the sister or brother to enter into the sort of self-contradiction that imperils his or her own project of realizing what he or she takes to be essential to the Christian life. The point of such an exercise is to discover the pitfalls of an attempt to develop an evangelical economics against which we may be both forewarned and forearmed.

HEDGES AND QUALIFICATIONS

We will first consider some of the ways Wesley may have so qualified and hedged his presentation of evangelical economics as to make it possible, if not excusable, for the Methodists to hear what they wanted to hear and ignore the more challenging thrust of Wesley's position. At a number of points we may notice a certain hesitancy in Wesley, a hesitancy that, to be sure, is always corrected, but appears to leave room for the hearer or reader to squirm out of the application of Wesley's position to her or his own circumstance. A few instances may indicate the character of this hesitancy.

> And it is no more sinful to be rich than to be poor. But it is dangerous beyond expression. ("The Rich Man and Lazarus," VII:250)
> It is true, riches, and the increase of them, are the gift of God. Yet great care is to be taken, that what is intended for a blessing, do not turn into a curse. ("On the Danger of Increasing Riches," VII:355)
> He does not affirm this absolutely of the rich. . . . But he affirms it of . . . *those who desire* or *seek to be rich.* Riches, dangerous as they are, do not always "drown men in destruction and perdition;" but the *desire of riches* does. ("Sermon on the Mount, Discourse VIII," V:369)

Now, in each of these cases Wesley's position seems clear and balanced. But the tendency of a reader not antecedently convinced of Wesley's evangelical economics is to read here only that it is not sinful to be rich, that riches are the gift of God, and that all is well so long as we aren't too greedy. Thereafter it is an uphill battle for Wesley to persuade people that they really have set their hearts on riches, that riches are for them a curse, and that the only way to escape the threat is to give abundantly more to the poor. That he exerts himself to persuade them of all this is quite true. But meanwhile they are wriggling out of the loopholes in the rhetoric.

Another sort of difficulty arises from Wesley's attempt to show that he is not a dreamy idealist, that he does know the value of money.

> Not that money is an evil of itself: It is applicable to good as well as bad purposes. But, nevertheless, it is an undoubted truth, that "the love of money is the root of all evil;" and also, that the possession of

riches naturally breeds the love of them. ("The Mystery of Iniquity," VI:265)

Above all, he has committed to our charge that precious talent which contains all the rest,—money: Indeed it is unspeakably precious, if we are wise and faithful stewards of it; if we employ every part of it for such purposes as our blessed Lord has commanded us to do. ("The Good Steward," VI:139)

Let the world be as corrupt as it will, is gold or silver to blame? "The love of money," we know, "is the root of all evil;" but not the thing itself. The fault does not lie in the money, but in them that use it. It may be used ill: And what may not? But it may likewise be used well: It is full as applicable to the best, as to the worst uses. It is of unspeakable service to all civilized nations, in all the common affairs of life: It is a most compendious instrument of transacting all manner of business, and (if we use it according to Christian wisdom) of doing all manner of good. It is true, were man in a state of innocence, or were all men "filled with the Holy Ghost," so that, like the infant Church at Jerusalem, "no man counted any thing he had his own," but "distribution was made to every one as he had need," the use of it would be superseded; as we cannot conceive there is any thing of the kind among the inhabitants of heaven. But, in the present state of mankind, it is an excellent gift of God, answering the noblest ends. In the hands of his children, it is food for the hungry, drink for the thirsty, raiment for the naked: It gives to the traveller and the stranger where to lay his head. By it we may supply the place of an husband to the widow, and of a father to the fatherless. We may be a defence for the oppressed, a means of health to the sick, of ease to them that are in pain; it may be as eyes to the blind, as feet to the lame; yea, a lifter up from the gates of death! ("The Use of Money," VI:126)

The bulk of this is unexceptionable as it stands. But why the need to reassure readers and hearers of what they know only too well and already ardently believe? Why an entirely gratuitous praise of the virtues of money? Of course, any reader, not only of Wesley as a whole, but also of these very sermons, will know that for Wesley the only justification for having money is that we may do the sort of good he has mentioned in the last quotation. Wesley in every case immediately supplies all those qualifications that open up the themes of his evangelical economics. But by demonstrating his sophistication about money, he opens the

161

door, if only a crack, to those who suppose that they too know the value of money and that there is no need to make such a fuss about the misuse of something so obviously beneficial. It is as if Wesley is giving something of a double message, despite his clear intention to sound the trumpet for a truly evangelical economics, which does more than echo worldly wisdom.[4]

Even more serious are those points at which Wesley's evangelical economics is compromised by a traditionalist interpretation of Scripture, which leads him to propound notions that are "pleasing to flesh and blood," but that are in fundamental tension with what he otherwise sees to be the case. An illustration of this is the interpretation of the story of the rich young ruler. While Wesley wants to take seriously the position that a rich person is prevented by the fact of wealth itself from entering into the kingdom of God, and that the only remedy for this is giving all surplus (all above what is necessary for food and raiment) to the poor, he nevertheless adopts the traditional evasion that seeks to limit the applicability of this story to a particular case. Thus he writes:

> God doth not say to thee, "Sell all that thou hast." Indeed, he who seeth the hearts of men saw it needful to enjoin this in one peculiar case, that of the young rich ruler. But he never laid it down for a general rule, to all rich men, in all succeeding generations. ("Sermon on the Mount, Discourse VIII," V:370; see V:376)

It is quite extraordinary for Wesley to thus limit the applicability of an episode from the Gospels to just the particular case in the past. I know of no other instance of this in Wesley's biblical interpretation. He is clearly repeating the common wisdom of the tradition he has inherited, a tradition formed by the very Constantinianism he is so concerned to expose. Moreover, the interpretation Wesley proposes here is not only contradicted by Luke 14:33 and 18:32, but it is also contrary to Wesley's own view of the gravity of the problem of wealth and of the necessity of giving one's substance to the poor as the only remedy—theses which this sermon develops at some length. Unfortunately, then, the appearance of this interpretation of the story of the rich young ruler in one of Wesley's

"Standard Sermons" provides those who wish to use Wesley to overturn Wesley with an irresistible opportunity.

A similar opportunity is provided by Wesley's interpretation of the teaching in the Sermon on the Mount about anxiety over material security (Matt. 6:25-34). Concerning this, Wesley writes:

> It is the will of God, that every man should labour to eat his own bread; yea, and that every man should provide for his own, for them of his own household. It is likewise his will, that we should "owe no man anything, but provide things honest in the sight of all men." But this cannot be done without taking some thought, without having some care upon our minds; yea, often, not without long and serious thought, not without much and earnest care. Consequently this care . . . our blessed Lord does not condemn. Yea, it is good and acceptable in the sight of God our Saviour. ("Sermon on the Mount, Discourse IX," V:385)

Whatever one may think of this as prudent advice, it is manifest that it is a total contradiction of the plain meaning of the text. Of course, Wesley does not invent this particular interpretation. It is the staple of tradition. But it is nonetheless false for all that. Moreover, Wesley sees that it is false in a practical sense as he berates, in the same sermon, those who use the question "What will we eat?" as an excuse to evade the necessity of obeying the instructions of this text: "They throw away their poor souls, lest they should, some time or other, fall short of what is needful for their bodies!" (ibid., V:390)

Clearly there is a fundamental tension here between an attempt to apply the text in a penetrating way so as to insist that a preoccupation with worldly goods is destructive of faith, and, on the other hand, an attempt to accommodate the prudential ethos of the reader. Thus the way is opened again to the sort of worldly prudence that Wesley wanted to oppose.

A final illustration of this tension in Wesley's exposition comes in his discussion of diligence in work to provide what is necessary for life.

> We ought, therefore, to use all diligence in our calling, in order to owe no man anything; this being no other than a plain law of

common justice, which our Lord came "not to destroy, but to fulfil." ("Sermon on the Mount, Discourse VIII," V:366-67)

We should note first that Wesley here uses two biblical passages as mere slogans with no regard for their context. "Owe no man anything" (Rom. 13:8) has nothing to do with financial solvency but with the command to love. The law that Jesus came "not to destroy but to fulfill," according to Matthew, has nothing to do with "common justice" but with the Old Testament. This superficial use of biblical texts is quite common in Wesley's earlier sermons and diminishes in the later ones. Much of the rest of his discussion of the aim of diligence in our work has the same character.

> This also it is our duty to do, even upon principles of heathen morality. Every man ought to provide the plain necessaries of life, both for his own wife and children; and to put them into a capacity of providing these for themselves, when he is gone hence and is no more seen. I say, of providing *these*; the plain necessaries of life; not delicacies; not superfluities . . . it is no man's duty to furnish them, any more than himself, with the means either of luxury or idleness. . . .
>   Lastly. We are not forbidden, in these words, to lay up, from time to time, what is needful for the carrying on our worldly business, in such a measure and degree as is sufficient to answer the foregoing purposes. ("Sermon on the Mount, Discourse VIII," V:367)

Who can doubt that Wesley has here opened up enough loopholes for those who desire accommodation to the world to drive through an entire caravan of camels? What amount of "laying up treasure" cannot be justified by the necessity of providing for our families or, especially, keeping our "worldly business" solvent? To be sure, Wesley tries to hold the gates against wholesale surrender with strictures about luxury and idleness, but it is to no avail. Even the Gettys and the Rockefellers can get past this one by training their heirs to be industrious as well. Moreover, Wesley has placed all this evasion on the footing of an obligation, the obligation of "heathen morality." Is it any wonder that he has so much subsequent difficulty in persuading the Methodists to take a different course, to choose a different way?

THE THREE RULES

The hedges and qualifications we have observed in some of Wesley's sermons appear to give license to those who search for ways to avoid the radical direction of Wesley's thought. The bulk of these passages are isolated fragments of Wesley's early sermons. None of these early sermons acquires the normative status of Wesley's sermon "On the Use of Money," which is also referred to by Wesley as the sermon "On the Mammon of Unrighteousness" because of the text from which Wesley launches the discourse (Luke 16:9). It is here that one encounters Wesley's "three rules" of gaining, saving, and giving "all you can." We have already encountered a number of texts in which Wesley refers to this sermon and laments that Methodists have proven all too willing to gain and even save, but have failed utterly to give with the same willingness.[5] Because these rules serve as one of the ways in which Wesley measures the failure of Methodism, it may be useful to take a closer look at the sermon to see to what degree it serves to permit the failure of which Wesley complains.

It does not require exaggerated attention to exegetical detail to see that, for Wesley, the aim of the discourse is to emphasize the necessity of giving to the poor. He says at the introduction to the third rule: "All this is nothing, if a man go not forward, if he does not point all this at a farther end" (VI:133). Clearly, for Wesley, the end of gaining and of saving is giving. The goal of diligence and frugality is the capacity to serve the poor. But the willful reader may say: "Here are three rules, and if I obey two . . . well, two out of three ain't bad." Wesley will say that two out of three will make you "twofold more the children of hell" than you were before ("Causes of the Inefficacy of Christianity," VII:286). But it will not be persuasive to those who fail to see (or refuse to see) the point of this evangelical economics.

Now, if we recall Wesley's own later diagnosis of the apparent self-contradiction in Christianity, we will see how this sermon plays a key role in the demise of the project of original Methodism. That diagnosis was as follows:

> Does it not seem (and yet this cannot be) that Christianity, true scriptural Christianity, has a tendency, in process of time, to undermine and destroy itself? For wherever true Christianity spreads, it must cause diligence and frugality, which, in the natural course of things, must beget riches! and riches naturally beget pride, love of the world, and every temper that is destructive of Christianity. Now, if there be no way to prevent this, Christianity is inconsistent with itself, and, of consequence, cannot stand, cannot continue long among any people; since, wherever it generally prevails, it saps its own foundation. ("Causes of the Inefficacy of Christianity," VII:290)

The question, then, is, in the first place, whether Christianity does necessarily produce that diligence and frugality that produces riches and catastrophe. What case does Wesley make for this diligence and frugality? What is the reason for encouraging Methodists to gain all they can? One is immediately struck by the fact that Wesley does not provide any real justification for this at all! Indeed, the bulk of this section of the sermon is devoted to qualifying the instruction so as to restrict it to forms of work that do no damage to one's own or one's neighbors' body, mind, or soul. Now all of this is quite appropriate and has served as the basis for some of the most important aspects of the Methodist Social Creed, for here we encounter the basis in Wesley's thoughts for the reform of the conditions of labor that go far beyond anything explicitly developed by Wesley himself. For example, the view that labor should not damage the mind or body can serve as the basis for opposition to child labor, to the abominable working conditions of miners, and so forth. The importance of this should not be underestimated. But at the same time we must ask, "But what is the basis for seeking to 'gain all one can' in the first place?"

We have already seen that Wesley regarded it as a duty to try to earn enough to provide the necessities of life for oneself and one's household. To be sure, this view itself is impossible to justify on the basis of the Sermon on the Mount or any other text from the four Gospels. But even if we waive this objection, how is this supposed duty in any way appropriately described as "gaining all you can"? Earning what is needful is not the same as gaining all you can. Wesley's use of a catchy phrase produces a ringing rhetorical effect. It also produces a catastrophic misunderstanding. Earning what you need does not produce riches. Gaining what you can does. Perhaps it is not Christianity (even the sort that encourages one to provide for one's family), but Wesley's rhetoric, that self-destructs.

The second rule is "save all you can." In other sermons, Wesley emphasizes that this means "Don't spend on yourself what God gives you to aid the poor." But here the emphasis falls on avoiding needless expense so as to hold oneself free of the sort of self-indulgence that leads to sin. The result is that the instruction about saving is here divorced from its ground in evangelical economics. It thus seems to stand apart from the subsequent instruction to give.

Although in Wesley's overall view gaining and saving are carefully related to the principles of his evangelical economics, that is not the case here. It is already too late when he attempts to show the necessary relationship between the first two rules and the third. He has himself developed them independently. The reader can understand what he says here about the first or second without referring to the third. Thus, despite Wesley's clear intention, it looks as if three independent rules are held together only by the theme of money.

On the whole, then, despite the virtues of some of what Wesley has to say about work, this sermon must be regarded as the source of most of Wesley's problems with the Methodists. It produces the very situation that Wesley so heartily laments: that Methodists increase in riches and so decline in holiness. The attempt to present Wesley's economic ethic using this sermon as its basis or outline is doomed to failure, for this sermon does not represent the center of Wesley's position, but an uncharacteristic deviation from it.[6]

THE MODEL DEED

The majority of sermons that contain evidence of Wesley's vacillation with respect to evangelical economics are those that are included in the "Standard Sermons," which provide one of the norms of Methodist doctrine. The main elements of Wesley's evangelical economics—including the demystification of wealth, solidarity with the poor, and the theory of stewardship—are also found there, usually in the same sermons. A fair reading even of his early sermons would confirm that Wesley is far more concerned to emphasize these features than he is to accommodate them to the worldly wisdom of his readers. But the fact remains that these sermons do provide loopholes that Wesley will later seek to close.

The difficulty of doing so is exacerbated by the fact that Wesley has in the meantime made these sermons the legal norm of doctrine for the Methodist preaching houses through the establishment of the Model Deed (1763) and, subsequently, of the Deed of Declaration (1784). These steps, which were taken to secure continuity and order in the connection, had a distorting effect on Methodist perceptions of Wesley's preaching. Wesley's views on nearly every point of theological importance—including the results of regeneration, the permanence of perfection, the nature of the law, and so on—underwent significant modification in the years following 1763. Still, the "Standard Sermons" have continued to occupy the main place in the study of Wesley. Only the first volume of the *Journal* and Wesley's *Appeals* have anything like a similar standing. Thus the first half of Wesley's theological development as leader of the Methodist movement typically eclipses the second half![7]

The result is that only that portion of Wesley is generally read which opens the door to an anti-Wesleyan ethic! If we are to understand how Wesley himself contributes to the collapse of the Methodist project, then we must give a role to the establishment of that very Model Deed whereby Wesley sought to secure Methodism from decay. Perhaps there is more wisdom than Wesley suspected in his Master's injunction to "take no thought for the morrow."

THE DEFENSE OF METHODISM

The establishment of the Model Deed tells us why Wesley's most equivocal statements acquire canonical status and so place in obscurity his more decisive and mature statement of evangelical economics. But this does not explain how Wesley came to make such equivocal statements in the first place. The effect of such statements is to accommodate Wesley's views to the then prevailing "common-sense" thinking about Christian participation in economic life. Why was Wesley concerned to do this? What leads him to compromise his own insights in ways that ultimately prove fatal to his own project of spreading scriptural holiness throughout the land? (We must remember that this is Wesley's own judgment, not one that is imposed from outside his thought.)

I think that we can come to a better understanding of the dynamics that produce equivocation in some (though by no means all) of Wesley's formulations of evangelical economics in this early period if we remember that Methodism was under concerted attack during this time by those who sensed in the movement a vaguely defined, but nonetheless monumental, threat to their ideology and privilege. The groups and interests who felt themselves threatened by Wesley's project mounted an intense campaign to discredit Wesley with the government, with the Church, and with the people. Nor did things stop with propaganda. The accounts of violence directed against Methodists in general and Wesley in particular is no invention of Methodist legend. The sheer physical courage, especially of Wesley, makes gripping reading even today. What hagiographic legend does do, however, is to render all of this conflict utterly unintelligible to us. Why did these powerful interests feel so threatened by Wesley's movement that they resorted to a campaign of concerted violence and intimidation?

Surely these interests are not enraged by being told that God loves them! When we recall the main points of Wesley's evangelical economics, however, that outrage becomes somewhat more intelligible. The denial that wealth and privilege are the sign of God's favor; the assertion that all of this is instead a robbery of God and the poor; the insistence that the poor have a

169

particular place in God's action and that concern for the poor be made the litmus test of our action; the articulation of a notion of stewardship that undermines the sacred character of private property—these are themes that are quite capable of enraging powerful interests and of leading them to incite violence and campaigns of attempted intimidation, to denounce the proponents of such views as insurrectionists in the employ of sinister foreign powers.[8] No one who has the slightest acquaintance with the history of the Church in Latin America in the last few decades particularly would find the reaction of the powerful to this sort of message in the least bit strange. That sort of persecution characterizes the life of the Church wherever it is a Church of and for the poor.

Wesley was accused of amassing an army of the poor and of being in the employ of Spain (*Journal*, 1:322-33), or of fomenting insurrection (*Journal*, I:199). Wesley responded to these political charges by making himself and the Methodists out to be super-patriots. He won that battle—and lost the war. He had produced the very sort of position that makes his political ethic unusable for any situation, save that of monarchy. Much the same dynamic is at work on the economic front.

Wesley was accused of preaching a doctrine that results in economic irresponsibility on the part of the poor and the laboring classes. To his credit, Wesley's first response to this accusation is to admit a part of the force of the objection by boldly asserting some of the principles of his evangelical economics:

I believe many of those who attend on my ministry have less of this world's goods than they had before, or, at least, might have had if they did not attend it. This fact I allow; and it may be easily accounted for in one or other of the following ways:—

First. I frequently preach on such texts as these: "Having food and raiment, let us be content therewith." "They who desire to be rich, fall into temptation and a snare. . . ." "Lay not up for yourselves treasures upon earth. . . ." (*A Farther Appeal to Men of Reason and Religion*, VIII:125)

Some cannot follow their former way of life at all; (as pawnbrokers, smugglers, buyers or sellers of uncustomed goods;)—others cannot follow it as they did before; for they cannot oppress, cheat, or defraud their neighbour; they cannot lie, or say what they do not mean; they must now speak the truth from their heart. On all these accounts, they have less of this world's goods; because they gain less than they did before. (Ibid., VIII:126-27)

This response is in general rather forthright. It does, however, pass over in silence the whole notion of stewardship for the poor.

Whatever may be said for Wesley's response, it turns out to be ineffective. The attacks at this point are not deflected. Thus Wesley is led to make even more concessions in his defense of Methodism, concessions that play directly into the hands of the precursors of what I have called the gospel of wealth and success. Here are some examples:

> You affirm, Sixthly, that I "rob and plunder the poor, so as to leave them neither bread to eat, nor raiment to put on." (Page 8.) An heavy charge, but without all colour of truth. Yea, just the reverse is true. Abundance of those in Cork, Bandon, Limerick, Dublin, as well as in all parts of England, who, a few years ago, either through sloth or profuseness, had not bread to eat, or raiment to put on, have now, by means of the Preachers called Methodists, a sufficiency of both. Since, by hearing these, they have learned to fear God, they have learned also to work with their hands, as well as to cut off every needless expense, to be good stewards of the mammon of unrighteousness. (Letter to the Rev. Mr. Baily [1750], IX:81-82)

> We, on the contrary, severely condemn all who neglect their temporal concerns, and who do not take care of everything on earth wherewith God hath entrusted them. The consequence of this is, that the Methodists, so called, do not "neglect their affairs, and impoverish their families;" but, by diligence in business, "provide things honest in the sight of all men." Insomuch, that multitudes of them, who, in time past, had scarce food to eat or raiment to put on, have now "all things needful for life and godliness;" and that for their families, as well as themselves. (Letter to the Rev. Mr. Downes [1759], IX:99)

In these passages, Wesley boasts of the very industry and frugality that are to lead the Methodists into fatal contradiction to the project of scriptural holiness. To be sure, Wesley does not go so far as to commend prosperity. He does not simply say one thing here and quite another when he speaks of the dangers of growing prosperity. But he does not make it easy for Methodists to see that they are doing anything wrong when the very results here commended are later the subject of warnings and admonitions. It looks like no more than a matter of degree rather than one of principle. And if so, why not use the dodge that one is not nearly so rich as so-and-so?

It seems likely that some of the tensions in Wesley's presentation, at least in the early period, are produced by his response to critics of Methodism. In these responses, Wesley chooses to emphasize those elements of his teaching that are most innocuous in order to make the critics appear ridiculous. Wesley seldom could resist a rhetorical knock-out punch. And the prospect of defusing these critics may have caused him to so formulate his position as to appear to accommodate the worldly wisdom he otherwise attacked. It certainly appears that Wesley gives way before the very sort of prudential reasoning he knew to be destructive of the life of faith.

THE WEIGHT OF TRADITION

It is noteworthy that those critics who attack Wesley for encouraging economic irresponsibility, and so elicit from him the responses that make difficulties for his own view of evangelical economics, are members of the clergy. They were not likely to have been the only persons to have raised these objections. But they are the ones to whom Wesley responded— in such a way as to insist on the Protestant work ethic. This is by no means fortuitous, for the clergy were expected to enforce the virtues of diligence and frugality and general economic "responsibility." This was an essential part of the doctrine of the Church of England as represented by the official Homilies.

Now, this placed Wesley under a particular difficulty. According to him, Methodists preached only the received doctrine of the Church as contained in the Articles of Religion, the Book of Common Prayer, and the Homilies.[9] This was the core of the case made by Wesley in defending his teaching about faith, about the witness of the Spirit, about empowerment by the Spirit, and so on.[10] Thus when the establishment accused Wesley of "enthusiasm" he would turn the tables to show that he, and not they, adhered to the doctrine of the Church. This may have been an especially effective ploy where bishops were concerned.

The same rhetorical ploy used to combat the political charge of insurrection and to combat the ecclesial charge of "enthusiasm" is used to deflect the charge of economic irresponsibility (a kind of insurrection and enthusiasm). Wesley is especially sensitive to this charge when it is made by clerics, since to be found in opposition to the Homilies, for example, would result in the unraveling of his defense of core doctrines. Thus Wesley has a strong incentive to make his teaching appear to be as much in harmony with the Homilies as possible, using the very language of the Homilies wherever possible. This is precisely what Wesley appears to be doing at those points where we have noticed tensions and hesitations in the treatment of evangelical economics.

The Homily "Against Idleness" emphasizes the sort of "diligence" that Wesley believed is necessary to Christian existence, but that also results in the dilemma of "increasing riches," which destroys "true religion." The Homily maintains:

> . . . every one ought, in his lawfull vocation and calling, to give himselfe to labour: and that idlenesse, being repugnant to the same ordinance is a grievous sinne. . . . [Therefore] earnestly apply yourselves, every man in his vocation, to honest labour and businesse, which as it is enjoyned unto man by God's appointment, so it wanteth not his manifold blessings and sundry benefits. . . . It is the appointment and will of God, that every man, during the time of this mortall and transitorie life, should give himselfe to such honest and godly exercise and labour, and every one follow his owne business, as to walke uprightly in his owne calling. (*Certaine Sermons or Homilies*, p. 249)

Many of the phrases of this Homily are used by Wesley in the responses to attacks we have cited above. As we have seen in Wesley's discussion of the poor (chap. 3), he does draw the line at agreeing to the Homily's observation that "a great part of the

173

beggary that is among the poore, can be imputed to nothing so much as to idlenesse " (Ibid, p. 251). Indeed, Wesley maintains that the view that idleness is the chief cause of poverty is "wickedly, devilishly false" (*Journal,* Feb 9, 1753, II:280).

That the Homilies should teach something other than evangelical economics should not be too astonishing. After all, Wesley has himself developed the idea of the Church's fall "when Constantine called himself a Christian." And what is the established Church but a perpetuation of that very corruption? If this is so, then is it so very surprising that such a Church's official economic teaching should be at variance from the gospel? Yet, Wesley's determined loyalty to the Church prevented him from seeing this contradiction. He was determined, as he said, to be a "churchman" first and last. This served as a final barrier to his development of a truly thoroughgoing evangelical economics.

This conflict becomes especially acute at the point of Wesley's growing sense of the importance of the description in Acts of the pentecostal community. We have seen that the recognition of the significance of pentecostal commun(al)ism is a direct consequence of the development of his view of stewardship. It is, then, the culmination of Wesley's evangelical economics.

But precisely at this point the prospect of a definitive break with the established Church appears, for what is in question here is not the content of one or another Homily, but one of the Articles of Religion. Article XXXVIII, "Of Christian Men's Goods, Which Are Not Common" reads:

> The Riches and Goods of Christians are not common, as touching the right, title, and possession of the same; as certain Anabaptists do falsely boast. Notwithstanding, every man ought, of such things as he possesseth, liberally to give alms to the poor, according to his ability.[11]

We need only compare this with Wesley's view, expressed, for example, in the sermon on "The General Spread of the Gospel," to see the conflict:

> The natural, necessary consequence of this will be the same as it was in the beginning of the Christian Church: "None of them will

say, that aught of the things which he possesses is his own; but they will have all things common. Neither will there be any among them that want: For as many as are possessed of lands or houses will sell them; and distribution will be made to every man, according as he has need" (VI:284)

Nor is this merely an eschatological dream, for:

If the whole church had continued in this spirit, this usage must have continued through all the ages. To affirm, therefore, that Christ did not design it should continue, is neither more nor less than to affirm that Christ did not design this measure of love should continue. (*Notes*; note to Acts 2:45)

Thus the inevitable consequence of the view of evangelical economics developed by Wesley is a direct contradiction of one of the Articles of Religion!

This conflict is also seen in the Homilies, where the "having all goods in common" is treated exclusively as a consequence of the chaos that would result if there were no obedience to kings. Thus the early "Exhortation Concerning Good Order, and Obedience to Rulers and Magistrates" warns:

Take away Kings, Princes, Rulers, Magistrates, Judges and such estates of God's order, no man shall ride or goe by the high way unrobbed, no man shall sleepe in his owne house or bedde unkilled, no man shall keepe his wife, children, and possession in quietnesse, all things shall bee common. (*Certaine Sermons or Homilies*, p. 69)

The third part of the later Homily "Against Disobedience" speaks of the rebels "who by their willes would leave unto no man anie thing of his owne" (p. 293). It is easy to see how Wesley's teaching about stewardship could alarm an establishment that views this only as inciting rebellion against the divinely sanctioned orders that protected their position and privileges.

Did Wesley see this conflict? It is possible that he did and that this was the reason he persuaded himself to forego the reference to pentecostal commun(al)ism in the rules for the select societies.[12] It is clear that Wesley stopped short of such a break, even though his views were sufficiently well known on this subject that it was the occasion of public rebuke of the Methodists.[13] After Wesley's death it fell to Coke to officially deny that Methodism taught any such thing.[14]

Wesley himself let stand the offending Article in his revision for the American Methodists, with the result that a somewhat less polemical version of the original is part of the Articles of Religion of American Methodism. Therefore, Article XXIV reads:

> The riches and goods of Christians are not common as touching the right, title, and possession of the same, as some do falsely boast. Notwithstanding, every man ought, of such things as he possesseth, liberally to give alms to the poor, according to his ability.[15]

All that is lacking is the reference to the Anabaptists. Did Wesley surrender his convictions at this point? Did he suppose that a sufficiently radical (consistent) interpretation of the second sentence would obviate the need for a definitive break with established Church tradition? Did he simply fail to see the contradiction? Was he persuaded by Coke, who obviously opposed the implications of Wesley's evangelical economics, to retain the offending Article? Or is there some other explanation?[16]

In any case we should note that while the American Methodists were let comfortably off the hook of Wesley's views about stewardship, there were still Wesleyans who did not wholly forget. Article XV of The Confession of Faith of the Evangelical United Brethren Church reads as follows:

> We believe God is the owner of all things and that the individual holding of property is lawful and is a sacred trust under God. Private property is to be used for the manifestation of Christian love and liberality, and to support the Church's mission in the world. All forms of property, whether private, corporate or public, are to be held in solemn trust and used responsibly for human good under the sovereignty of God.[17]

This is clearly a compromise formulation, which is not a fully adequate expression of Wesley's teaching.[18] Nevertheless it is manifestly more adequate than the formulation of either version of the Articles of Religion.

The consistent application of Wesley's view of stewardship leads to an acceptance of pentecostal commun(al)ism as the model for the new society of scriptural holiness. But Wesley's movement in this direction runs up against the protection of the established economic order as enshrined in The Articles of Religion. Thus Wesley's determination not to break with the Church of England in any point of doctrine means that irreconcilable equivocations are introduced into his economic ethic. The price of maintaining a doomed relationship with the Church was the weakening of Wesley's evangelical economics to the point that it could be largely forgotten following his death. The failure of the Methodist project was the price paid for an illusory continuity with official tradition.

CONCLUSION

Wesley knew that, in this respect, Methodism was a failed enterprise. He also knew that the point of failure was the abrogation in practice of the evangelical economics he tirelessly supported. As we have seen, this recognition led Wesley to cry out:

I am distressed. I know not what to do. I see what I might have done once. I might have said peremptorily and expressly, "Here I am; I and my Bible. I will not, I dare not, vary from this book, either in great things or small. I have no power to dispense with one jot or tittle of what is contained therein. I am determined to be a Bible Christian, not almost, but altogether. Who will meet me on this ground? Join me on this, or not at all. . . . But, alas! the time is now past; and what I can do now, I cannot tell. ("Causes of the Inefficacy of Christianity," VII:287)

Any attempt to rethink the practicability of an evangelical economics must take this question seriously if it is to profit not only from Wesley's teachings but also from his mistakes.

177

It is clear that Wesley himself recognized that he had not enforced these precepts with adequate rigor. What I have attempted to demonstrate is that some of Wesley's own formulations, especially in the early years of the revival, introduce ambiguity and equivocation between the demands of the gospel and the ethos of "worldly prudence." These very formulations become "canonical" through the effect of Wesley's attempt to legally secure the future of Methodism by the Model Deed and the Deed of Declaration. Moreover, these dubious formulations also appear to be motivated, at least in part, by the attempt to deflect the hostility of the powerful toward the Methodists. Despite Wesley's recognition that persecution was the inevitable consequence of true Christianity, he nevertheless shrank from a direct confrontation with vested interests over the principles of an evangelical economics. This accommodation may have been motivated in part by Wesley's reluctance to open a breach between his movement and the Church of England.

Now there is good reason to believe that Wesley himself could have been persuaded of the cogency of something like this analysis. It is not an external critique but an internal one. It holds Wesley accountable not to alien norms but to those he himself propounded and insisted upon. In plain terms, Wesley compromised with worldly prudence and so opened the way to a wholesale abandonment of his own principles on the part of the Methodists.

Of course, when we consider the enormous weight of official Church tradition and the violence of the persecution unleashed against the Methodists, we may be astonished not that Wesley compromised, but that he did not capitulate. The equivocations in his position are, in fact, few and far between, the articulation of principles generally clearly and vigorously expressed. Whatever his faults, he sounded the trumpet far more clearly than his successors have done, ourselves included.[19] Were we to be only half so radical in our proclamation and practice, Methodism in its various forms would be utterly transformed.

But if we were to seek such a transformation, we would have to learn from Wesley's mistakes that evangelical economics means that we must forego any attempt to ensure the survival of

Methodism, that we must be prepared to subject the traditions of a Constantinian Church to relentless criticism on the basis of the gospel, that we must be prepared to accept virulent opposition from vested interests as the price and seal of our discipleship. None of this should seem extraordinary. It is the character of any "scriptural Christianity."

CHAPTER NINE

THE RELEVANCE OF WESLEY

The aim of the Methodist movement as conceived by Wesley was not to generate a prosperous and successful denomination, or even several of them, but "to spread scriptural holiness throughout the land" and thence throughout the earth. The success or failure of this project depended not on increase of numbers and influence, but on an increase in faithfulness, in holiness of life. And that holiness of life had as its test or criterion the fact that the people called Methodists practice the tenets of what I have called here "evangelical economics."

By Wesley's own standard, the Methodist movement must be reckoned a failure.[1] Despite all that may and must be alleged to its credit, it has, as a movement, become a mirror and an instrument of the reign of mammon. In spite of the intentions of its founder, it has basked in the upward socioeconomic mobility of its members, making the middle class the object of its solicitous regard, the norm of the efficacy and relevance of its programs. It has made itself hostage to the dream of denominational success and influence, perverting stewardship into a new temple tax and appropriating the management and organizational models of institutional maintenance and growth. The concern for the destitute and oppressed has not been silenced, but it has been marginalized, placed not at the center, but at the periphery of institutional life and commitment.

In this the Methodist churches are not in worse condition than are other denominations. We merely echo the general forgetfulness of the evangelical call for sacrificial solidarity with the poor. But to admit this much is to see the enormity of our failure, for Methodism does not have the excuse of other denominations, which were founded on other than Wesleyan principles. If we are not centrally committed to the actualization of evangelical economics, then we are no more Methodists than we are Rosicrucians.

Although our situation is desperate, it need not be without hope. The grace we once received in the call to scriptural holiness, the grace we have squandered away in our concern for institutional survival and even success, may not be utterly withdrawn. We may yet turn and live. And if we do, we may yet be a source of life for those who are perishing, a serviceable instrument of the divine mercy.

For some, the study of Wesley may be an instrument of this turning. Others may find the study of contemporary liberation theology, with its reflection upon the experience of the poor gathered together in base communities, an impetus to turn toward something like the practice of evangelical economics. Still others may find a rereading of the Bible, the same Bible that nourished Wesley and that illumines the lives of the poor in base communities today, the most effective prod to a turn toward evangelical economics.

But however and by whomever it is done, the turn to an evangelical economics is an urgent task. Just as it mattered little to Wesley whether the members of his societies were Anglicans like himself or Quakers or Presbyterians or Congregationalists or even Catholics, so also what matters today is not so much whether Methodists rediscover evangelical economics but whether Christians do.

THE ECONOMIC CRISIS

It is becoming increasingly clear that the anti-evangelical economics of institutionalized greed and violence is destroying the earth and its inhabitants. During the Nazi horror twelve million victims, half of them Jews, were sacrificed to national pride and institutionalized insanity. But in the decade of the 1980s, one hundred million children worldwide died of poverty. *One hundred million!* Each year of the past decade, more children have died of poverty—of starvation, malnutrition, and the diseases that feed on the starving—than the Nazi horror machine could exterminate in all the years of its feverish and fiendish activity. Each year there is a new holocaust, a new sacrifice to the Moloch of greed and indifference. And like the good German neighbors of Dachau, we scarcely notice.

This slaughter of the innocents is no fortuitous calamity but the direct result of economic arrangements that blind us to reality by making us complicitous in calamity. Mortal poverty is not due, as some blasphemously maintain, to an act of God. It is the work of our economic idolatry.[2]

The earth, reeling as it is, produces more than enough food to feed plentifully every man, woman, and child on the planet. There is enough food; yet, our economic system produces murderous scarcity. A few have more than they can consume, so much that garbage disposal is a critical problem; while millions perish in sight of plenty. One nation, containing a tiny fraction of the earth's population (the majority of whom think of themselves as Christians), consumes half the earth's resources; yet, it still manages not to feed its own hungry.

If we make proposals to remedy this iniquitous hoarding and waste by the few at the expense of the many, we are told that this would destroy the economy. The economy of death. That is an economy worthy of destruction. It is open contempt of God.

This same economy of death imposes upon poor nations the crushing burden of debt, extorting interest payments by which poorer nations subsidize the excesses of richer nations. Thus the countries of Latin America, for example, so far from receiving aid from their immensely wealthy neighbor, actually export capital. And the banks and international lending agencies propose that in order to solve the "debt crisis" the poorer countries should accept "loans," the effect of which is to increase their debt and their payments of interest to these same banks.

Then the United States dominated International Monetary

Fund has the audacity to demand as the price of this "aid" that the poor countries actually reduce their assistance to the poor of their own nation, cutting back food assistance to the hungry, medical care to the dying, and education for the illiterate in order to have the honor of continuing to subsidize the wealthiest nation on earth. Neither Latin American bureaucrats nor international bankers nor the technocrats who negotiate these "final solutions" pay a penny. On the contrary, they grow wealthy creating and solving the "debt" crisis. It is only the poor who pay. The solvency of the international financial market is the blood of the poor.

The labor of the poor cannot bear the burden. Their hope of avoiding for a time the starvation that threatens them is to produce, out of the bodies of poor women, more hands to work. Since many of these infants will die, it is necessary to produce more and more. It is the only "natural resource" to which they are permitted access, the only "social security" they have. The population explosion is a direct consequence of the economy of death. Rather than seek ways to distribute more equitably the abundance of the earth, the wealthy make the problem the fault of the poor and seek to control the last remaining economic lever still in the hands of the poor.

The same economy of death that hoards resources for the wealthy must protect their "rights" against both their greedy counterparts in other nations and the increasingly desperate masses of their own. In the name of "property rights," those who protest this iniquity are imprisoned, tortured, made to disappear, and executed. Human rights are sacrificed on the altar of property rights for the privileged. What some are pleased to call the "God-given rights of liberty and property" turn out to be the right of liberty for the propertied from the protest of the poor. But no such "rights" derive from the God known to the Bible. That God is not the god of property and security but of justice and compassion.

The same economy of death diverts human resources and those of the planet to the creation of weapons of death to ensure the security of the greedy and the complacent. Vast sums are squandered on unproductive arms industries even by the poorest nations, or rather by the elite of those nations, in imitation of their wealthier cousins of the north. Thus the instability generated by the greed of the few and the impoverishment of the many induces the greedy to protect themselves from the many, thereby reducing the resources available to redress the grievances of the many, further destabilizing the societies they pretend to protect. If the poor are not deterred, they are called "communists" for not respecting the rights of the exploiters to exploit, in the certain knowledge that wealthier nations (especially the most wealthy) will provide additional loans to purchase additional arms. The vicious cycle of impoverishment and violence feeds upon itself.

This same economy of death is masked as ideological conflict, pitting two great materialistic empires against each other for the "right" to possess the earth itself, each threatening the other with the capacity to destroy the planet itself, holding the entire earth hostage to their imperial demands. The economy of death produces international nuclear terrorism as the price for maintaining itself under the mask of self-defense.

This same economy of death, meanwhile, is rapidly destroying the earth itself. More than half the arable land of the globe has already been turned into desert by the agriculture of avarice, arrogance, and ignorance. The waters of the earth are becoming cesspools, the air poisonous. Where once forests stood to cleanse the air and make it healthful for all creatures, there is now drifting sand. Where grassy plains stretched to the horizons to feed the creatures of the earth, there is now only desert. The prophets promise that the deserts can be made to bloom like gardens, but the economy of death turns the garden that remains into a desert. Already the vast majority of the earth's plant and animal species have been exterminated.

Is there no remedy? Certainly no minor adjustments in this mechanism of death will transform it into something that nourishes life. Without a radical transformation of our ways of dealing with one another and the earth, God's teeming creation may become a lifeless rock hurtling through the void of space. But from whence can such a radical transformation come?

IS THE GOSPEL RELEVANT?

Of course, we have heard that the gospel has something to say about radical transformation. Perhaps we have even heard that this transformation extends to the renewal of all creation, a new heaven and earth. But too often that very gospel has been subverted. Instead of producing a real and visible transformation, it has settled for an invisible and only nominal change. It has seemed content to produce only the religious trappings to decorate the same old greed and violence, becoming indeed a distraction from the tasks of genuine transformation by which the earth can be renewed.

How shall we explain to ourselves that nearly one-third of the earth's inhabitants claim to believe the gospel, while leaving human relationships as much characterized by greed and violence as ever they were before the gospel was first sounded forth among the poor of Galilee? If the gospel is about transformation, how is it that two thousand years of proclamation have had so little effect? How is that the wealthiest nations on earth, and the greediest and most violent, are those that claim the highest proportion of "Christians"? How is it that the gospel of Jesus Christ, so far from producing radical change, has instead become a cloak for avarice and arrogance, for a willful deafness to the cry of the poor and of the earth itself? How is it that the message of good news for the poor has become a sedative for the privileged while the poor perish?

Those who claim that the world can only be changed by converting persons one by one (or stadium by stadium) must ask whether the gospel they are preaching in fact produces any real transformation at all. Does it produce more than a nominal change, a change only in the name of the god in whose honor we continue to make the bloody sacrifice to Moloch? And in particular we "Protestants" must ask whether we have not so emphasized the sovereignty of grace as to make it impotent, so extolled its sufficiency as to render it invisible, while "faith alone" has been so stressed as to make faith a collaboration in the dominion of sin rather than liberation from it. And if we also speak of love, have we so emptied it of reality as to render it a pretty sentimentality that no longer has any idea what it would mean to lay down one's life for one's neighbor?

It is only possible to speak of the gospel as a source for a remedy of the planetary crisis that we face if we are talking about a gospel that makes possible, indeed requires and in fact produces, a radical and visible transformation in all dimensions of life. Only a gospel that produces holiness, scriptural holiness, can transform the economy of death—or rather, abolish it and give in its place something that can really be "good news to the poor."

In his own place and time, and with his own limitations and failings, Wesley sought to sound the call for just this gospel. He resolutely opposed the so-called gospel preachers who spoke of conversion without holiness, of justification without sanctification, of the vacuous sovereignty of an impotent grace.[3] These pseudo-evangelicals preach a forgiveness of sins that leaves us still enslaved to the power of sin, removing the guilt without touching the reality of sin, thus making their savior a collaborator in the dominion of Satan. But Wesley knew that the grace of God was the power to abolish the dominion of sin in human life. He had no more use for a grace that left lives and relationships unchanged than he did for the Deist's god.

Because Wesley insisted on the efficacy of grace, on its power to transform human life here and now, he was able to generate an evangelical economics. And this, not as an addendum or an extra, but as the center and the norm of the Methodist project as such. If the gospel is to be brought to bear in a meaningful way on the global economic crisis, this will occur through the development of just such an evangelical economics. Thus it may be that Wesley's reflections and practice in this sphere will at least point us in the direction of an appropriate response to the economic holocaust of our time.

THE CHALLENGE

What if the Methodists had heeded Wesley's call? What if the project of Methodism had not shattered on the rocks of prosperity and hardness of heart? What if the people called Methodists had demonstrated by the empirical evidence of their lives the truth of this gospel, the power of this grace?

A century after Wesley, a German empiricist sat writing in the British Museum, a few city blocks from the places where Wesley had preached. He wrote a description of the economic reality of England. What reality would he have described had the Methodists so-called been Methodists indeed? What if evangelical economics had triumphed over the economy of death or had at least taken the field in unswerving commitment?

When Karl Marx wrote a description of the economy of death, there was no empirical evidence that Christian commitment made any difference whatever to the course of history or to the development of the economy of death. Marx, like Wesley, was an empiricist. He looked for evidence, the evidence of altered interests, of altered relationships, of transformed society. If, several decades before, Wesley had already found Christianity generally and Methodism in particular lacking in evidence of real transformation, is it any wonder that Marx concluded that religion changed nothing, that it only distracted people from the concrete task of transforming reality? To what extent is Marxism the product of the failure of the Methodist project?

What wonder is it, then, that Marx did not conclude that Christian conversion would produce a just world? Where was the evidence? Like Wesley, Marx looked at economic reality from the perspective of the poor. Like Wesley, he was committed to the realization of a society in which all things were common, in which need was the sole criterion of possession. But if there was no evidence that the fire of economic injustice could be combated with the pentecostal flame of a renewed humanity, then some other means would have to be found to fight fire with fire. If the study of the Bible would not make people just, then perhaps the study of economic reality would. If class meetings failed, perhaps party discipline would not. If the message of divine love yielded nothing, perhaps class warfare would work. If grace proved impotent, perhaps a totalitarian state would be less impotent.

Marx chose a different path to reach a goal something like that envisioned by Wesley. Despite all of Marxism's historical achievements, it cannot be said to have succeeded. Indeed, it appears with each passing year that the Marxist experiment is yet another long and bloody detour on the road to justice. In its "orthodox" forms, it has only further postponed and even evaded and finally subverted the hope of the poor.[4] If anything, the experiments with Marxism should at least have taught us that one cannot produce justice by the means of injustice, that ends justify only those means that are themselves expressions of the ends.

Is there then no hope? Is there no real alternative to the economy of death? Was Marx right to suppose that Christianity is incapable of producing justice? Or was Wesley right after all?

There are many who will say that both Wesley and Marx were wrong to suppose that there is an alternative to the economy of death. Meanwhile, the planet is perishing. Those who share with Wesley the view that the gospel does mean a real and radical transformation, capable of transforming history, have the opportunity and the challenge to prove it. We hope for the reign of justice and joy. Can we give any evidence that this hope is well founded? Can we offer to our dying planet any sign of hope, any visible evidence of things not yet seen? That is the challenge to which we are put by our Wesleyan heritage and by the urgency of the global economic crisis.

AN AGENDA FOR METHODISTS

If Methodists are to respond to this challenge, we must seek to embody a truly evangelical economics; we must show by our lives together that grace is not impotent. In the global economic crisis that confronts us with the slaughter of the poor and the rape of the earth, there are many levels of response that may have validity. Here I want only to focus on some of the ways in which Methodist churches may seek to embody an evangelical economics. All of our calls for justice will ring hollow if we as a people do not embody the gospel that motivates these calls. What, then, would it look like for the visible and public entities known as Methodist churches to embody, if only in a partial way, this evangelical economics?

Of course, this will mean that we place the fate of the poor at the center and not at the edge or margin of our concern. It will mean that every program, every policy, every board or agency will have to justify itself in terms of the welfare of the poor. This is to say nothing more than that the gospel must be our norm and criterion.

But to do this would mean some dramatic changes in the way in which we operate. Take the way we talk about *stewardship,* for example. We should begin with a revision of our Social Principles to make clear that stewardship is not only from God but for the poor, thereby giving a more clearly Wesleyan basis to our reflections on the economic order.[5] We will have to consign to oblivion all the stewardship literature and campaign strategies that make of stewardship and of tithing a new temple tax. It will mean that we declare forthrightly that stewardship means restoring to God *in the poor* all that we have above what is necessary for life and holiness. **All.** It will mean that we banish forever the vain superstition that one can give to God by giving to the church. God has appointed the proper recipients: the poor. We must forswear all this ecclesiastical diversion of funds for our own institutional maintenance.

Of course, if we begin here some may claim that the church needs the money. But why should this be so? Is it not so because we have somehow deluded ourselves into thinking that it is good and right to build not just one temple in Jerusalem, but hundreds of them in every town and village? Do we anywhere read that Jesus or his disciples launched a building campaign? That we are commanded to build temples in the name of the gospel? Do we not, in fact, encounter the opposite on nearly every page of the Gospels? Are we not told that if we desire to identify ourselves with Jesus we may do so not by constructing temples or even social halls, but by feeding the hungry? And is it not plain that our commitment to building serves to divert a vast proportion of our resources that otherwise might be used to feed the hungry and clothe the naked? Are these temples, then, anything other than open defiance of God?[6]

But perhaps we are not yet ready even as a church to sell off all these white elephants (or camels) and give to the poor. If this seems too hard, perhaps, we could take only a modest first step: We could establish a moratorium on all new church construction until the hungry are fed. We don't have to raise an extra dime or part with a single beloved building. We just won't build anymore until children stop dying for want of food and medicine. Everything that we might have spent on pews and brass candlesticks, on bricks and glass and steel, will go for food and medicine. It might not be enough to solve the problem, but it would be a concrete sign of hope, visible evidence of our good faith. If we don't do this, can we expect that anyone will take us seriously?

Why is it that there are still some Methodist churches that have a gap, indeed a chasm, between the salaries of the highest and the lowest paid pastors? Have we so utterly sold ourselves to mammon that we must measure achievement and responsibility by the salary structure of the economy of death? Perhaps we are not yet ready to serve as Jesus commanded his disciples to serve, without a shekel in their pocket or a change of underwear (Matt. 10:9-10; Mark 6:8-9; Luke 9:3; 10:4). But surely we can agree that all those who are devoted to the gospel will receive a living wage and not a penny more. Do we imagine that anyone will believe that economic justice is possible if we do not take even this small step? The Methodist churches, descended from British Methodism, have long had the practice of uniform salaries. But wherever American Methodists have gone, we have introduced the salary system, which mirrors a corporate, rather than a Christian, standard.

We need not restrict ourselves to clergy here. Why is it that we do not insist that all who are employed by the church receive the same salary: janitors, secretaries, pastors, bishops, professors, administrators? It is often said that the greater responsibility of some justifies a greater reward. Is not the responsibility itself the reward? That some have the privilege of education, which opens the mind, of work, which gives them rewarding contact with other people and the exhilaration of relating complex ideas or institutions, ought to suggest that those who do not have these benefits should be compensated. But to suppose that because I have all the fun and glory I should also get all the money is mind boggling in its sheer perversity. How shall we give evidence of a countereconomics of the gospel, an economics of solidarity with the poor, if we are not prepared for solidarity even with our secretaries and janitors?

And what of *evangelization* and *church growth*? Can these be reformed along Wesleyan lines so that we are committed to preach good news to the poor? Can we rid ourselves here once and for all of our preferential option for the affluent? Of course, it will help if we have committed ourselves to the building moratorium; the affluent have shown an insatiable desire for temples since the days of Solomon. But can we, like Wesley, seek out only the poor, and so disentangle ourselves from the embrace of the wealthy and the influential? The California-Nevada Annual Conference sought denominational advice on how to start new churches in 1987. It was told to appoint an advisory council to the bishop of "rich men." How remarkable that the Conference did not return the proposal with the explanation that they had really had in mind churches of Jesus Christ, not temples of Baal! Why can we not ask, as Wesley did, what will enable the poor to hear good news; what will enable them to join in community? If this is not at the center even of evangelization, how can we think that we are talking about the same gospel as the one Wesley proclaimed?

And what of our institutions? We have founded hospitals and schools and homes for the elderly. But are they really oriented to the poor? How is it that Methodists build hospitals that the poor can enter only as the exceptional charity patient, homes for the elderly that only the wealthy can afford, universities that cater to the affluent? Can we not say that at least from now on we will support institutions that are primarily, centrally, perhaps even exclusively, devoted to the welfare of the poor? Hospitals that provide the least expensive care possible for the indigent, schools that meet the needs of the poorest children and youths—this is quite different from institutions that are primarily directed toward the affluent, but as a kind of charity make space for a few of the "deserving poor."

These suggestions are intentionally very modest. They only ask what would be the first steps we could take as a people to embody an evangelical economics. Surely other proposals might be advanced. But above all it is urgent that we begin to raise this sort of question, that we begin to take some steps, however faltering, toward the actualization of scriptural holiness as evangelical economics. As Methodists, we have the possibility of learning something about evangelical economics from the practice and the teaching of Wesley. But as Wesley saw, far more is at stake here than the faithfulness of the people called Methodists. What is at stake is the truth of the gospel and the healing of the earth.

THE THEOLOGICAL TASK

Although I have argued throughout this book that Wesley provides us with an important challenge both to understand and to practice an economics worthy of the gospel, I do not suppose that this can be accomplished through a simple repetition of what Wesley said and did. Rather, his thought and practice provide an impetus for attempting to do in our time and situation what he attempted to do in his. In this section, I want to indicate some of the ways in which it seems necessary to alter or transform Wesley's project if it is to become a project for us.

One of the most important advances to be made over Wesley lies in the area of biblical interpretation. Wesley sought to be, as he said, "a man of one book." That is, it was his intention, especially following his return to Oxford in 1729, to base his thought on the Bible. But Wesley was often prevented from adequately understanding the Bible by the lack of an appropriate manner of reading it. In the early days especially, Wesley tended to read the Bible as a heap of "quotable quotes," as a fund of learned citations, or as enigmatic counsel rather than as a connected whole. Thus Scripture early served for him simply as a pretext for the development of an idea.[7] Later, especially in the course of preparing his *Explanatory Notes Upon the New Testament* and under the necessity of defending his views from those of others, Wesley came to a far more contextual reading of the text. As he did so, his doctrine of the Christian life became more adequate both to the New Testament and to experience.

Never, however, does Wesley attain to a way of reading the Bible in general or the New Testament in particular that succeeds in seeing it as a whole. In the case of his evangelical economics and social ethics generally, this means that Wesley does not really succeed either in freeing himself from the remnants of traditional exegesis (as in the case of the "rich young ruler") or in seeing the connection between a concern for the poor as the fulfillment of a dominical command and the prophetic tradition of the divine judgment upon the failure to justly deal with the weaker and more vulnerable.

In this respect, it seems to me, modern biblical scholarship, especially the work of liberation theologians, provides a more ample framework of biblical reading and interpretation than was available to Wesley (or to the eighteenth century in general). One of the ways in which it is important for a contemporary Christian ethic, and especially an evangelical economics, to improve upon Wesley is precisely in the grounding of this in a more ample understanding of the biblical witness to the way and will of God. In this way it will be possible, I think, to make clearer to ordinary Christians than Wesley did the place of such a commitment to the poor.

A second area in which it seems to me to be necessary to "go beyond" Wesley is the area of anthropology. Wesley is often accused of being too individualistic in his view of human sin and salvation. Of course, in this way Wesley was simply reflective of his time, insofar as this refers to an inability to think clearly about institutions and structures. The eighteenth century was the century of the individual. But this does not mean that Wesley should be held responsible for the sort of individualism that came to characterize nineteenth-century piety or that characterizes the secular pietism of the "me" generation. Wesley did not imagine that the self in isolation could be either a Christian or a human being. Nor did he imagine that the inner drama of the interior life was more important than the transformation of relational behavior. In many ways, Wesley was far less tied to an individualistic anthropology than most of us are.

But it is the case that Wesley focused on the personal level of relationships rather than on the institutional level. He did attempt to move beyond this. He did recognize the role of social forces, for example, in the essay "On the Present Scarcity of Provisions," and he did see the interlocking interests that implicated a whole society in the slave trade. But precisely when he was operating at this level of analysis he did not think, or at least write, theologically. The categories of sin and righteousness, of grace and mercy, deserted him when he did get to the level of institutional reflection. And he was certainly at his best when he was using this theological language to illuminate the life of the person and his or her immediate relationships.

I do not think that it is fair to fault Wesley for this. But I do think it is possible and necessary to do differently. This possibility is, in part, provided by a greater clarity about the way in which biblical language and categories themselves exceed the domain of the individual and personal in order to direct themselves to the social, and even political (indeed cosmic), levels of meaning.

At the same time, it has become increasingly clear as we struggle with forces like racism, poverty, and nationalism that it is not adequate to speak of these things as simply the accumulation of personal sins. We are learning that the social reality is more than the sum of individual realities. Again, it seems to me that the attempt of liberation theologians to deal with the social character of our existence, the social character of sin and of salvation, is of great help here. In doing this, they in fact do what Wesley also did: use the best insights of the available human sciences to clarify the character of our existence.[8]

There are two contributions that Wesley may make to this attempt to take more seriously the social and institutional dimensions of our life. In the first place, Wesley's emphasis on the sinfulness of the human condition, combined with his strong confidence in the efficacy of grace in overcoming that condition, may be of help. It helps to clarify how we can really hope for a new humanity without falling into self-delusion. Capitalists tend to dismiss socialists as mere dreamers. Socialists tend to regard the defense of capitalism as a justification of sin. Surely a

Wesleyan view would enable us to acknowledge the depth of human captivity to avarice and arrogance without this acknowledgment's becoming a way of excusing the inexcusable. Similarly, it should be possible for a Wesleyan view to affirm the vision of Christian perfection and the disciplines of approximating to this end without falling into fanaticism or idle dreaming.

The resources of the Wesleyan tradition—worked out, to be sure, on the plane of the personal—may nevertheless be helpful in clarifying the way in which it is possible to speak of social transformation. We should note that Wesley certainly intended this. He certainly supposed that the gospel would transform not only individuals but also the nation. And he certainly came to see the point of Methodism as just this transformation of social reality.[9] He lacked the categories and language to make this case compellingly to his own followers. Perhaps we may be more fortunate.

The other contribution of Wesley to the project of a liberation theology lies precisely in the area of his emphasis on personal transformation. There are, to be sure, ways of speaking about faith that preclude any real or social transformation. Thus some kinds of contemporary evangelicalism do preach a faith that does not issue in any real transformation, especially not in our participation in economics. Certainly Wesley has nothing in common with this. Thus he provides a way of speaking about personal transformation that is not inimical to social transformation.

This is important because the project of liberation cannot be sustained without the transformation of persons. If arrogance and avarice are not rooted out of our lives, then so-called structural changes become merely changes in the personnel and ideology of those who occupy the same old place in the socioeconomic pyramid. This is recognized, I think, by a number of liberation theologians, perhaps with special clarity by Gustavo Gutierrez.[10] We cannot hope to have more just societies without having persons who are prepared to forgo vengeance, personal security, gain or privilege, and so on. Wesley's version of Methodism may offer a model for the development of such personal transformation.

It also seems to me that it is necessary to move beyond Wesley in the readiness to see a fundamental conflict between the gospel and the world. Certainly, Wesley recognized that powerful forces are at work in the human heart, struggling against the birth and growth of faith. He also rightly recognized that these forces are not confined to the heart but can be expected to oppose true Christianity wherever it presents itself. He thought of persecution as the normal condition of Christian existence, and in this certainly had the New Testament on his side. He also knew that the new life he proclaimed meant coming into conflict with the ways of the world, and he roundly attacked conformity with worldly standards, not least of all in economics. Nor did he yield to the temptation to withdraw from the world despite the attraction of the secluded life at Oxford. The business of the Christian was to be in the world while rejecting worldliness. These are very important insights.

But Wesley did not succeed in making clear to his followers the true danger of worldly prudence, especially in economics and politics. As we have seen, he was far more insistent on this in the economic sphere than in the political. But even there his compromises with the language of prudence were enough to permit his followers to ignore the core of his ethic. But this problem really comes to the fore in his political ethic. Wesley was not able to see that political structures could themselves be expressions of injustice, of avarice, of sin. To be sure, he sensed this in biblical language and could employ it at times in the supposition that national calamities could be seen as punishment not simply for individual but also for national sin.

Still, in order to go beyond Wesley here, it will be necessary to see more clearly the ways in which political structures are or may be demonic, idolatrous, enslaving. This again is one of the important contributions of liberation theology. These contributions do not mean a rejection of Wesley; indeed, one could argue that they do more consistently what Wesley himself recognized must be done. They make clear how it is that persecution, for example, really is ingredient to Christian existence. They suggest how it is that wealth and power are, as Wesley intuited, really hostile to Christian faith.

These are some of the elements that I believe are important if

197

we are to seek to develop an evangelical economics (and politics) that builds upon Wesley's best insights without falling into the snares that threatened even in his day to render the Methodist project unintelligible or a "dead sect." Insofar as we are prepared to develop for our own day an economics worthy of the gospel, we may yet make good Wesley's claim that never before since the days of the apostles has it been so true as it is for us that the poor hear "good news."

WESLEY ON POLITICS

Any attempt to deal constructively with Wesley's social ethic must face the conflict between Wesley's concern for the poor and oppressed on the one hand, and his apparently reactionary politics on the other. Wesley's political views threaten to make any attempt to grapple with his more radical socioeconomic views seem arbitrary.

Wesley's political views seem to make him a most unlikely advocate of anything remotely like a radical social ethic. He was devoted to the king, wrote vigorously in favor of the institution of the constitutional monarchy, opposed democracy, attacked the American Revolution—even appears to have offered to raise an army in support of the king when the revolution threatened to spread to England—and maintained that his preachers should deal with politics only to defend the king against slander. These are not the sort of views that are likely to commend Wesley to the attention of even the most reactionary Tory (who presumably accepts democracy at least as a fact of life), let alone more mainstream, liberal, or radical points of view. When it comes to working assumptions about political life, Wesley is not merely of a different era, he seems to be from a different planet.

Since appeal to Wesley's political views is sometimes made by those who desire to deflect attention from some of the more radical elements of Wesley's social ethic,[1] it is important to attend to these views in order to make possible a more clear-sighted reading of Wesley's socioeconomic ethic. In what follows I will attempt to present Wesley's political views in the context of the Anglican political theology to which he held himself accountable and in relation to the specific issues that led him to assert his own loyalty to the king. This will then open the way to a consideration of some of the more theoretical aspects of Wesley's political ethic, especially as they bear upon the question of democracy versus monarchy. This discussion will show that for Wesley the question of human rights is the decisive norm for the development of a political ethic. It is this principle, rather than its specific application in terms of constitutional monarchy, that is Wesley's lasting contribution to a Christian political ethic.

WESLEY AND ANGLICAN POLITICAL THEOLOGY

An attempt to understand Wesley's political views and their connection to the Methodist project must take into account the political theology that was the official teaching of the Church of England. Wesley took very seriously his position as priest of the Anglican Church. Among the rules of the first Methodists at Oxford was a strict adherence to the doctrine and the rubrics of the church. This included the strict observation of all fast days and regular (at least weekly) participation in the Eucharist. When he was a priest in Georgia, he was regarded as far too strict in his rigorous application of the rubrics of the church with respect both to baptism and to admission to communion.

This rigorous adherence to Anglican doctrine and polity was to a certain extent weakened by the necessity (as Wesley saw it) of preaching in the fields and, later, of designating lay preachers to care for the rapidly growing societies. This departure from settled polity brought with it the suspicion, indeed the frequent charge, that Wesley's preaching and teaching were contrary to the doctrine of the Church of England as well. Wesley vehemently denied this. Indeed, it became his practice to defend Methodist doctrine as the true teaching of the Church of England, especially as that doctrine was formulated in the *Book of Common Prayer*, the Articles of Religion, and the Homilies.

In order to see the normative place the Homilies played in Wesley's theology, it is only necessary to look at the way in which he buttresses key arguments by appeal to them. The early sermons, which lay out the basic doctrines of Methodism, contain frequent references to the Articles of Religion, the Liturgy (especially that for ordination), and the Homilies. So, for example, the sermons "The Almost Christian," "Justification by Faith," and "The Marks of the New Birth" all demonstrate the conformity of Wesley's teaching to that of the Homilies.

The reference to the authority of the Homilies is central to Wesley's defense of Methodism in the Appeals. Thus in *An Earnest Appeal to Men of Reason and Religion* Wesley defines the church in accordance with Article XIX and then defines faith in terms of the Homilies (VIII:31) in order to show that Methodism in fact strengthens the church through the true proclamation of faith. This case is then clinched in *A Farther Appeal* by extended quotations from the "liturgy, Articles or Homilies" (VIII:51). He then proceeds to show that his proclamation of justification by faith conforms to this norm (VIII:51-55). He makes extensive use of quotations from the same sources to justify his preaching of an assurance of pardon (VIII:73-75), and for his teaching on the testimony of the Holy Spirit (VIII:103-5). He concludes this defense of Methodism by saying that if he and the Methodists are enthusiasts for teaching these doctrines then so were

> Archbishop Cranmer, Bishop Ridley, Bishop Latimer, Bishop Hooper; and all the venerable compilers of our Liturgy and Homilies; all the members of both the Houses of Convocation, by whom they were revised and approved; yea, King Edward, and all his Lords and Commons together, by whose authority they were established. (VIII:110)

Wesley's apology for Methodism is, then, a bravura performance that shows that Wesley, rather than his episcopal critics, is the true defender and exponent of orthodox Anglicanism. By this means the "legitimacy" of Methodism was tied to the official teaching of the Church of England. As a national church whose head was then and is now the English monarch, the Church of England has a certain obligation to the sovereign, whose responsibilities include the selection and appointment of bishops charged with the oversight of the normal functioning of the church. In short, commitment to the Church of England entails a certain kind of political theology.

This is especially clear in the very Homilies to which Wesley appealed in defense of the legitimacy of Methodism. The *Book of Homilies* is composed of two sets of addresses written to be used by the priests in explaining the nature of true doctrine. The first set was published at the beginning of the reign of Edward VI and sets out the basic doctrine of the Church of England. The second set was written at the direction of Elizabeth I and has the task of extending the rather scanty instruction of the first set.

These officially approved sermons, then, occupy an important place in the development of the doctrine of the Anglican Church. Moreover, they may have been the model for Wesley's much longer series of doctrinal essay-sermons, which were made to be the basis of official Methodist doctrine. These Homilies treat not only of doctrinal themes like grace and faith, and of such practical themes as almsgiving, excess of apparel, and drunkenness, but they also deal prominently with the royalist political theology appropriate to a State church. Thus one of the longest of the Edwardian Homilies is entitled "An Exhortation Concerning Good Order, and Obedience to Rulers and Magistrates." And by far the longest of the Elizabethan sermons (actually six homilies in one) is entitled "An Homilie Against Disobedience and Wilfull Rebellion."[2]

Wesley, as a priest of this church, felt himself obligated to uphold its doctrine. And his apologetic stratagem of insisting on the legitimacy of Methodist teaching by reference to these Homilies means that the political theology of the Homilies plays a privileged role in the articulation of his own political views.

In order to see how this material presents Wesley with a ready-made political theology, let us first look briefly at the earlier Homily, produced under Henry VIII. The sermon begins with the notion of the ordaining will of God, which is evident in creation. This is then applied to the stratification of society on the basis of a somewhat Lutheran view of "office."

> Every degree of people in their vocation, calling and office, hath
> appointed to them their duty and order: some are in high degree,
> some in low, some Kings and Princes, some inferiors and subjects.
> (*Certaine Sermons or Homilies,* p. 69)

This notion of the stratification of the social order plays a small
role in Wesley's thought generally. It would be unthinkable for
Wesley that abject poverty (what we today call "marginalization") could be considered a specific status ordained by God. But
he could use this view to encourage people not to seek to
overturn the essential distinctions between groups or classes.

One indication of the difference between a right-wing
interpretation of this political theology and that of Wesley is
evident in one of the examples adduced in the sermon itself of
the mischief that would follow if the established orders were
overturned. In addition to the reign of lawlessness and violence,
"all things shall be common." So, far from being a sign of chaos,
this would be for Wesley a sign of scriptural holiness.

But the point of this first part of the Homily is that religion
compels us to be obedient to kings.

> [The Bible commands us] all obediently to bee subject, first and
> chiefely to the Kings [Majesty], supreme governour over all, and
> the next to his honourable counsell, and to all other noble men,
> Magistrates, and officers, which by GOD'S goodnesse, be placed
> and ordered. . . . That the high power and authoritie of kinges,
> with their making of lawes, judgements and offices, are the
> ordinances not of man, but of GOD. . . . That this good order is
> appointed by GOD'S wisdome, favour, and love, especially for
> them that love GOD. . . .That a Kinges power, authoritie, and
> strength, is a great benefite of GOD, given of his great mercie, to
> the comfort of our great miserie. (p. 70)

It is here, then, that we encounter the explicit basis of a pious
monarchism.

The second part of the Homily (actually the second
mini-sermon in a series of three with the same subject and title)
emphasizes that the duty to obey the king is an absolute one, not

dependent on the goodness of the king's rule. The thesis is "that all Subjects are bound to obey them as God's ministers, yea, although they be evill, not onely for feare, but also for conscience sake" (p. 72). From this it follows:

> It is an intolerable ignorance, madnesse, and wickednesse for subjects to make any murmuring, rebellion, resistance, or withstanding, commotion, or insurrection against their most deare and most dread Soveraigne Lord and King, ordained and appointed of GOD'S goodnes for their commodity, peace, and quietnesse. (p. 74)

But this duty is not absolute, for "we may not obey Kings, Magistrates, or any other, (though they bee our owne fathers) if they would command us to doe any thing contrary to GOD'S commandments. In such a case wee ought to say with the Apostle, [We] must rather obey GOD [than] man."

Even in this case, however, there is no justification for rebellion, but only for passive disobedience.

The third mini-sermon in this Homily emphasizes the view that kingly authority does not derive from, nor may it be superseded by, ecclesial authority, but comes directly from God. This serves as the legitimation of the separation of the Church of England from Rome.

The Homily as a whole presents a rather beneficent view of the institution of monarchy and of the place of that institution in the scheme of God's ordering of the world. To be sure, a modern reader will find some of its statements rather self-serving in the light of the royal authority that "authorizes" the teaching. But there is not to be found here the more blatant apologetics for absolutism that come to prevail in much of Continental political theology, especially during the time of Wesley.

Even the much longer Elizabethan Homily does not warrant absolutism, though it is almost entirely directed to the theme of the second part of the first Homily—the impiety of rebellion— and does make a more detailed and forceful case for obeying the prince than the Homilies in general make for, say, the importance of reformed doctrine. Some idea of the rather more forceful language of the Elizabethan Homily may be conveyed by the following quotations.

> It is evident, that obedience is the principall vertue of all vertues, and indeed the very root of all vertues, and the cause of all felicitie. . . .
>
> . . . Thus became rebellion, as you see, both the first and the greatest, and the very root of all other sinnes, and the first and principall cause, both of all worldly and bodily miseries, diseases, sickenesses, and deathes, and which is infinitely worse [than] these, as is said, the very cause of death and damnation eternall also. . . .
>
> . . . For he that nameth rebellion, nameth not a singular or one onely sinne, as is theft, robbery, murder, and such like, but he nameth the whole puddle and sinke of all sinnes against GOD and man, against his Prince, his country, his countrymen, his parents, his children, his kinsfolkes, his friends, and against all men universally, all sinnes I say against GOD and all men heaped together nameth he, that nameth rebellion. . . .
>
> . . . Heaven is the place of good obedient subjectes, and hell the prison and dungeon of rebels against GOD and their Prince. (*Certaine Sermons or Homilies*, pp. 275-76, 292, 296)

This Homily makes loyalty to the prince the sum of all virtues and disloyalty the sum of all evil. The Crown, then, is given ultimate sanction, and monarchism is made the absolute criterion of temporal and ultimate salvation.

The remarkable thing about the much longer and more monarchist Elizabethan Homily for our purposes is the insignificant role it plays in Wesley's own thought. He seems to have been content, as Elizabeth I obviously was not, with the more temperate royal theology of the first Homily. Even when Wesley deals directly with the question of the rebellion of the American colonies, he stays away from the more extreme Elizabethan language and favors the more benign and balanced view of the earlier Homily. This may also be related to Wesley's evident disapproval of Elizabeth I and his championing, in a purely scholarly way, of course, the revisionist view that Mary Queen of Scots had been unfairly and even outrageously mistreated by Elizabeth and by subsequent royalist historiographers (see, for example, III:317-18; III:383; IV:326).

It was to this royal theology, or at least some version of it, that

205

Wesley felt himself bound as a priest of the Church of England. To oppose this monarchism on any other ground than the originally sanctioned loophole (for conscience's sake to obey God rather than humans) would mean that Wesley would, in his rather strict view, have perjured himself. We shall see that Wesley was not persuaded by the American rebels that this loophole applied to their case. Still, when one considers the prominent place that this royalist theology plays in the Homilies, it is remarkable how little use Wesley makes of it. It is to a consideration of the occasions of that use and its manner that we next turn.

THE CHARGE OF SEDITION

It is remarkable that Wesley's monarchism has so little place in his sermons. Certainly it is not the case that this doctrine has anywhere near the function in Wesley's thought that it does in the Homilies of his church. For Wesley to advert to this royalist political theology, some particular crisis or catalyst appears to be necessary. This is true in spite of the fact that this political theology is not just "politics" in the modern secular sense, but is the official doctrine of the church of which Wesley was a priest.

The first crisis that leads Wesley to invoke Anglican political theology coincides with the rise of Methodism as a popular movement. Wesley's habit of preaching in public squares, marketplaces and fields meant that he was able to draw great crowds of the poor, most of whom had never voluntarily entered a church (except, perhaps, for baptisms, weddings, or funerals). These crowds generally heard him gladly, if only for the novelty of the occasion. But as they were persuaded by his message and became not only hearers, but also followers, they left off former habits of drunkenness and gambling, to the great displeasure of those who gained their living from the vices of the poor.

Clergy, too, were outraged that the Methodists reached far many more members of the parish than attended church. The "spiritual populism" of Wesley's offer of free salvation to all by grace through faith offended more aristocratic sensibilities, while it attracted growing numbers of the poor and marginalized of England. Add to this the not uncommon view of the comfortable and powerful that any stirring of the masses could only bode ill, and we begin to get an idea of the vested interests who were alarmed by the Methodist phenomenon.

The response of many, not unnaturally, was to launch a vigorous campaign of persecution against the Methodists. The decade of the 1740s, especially, witnessed a violent campaign against the Methodists. Frequently mobilized and led by the wealthy, the middle class, and the conventionally pious, mobs would attack Methodist meetings, stone the preachers, and destroy the homes and threaten the lives of ordinary Methodists. A particularly full description of one such incident is found in Wesley's *Modern Christianity Exemplified at Wednesbury* (XIII:169-93), which consists of a series of depositions taken by Wesley of the victims of this persecution. In addition, there appears to have been something of a campaign to round up Methodist preachers by "press-gangs" to be put aboard naval vessels as virtual slaves (see *Journal*, July 21, 1743, I:212; and *Journal*, July 3, 1745, I:503).

As is not uncommon in the world even today, the victims of that orchestrated mob-violence were held responsible for having caused it! After recounting his own experience at Wednesbury, Wesley notes that the Methodists have now been charged with sedition and are to be hounded out of the country. He laments: "The Christian country, where His Majesty's innocent and loyal subjects have been so treated for eight months; and are now, by their wanton persecutors, publicly branded for rioters and incendiaries!" (*Journal*, Feb. 6, 1744, I:454; see also Oct. 20, 1743, I:436-41) To add further insult to injury, Wesley himself was accused of leading an insurrection (*Journal*, Feb. 6, 1744, I:453), of organizing conventicles of sedition (*Journal*, June 4, 1739, I:199), of being in league with the pope, and of conspiring with England's enemies. Thus he reports the charge that "Mr. Wesley had large remittances from Spain, in order to make a party among the poor; and that as soon as the Spaniards landed, he was to join them with twenty thousand men" (*Journal*, June 26, 1741, I:322-23). This array of charges, if translated into contemporary idiom, will not seem unfamiliar to those Christians whose principal work it is to serve the poor.

How should one respond to this crisis, which threatened to destroy the Methodist movement before it had been fairly launched? Certainly, Wesley was not one to back off in the face of a threat of this magnitude. Tiny, even dainty, he may have appeared, but his courage was legendary. Time and again he would face down the mob, seek out its leader, and confront him face to face. That was one level of response.

Another was to appropriate the biblical themes of the conflict between the kingdom of Satan and the kingdom of God, of the inevitability of persecution, and of the requirement of unflinching witness, even to the point of martyrdom. Time and again he reminds himself and his reader that persecution must ever be the lot of those who are committed to true Christianity. Perhaps his most extended treatment of this theme is found in his sermon on Matthew 5:8-12 ("Sermon on the Mount, Discourse III," V:286-90). But this is by no means an isolated theme in Wesley's preaching. He returns to it again and again.

Yet, however powerful this theme is in his own reflection and preaching, Wesley did not, indeed could not, bring himself to draw from it the consequences for an evangelical political theology that would have placed him in flat contradiction to the political theology of his beloved Anglican Church.

Instead, Wesley appealed for justice. And it is in connection with this appeal for justice that Wesley invokes the Anglican political theology. He insists that his doctrines "do not tend to weaken either the natural or civil relations among men; or to lead inferiors to a disesteem of their superiors, even where those superiors are neither good nor sober men" (A Farther Appeal to Men of Reason and Religion, VIII:65). Nor are the Methodists seditious: "We do nothing in defiance of government: We reverence Magistrates, as the Ministers of God" (Ibid., VIII:114). In these contexts, indeed, Wesley is driven to equate the Methodist project with support for the king. Thus he writes: "If he does not love the King, he cannot love God" ("A Word to a Freeholder," XI:197). And he describes the results of the Methodist revival as follows: "Thousands of sinners in every country [have] been brought to 'fear God and honour the King' " (*A Farther Appeal*, VIII:238). Wesley writes in his *Journal*

> All I can do for his Majesty, whom I honour and love,—I think not less than I did my own father,—is this, I cry unto God, day by day, in public and in private, to put all his enemies to confusion: And I exhort all that hear me to do the same; and, in their several stations, to exert themselves as loyal subjects; who, so long as they fear God, cannot but honour the King (*Journal*, Sept. 21, 1745, I:519)

Taken in isolation, these and similar texts would persuade the unwary reader that Anglican political theology was a central and regular theme of Wesley's preaching and teaching. Such a view would be mistaken. This political theology only appears in responses to charges made against the Methodists. Wesley deploys it here for purely defensive purposes. This is not to say that Wesley was insincere. He accepted, as a matter of course, the authority of the *Book of Common Prayer*, the Articles of Religion, and the Homilies. Indeed, he felt obliged to do so as a priest of the church, and he regarded those priests who did not as being guilty of perjury—a crime to which he was particularly sensitive and against which he inveighed so strongly in a famous sermon for Oxford ("True Christianity Defended," VII:452-62; see also "Scriptural Christianity," V:51). Wesley accepted the tenets of this political theology, but he never made them central themes.

As it happened, events turned out to justify this theology. Despite pressure from powerful and influential figures in church and politics, the king let it be known, as Wesley would phrase it, that there was a law even for Methodists. Much later, Wesley gave this account:

> God stirred up the heart of our late gracious Sovereign [George II] to give such orders to his Magistrates as, being put in execution, effectually quelled the madness of the people. It was about the same time that a great man applied personally to His Majesty, begging that he would please to "take a course to stop these run-about Preachers." His Majesty, looking sternly upon him, answered without ceremony, like a King, "I tell you, while I sit on

the throne, no man shall be persecuted for conscience' sake. ("On God's Vineyard," VII:210)

The protection of the king meant that Methodists were granted equal protection under the laws. This was enough for Wesley. When ordered to stop preaching in Shaftsbury, Wesley replied: "While King George gives me leave to preach, I shall not ask the leave of the Mayor of Shaftesbury" (*Journal*, Sept. 3, 1750, II:207). The irony that the king's position was based not on his role as head of the Church of England but on his Deistic principles was not entirely lost on Wesley. But that is another story.[3]

In any event, the king had acted in such a way as to fully justify Anglican political theology. The necessity of developing a counter political theology on the basis of the theme of persecution had passed. To be sure, these themes continue to play an important part in Wesley's theology; they are, after all, relatively prominent in the New Testament. But Wesley was able to account for the suspension of the persecution on the basis of the extraordinary providence of God in restraining the hand of Satan (see again his sermon on Matt. 5:8-12, V:290).

Wesley was naturally grateful to the king for this intervention. He had received justice. And this strengthened both his personal loyalty to the sovereign and his confidence in the institution of the constitutional monarchy, established by the Glorious Revolution of the previous century. While this by no means resulted in an uncritical attitude toward government policy (see chap. 4), it did mean that Wesley concerned himself with the question of making the system work. Thus he attacked the smuggling that was rife in Cornwall as robbery of the king ("A Word to a Smuggler," XI:174-78), inveighed against corruption and fraud in elections ("A Word to a Freeholder," XI:196-97), and urged his preachers to counter slander against the king ("How Far Is It the Duty of a Christian Minister to Preach Politics?" XI:154-55). Such was the result of the first crisis. Wesley was publicly committed to a moderate constitutional monarchism and thus to the political theology of the early Homilies.

AGAINST THE REBELLION IN AMERICA

Wesley, ever the pragmatic empiricist, had learned from experience that the constitutional monarchy of George II and George III justified by its policies the moderate royalism of the early Homilies. In spite of this, when unrest was reported in Britain's North American colonies, Wesley was prepared to take seriously the grievances of the colonists. Indeed, he makes clear that he initially believed them to be in the right over against the king's ministers. Thus writing in 1768 in his "Free Thoughts on the Present State of Public Affairs," he avers: "I do not defend the measures which have been taken with regard to America: I doubt whether any man can defend them, either on the foot of law, equity, or prudence" (XI:24).

But when protest turned to outright rebellion, Wesley had second thoughts. Now what was at stake was not the reform of the system but the rejection of the system—the repudiation of the very principle of monarchy and thus the heart of Anglican political theology. Nor was this threat limited to the colonies. They were Englishmen after all. And there was sympathy for the cause of these seditious republicans in England itself, where the economy had been battered by a severe depression (which had occasioned Wesley's "Thoughts Upon the Present Scarcity of Provisions" in 1772).[4] Moreover, the "German" king had no automatic base of nationalistic fervor from which to draw as a defense of the throne.

Now this crisis could have been regarded as an entirely secular matter in which an evangelist need not interest himself. But Wesley threw himself into the political debate with characteristic zeal and thoroughness. For the sake of clarity, we may distinguish three levels of Wesley's response: (1) a personal defense of the king, whose father had saved the Methodists from persecution; (2) a consideration of the justice of the claims of the colonists; and (3) a theoretical discussion of the relative merits of constitutional monarchy versus republican democracy. A consideration of each of these levels is necessary if we are to see that Wesley's response to the American Revolution was by no means the knee-jerk reaction of an ideological monarchist but a careful and measured reflection.

Defense of the King

Wesley first comes to the defense of the king whom he believed to be unfairly and personally attacked. Thus Wesley writes of the monarch's being pilloried in the colonial press: "His whole conduct, both in public and private, ever since he began his reign, the uniform tenor of his behaviour, the general course both of his words and actions, has been worthy of an Englishman, worthy of a Christian, and worthy of a King" ("Free Thoughts on Public Affairs," XI:20). In "A Word to a Smuggler" (1766), Wesley writes: "King George is the father of all his subjects; and not only so, but he is a good father. He shows his love to them on all occasions; and is continually doing all that is in his power to make his subjects happy" (XI:174). Wesley even felt obliged to defend the king against those who derided his Germanic extraction:

> I was desired to go and hear the King deliver his speech in the House of Lords. But how agreeably was I surprised! He pronounced every word with exact propriety. I much doubt whether there be any other King in Europe, that is so just and natural a speaker. (*Journal*, Jan. 24, 1786, IV:325)

High praise indeed from one of the century's most noted public speakers!

Moreover, Wesley was in a position to counter alarmist views of the state of the nation (see "A Serious Address to the People of England, with Regard to the State of the Nation," 1778, XI:140-49; and "A Compassionate Address to the Inhabitants of Ireland," 1778, XI:149-54). His views on this matter were credible because of his earlier critical analysis of these conditions in his reflections "On the Present Scarcity of Provisions" (XI:53-59).

Perhaps the most bizarre episode in all this is Wesley's admission of having gone much further than mere political advocacy in defense of the king. By far the most astonishing testimony to the extent of Wesley's monarchism is found in a letter of 1782 in which he writes:

> Two or three years ago, when the kingdom was in imminent danger, I made an offer to the Government of raising some men. The Secretary of War (by the King's order) wrote me word, that "it

was not necessary; but if it ever should be necessary, His Majesty would let me know." (Letter to Joseph Benson, Aug. 3, 1782, XII:430)

Wesley himself seems to have realized that this may have been going too far, as he adds: "I never renewed the offer, and never intended it."

Debunking the Rebels

Those who take both the success and the justice of the rebels' cause for granted can only find Wesley's opposition to the rebel cause inexcusably reactionary. This is all the more true in the United States itself, where the cause of the revolution has come to be synonymous with "liberty and justice for all." How is it possible that Wesley—with his clear commitment to the cause of the poor and downtrodden as well as a commitment to justice, which led him to oppose both the slave trade and colonial policy in India—could have closed his eyes to the nobility of the revolution? The answer, of course, is that Wesley had a very different view of the rebels.

In the first place, he was suspicious of them precisely *because* of his opposition to slavery. When the rebel propagandists claimed that they had been deprived of liberty, that they were resisting tyranny, Wesley replied with massive sarcasm: "You and I, and the English in general, go where we will, and enjoy the fruit of our labours: This is liberty. The Negro does not: This is slavery" ("A Calm Address to Our American Colonies," XI:81). In short, the protestation that the rebels were fighting for the cause of liberty was pure humbug. Their interest was not in the cause of human liberty but in their own "independency."

And Wesley, the indefatigable champion of the poor, had even more cause for regarding the rebels' cause with antipathy, for these rebels were not like the poor of Sligo, who had taken matters into their own hands to protest their exploitation at the hands of the wealthy (*Journal*, May 27, 1758, II:446), nor were they like the poor of Belfast, who had been driven to outright insurrection by similar exploitation (*Journal*, June 15, 1773, III:499). With these causes Wesley had expressed sympathy (as he had with run-away slaves; see chap. 4).[5] But the rebels in America seemed to Wesley to be cut of quite a different cloth.

Wesley gives some idea of who he takes these rebels to be in his sermon "Some Account of the Late Work of God in North-America," written in 1778. After recounting the spread of the gospel, he writes:

> But now it was that a bar appeared in the way, a grand hinderance to the progress of religion. The immense trade of America, greater in proportion than even that of the mother-country, brought in an immense flow of wealth, which was also continually increasing. Hence both merchants and tradesmen of various kinds accumulated money without end, and rose from indigence to opulent fortunes, quicker than any could do in Europe. Riches poured in upon them as a flood, and treasures were heaped up as the sand of the sea. (VII:412)

He goes on to link this wealth to the increase of pride, sloth, and luxury and thus to the growth of a spirit of independence and a corresponding loss of concern for religion.

Now, is it so mysterious that Wesley would find little sympathy in his heart for the rebellion of slaveholders and merchant princes and Deists? These were the very sort of people whose injustice to the poor he so regularly denounced in England. Nor is it possible to dismiss Wesley's suspicions of the motives of these rebels as mere royalist propaganda. The great American historian Charles A. Beard discovered much the same when he investigated the authors of the Constitution a century and a half later.[6]

But there is more reason for Wesley to be suspicious of the motives of the rebels. They claimed that they were unjustly treated, since they had no representation in Parliament. One of their slogans had been "no taxation without representation." Wesley was not impressed: "Indeed you had no vote for members of Parliament; neither have I, because I have no freehold in England" ("A Calm Address to Our American Colonies," XI:89). At that time the vote was restricted only to those who held real estate. Wesley, of course, had none and wanted none. Of course, the rebels might reply, "But we are men of property and yet we have no vote." But then again we are back to the point above. These "freedom fighters" were not interested in human rights generally but in the rights of the propertied classes. Wesley was unmoved.

The rebels urged their cause by appealing for the rights of the people to elect their own governors. Two hundred years later it seems a reasonable request. But Wesley saw it differently, for in truth this rhetoric about democracy was simply moral imposture. The colonists argued that what was at stake was the inalienable right of all those created by God to liberty, to participation in government, and so on. But in truth these were mere empty words. They claimed that "a right of choosing his governors belongs to every partaker of human nature." But if this be so, Wesley notes, then consequences will follow, which the rebels will be most decidedly *not* prepared to draw:

> If this be so, then it belongs to every individual of the human species; consequently, not to freeholders alone, but to all men; not to men only, but to women also; nor only to adult men and women, to those who have lived one-and-twenty years, but to those who have lived eighteen or twenty, as well as those who have lived threescore. ("Thoughts Concerning the Origin of Power," XI:53)

Wesley makes the same point in another essay: "But who are the whole body of the people [who have this right]? . . . Every free agent. . . . [But] are not women free agents? Yea, and poor as well as rich men" ("A Calm Address to Our American Colonies," XI:81). All this talk of inalienable rights, then, is but the cover for insisting on the exclusive rights of the class of merchant princes and slaveholders!

It is difficult even two hundred years later to dismiss Wesley's arguments. After all, it took a century for the United States even to recognize the principle of extending the franchise to blacks (1870), and one hundred and fifty years before these rights were extended to women (1920), and two hundred years before real progress even began to be made in actually extending these rights to the descendents of slaves. Even today the idea of equal rights is controversial. And those who oppose things like the Voting Rights Act or the Equal Rights Amendment or the application of Constitutional rights to new cases of inequity are the ones who continue to insist that the most important rights are the rights of property. Even today Wesley's cynicism about the motives of those who talk grandly about rights as a cover for greed and arrogance has an unfortunate ring of truth.

Political Philosophy

Despite Wesley's loyalty to the king and his deep suspicion of the motives of the rebels, he was not inclined to let the case rest with these contingent issues. What if the king had been a tyrant? What if the rebels had been saints? Wesley's inquiring intellect could not let things go with an argument about cases; he wanted to get to principles as well. The principle issue is whether "democracy" is better than monarchy.

One of Wesley's arguments is based on the royal theology of the Anglican Church ("Thoughts Concerning the Origin of Power," XI:46-54). It is that the source of sovereignty is God, rather than the people. Thus the monarch's position is the one that reflects Paul's well-known argument in Romans 13 that our governors are servants of God. The notion that the people are sovereign utterly destroys the sense of Paul's argument. It is interesting in this regard that the flip side of Wesley's argument is that where sovereignty does reside in the people, then Romans 13 is no longer applicable, and the whole of Anglican political theology falls to the ground. This means that the only group who can appeal to Wesley's conservative argument that we ought to be obedient to our governors are those who deny that sovereignty flows from the people—that is, they deny the foundation of democracy. But where governments derive their legitimacy from the people, whether actually or rhetorically, then no appeal to this sort of political theology is possible. It is astonishing that even in that majority of nations where governmental legitimacy derives from the people, at least in theory, people continue to cite some version of a "divine right of kings" argument to forestall civil disobedience!

But Wesley seems to know that this is not a very good argument in any case. It begs the question. It proves the superiority of monarchy by reciting the theoretical basis of monarchy. But it is just this theoretical basis that must be justified. It may also be that Wesley was uncomfortable with this argument since it proved rather more than he wanted. It proved not only the superiority of the British monarchy but, even more, the absolutist claims of some European monarchies as well. But why should that bother Wesley? Because his main concern was not with monarchy at all but with a principle that today would be called human rights.

There was considerable common ground between Wesley and his opponents in this dispute. Both sides, at least in principle, agreed that the test for government was the principle of human rights. Which form of government really did best protect these universal rights? Wesley was persuaded that democracy was bad for human rights: "No governments under heaven are so despotic as the republican; no subjects are governed in so arbitrary a manner as those of a commonwealth" ("A Calm Address to Our American Colonies," XI:87). And when Wesley turns to rate the various options for government he finds: "There is most liberty of all, civil and religious, under a limited monarchy; there is usually less under an aristocracy, and least of all under a democracy" ("Some Observations on Liberty," XI:105). In all of this Wesley is simply working within mainstream political theory. Indeed, one of the severest problems faced by the framers of the Constitution was how to prevent democracy from becoming a dictatorship of the mob. It is a question as old as Plato and the beginnings of political theory.

As we know, Wesley was also an empiricist. It is not surprising, then, that one of his most telling arguments is based on experience. What is the actual state of civil and religious liberty in the rebellious colonies as opposed to monarchical England? In the colonies, he maintains:

> There is not the very shadow of liberty left in the confederate provinces[.] There is no liberty of the press. A man may more safely print against the Church in Italy or Spain, than publish a tittle against the Congress in New-England or Pennsylvania. There is no religious liberty. What Minister is permitted to follow his own conscience in the execution of his office? to put man in mind to be "subject to principalities and powers?" to "fear God and honour

the King?" Who is suffered (whatever his conscience may dictate) to "pray for the King, and all that are in authority?" There is no civil liberty. No man hath any security, either for his goods, or for his person; but is daily liable to have his goods spoiled or taken away, without either law or form of law, and to suffer the most cruel outrage as to his person, such as many would account worse than death. ("A Calm Address to the Inhabitants of England," XI:136)

The contrast to the situation in England is stark.

English liberty commenced at the Revolution [of 1688]. And how entire is it at this day! Every man says what he will, writes what he will, prints what he will. Every man worships God, if he worships him at all, as he is persuaded in his own mind. Every man enjoys his own property; nor can the King himself take a shilling of it, but according to law. Every man enjoys the freedom of his person, unless the law of the land authorize his confinement. Above all, every man's life is secured, as well from the King, as from his fellow-subjects. So that it is impossible to conceive a fuller liberty than we enjoy, both as to religion, life, body, and goods. (Ibid., XI:137)

For Wesley, the empirical argument concerning the actual state of human rights was devastating to the pretensions of the rebels.[7]

It is not necessary to rehearse here all of Wesley's arguments in justification of the view that limited monarchy, rather than democracy, is the best guarantor of human rights, of "religious and civil liberty." What is critical for our purposes is that Wesley makes this argument at all. Clearly for him the test of any government is how it protects these liberties, these rights. It is here, rather than in his use of Anglican political theology (which in any case applies, in Wesley's view, only to monarchical governments), that we find the relevance of Wesley's political thought for the altered circumstances of our era.

Now it must be clear that Wesley does not simply talk about the criterion of liberty as a concession to his opponents. While it is true that Wesley only invokes Anglican political theology in times of crisis (as in the persecution of the Methodists or the defense of the king from the propaganda of the American rebels) this is by no means the case with respect to the talk of liberty and human rights. This is not an *ad hoc* theme for Wesley but one that he employs in quite varied circumstances. It is for him a truly basic principle.

Thus Wesley uses this principle to show the unacceptability of slavery and of religious persecution. He uses it to oppose press-gangs early in his ministry and to oppose the corruption of legal institutions throughout his ministry. Early and late, in addressing a broad range of issues, Wesley defends and applies this principle. Thus he is more than prepared to admit its relevance to the discussion of political theory. It is his principle, after all, in a way that royalism never was. Wesley's talk of liberty is not a mere "flag of convenience" under which to protect the ship of monarchical state.

Moreover, it is a principle that is consonant with other of Wesley's constant theological themes. The doctrines of creation and of the image of God were directly linked to the aspiration for dignity and liberty. The doctrine of universal grace further emphasized the ultimate worth of individual persons in the work of God. Moreover, the principle of human rights fits neatly into Wesley's practice not only of reaching out to the poor with the gospel but also of championing their cause against the multitude of ways they were subjected to humiliation and exploitation. Indeed, on this basis Wesley had far greater claim to this principle than did the merchants and slaveholders who called for revolution.

We began this discussion of Wesley's response to the American Revolution by noting that it occasioned his use of the political theology of the Homilies. But we have seen that Wesley does not do this as a knee-jerk reaction. He does have reason to believe that the king is the friend of religious liberty; that has been proven by experience. He also has reason to believe that the American claims are simply a mask for special interests and have nothing to do with either liberty or justice. And he is persuaded that democracy is a poor protection for liberty and justice. None of these arguments can be simply dismissed as reactionary.

Wesley was prepared to come into conflict with official Anglican theology. We have seen him do so in the case of his appropriation of a radical economic ethic based on the New Testament. Thus the mere fact that the defense of monarchy was enshrined in Anglican political theology would not have absolutely precluded Wesley from reluctantly criticizing it. But the monarchy's defense of essential rights had been more than amply demonstrated by Wesley's own experience. He thus had no hesitation in making use of the Anglican political theology, which called for obedience to the king, and in calling for others to do so as well. It is against this background that we must understand the apparent "royalism" of passages like the following.

> It is my religion which obliges me "to put men in mind to be subject to principalities and powers." Loyalty is with me an essential branch of religion, and which I am sorry any Methodist should forget. There is the closest connexion, therefore, between my religious and my political conduct; the selfsame authority enjoining me to "fear God," and to "honour the King." (Letter to Walter Churchey, June 25, 1777, XII:435)

Assessment

We began this study confronted by what appeared to be a mystery: How was it that Wesley, with his radical economic ethic, could have held such a reactionary royalist political view? It turns out that where there appeared to be flat contradiction there is instead fundamental harmony. Wesley did not invent the monarchist political ideology that he sometimes employed. It was a key element in the theology of the Church of England. To break free of it would require compelling reasons. But Wesley had learned from experience that the monarchy protected religious liberty even for the Methodists. Those who were accused of rabble-rousing the poor were protected by the king over the objection of the powerful and the influential. That in itself was enough to earn Wesley's gratitude. And the very sympathy for the poor and down-trodden, which governed his economic ethic, made it impossible for him to find sympathy for a rebellion of the wealthy and, from his point of view, oppressors. And far from rejecting talk of human liberty and dignity as dangerous rubbish, there is every reason to say that Wesley took these things far more seriously than did many of the rebels.

This is not to say that Wesley's views of human rights are in every way like those of modern thinkers. He was passionately committed to the freedom of conscience and religion and, over time, came to be persuaded that slavery was an appalling deprivation of rights. But beyond this his views are, at best, embryonic. He does seem to support the freedom of the press, so long as writers are held accountable for veracity, but he obviously was not persuaded that liberty entailed active participation in government. In general his view of civil liberty was modest, claiming that people had the right not to be robbed, beaten, imprisoned, or killed by the powerful or the government. These rights were not absolute since he did suppose the government had a right to tax its subjects so long as this was done in conformity with constitutional standards. And government had the right to deprive criminals of their liberty (and presumably their lives) so long as this was done in accordance with law and did not serve to deny freedom of conscience. But Wesley saw no contradiction between this view and the support of constitutional monarchy. Indeed, he feared the loss of these liberties, especially the most basic freedom of conscience, if the existing order were overthrown. Thus he could defend the traditional Anglican political theology with a clear conscience and characteristic vigor.

In our time the Anglican political theology of kingship that Wesley supported has very little relevance. It has become very much a dead letter for most of the earth's population. But that does not necessarily mean that Wesley's political ethic has no relevance, for that ethic is far more than royalism. It tests the state by two inter-related criteria: (1) What is the consequence for the poor? and (2) What is the consequence for human rights? Wesley directs these to public policy and to political systems.[8] And they remain important questions today.

A Wesleyan political ethic may find ample room for development here. But it also has the added precedent of

Wesley's "hermeneutic of suspicion," directed against those who use talk of liberty as a cover for the promotion of special and limited interests, who use talk of democracy as a cover for avarice and arrogance.[9] The spiritual descendants of the slaveholders and merchant princes of Wesley's day have often acted in ways that have left many in the Third World more than a little dubious about the motives of those who promote "liberal democracy" or even "democratic capitalism." They may find that Wesley is a useful example of the sort of critique that may also be relevant today.

In many places in the world, it may also be fruitful to reflect on the "road not taken" by Wesley. Wesley's confidence in the king was not blind; it was not the product of royalist ideology. Rather, the king had earned his loyalty. The king had acted to defend the religious and civil liberties of his subjects. In consequence, Wesley had no need to develop an alternative to the Anglican political theology. But the means for doing so were readily at hand. He knew that the way of Christian witness was a way that always led to persecution, to the opposition of the powerful. He could maintain that "being despised is absolutely necessary to our doing good in the world" (Letter to His Father, Dec. 10, 1734, in *Journal*, I:184). And he could regard it as extraordinary that persecution had abated (*Journal*, II:222, 298).

As I have shown, Wesley did not need to develop his political theology on this basis. But for many Methodists in many parts of the world, the government does not thus protect the rights of its people. Instead the government itself launches the persecution of those who bring hope to the poor and who work in solidarity with the marginalized. In these circumstances the land is fertile for the development of a different political ethic, one based on, perhaps, a broader biblical foundation than the one Wesley was able to embrace in eighteenth-century England. That is the road not taken. But those who take it today are more "true" to Wesley than those who seek to do what Wesley never did: legitimate the rule of oppression and exploitation. The circumstances are right for Wesleyan theologians, on Wesleyan principles, to develop a thoroughly radical political ethic: a theology of liberation.[10]

NOTES

1. Introduction

1. See my *Life as Worship: Prayer and Praise in Jesus' Name* (Grand Rapids: Eerdmans, 1982), and *The Liturgy of Liberation: The Confession and Forgiveness of Sins* (Nashville: Abingdon Press, 1988).

2. The Demystification of Wealth

1. For a discussion of this problem, see Ana Maria Ezcurra, *Agresión ideólogica contra la revolución sandinista* (Mexico City: Nuevomar, 1983), and Cayetano de Lella, ed., *Cristianismo y liberación en América Latina* (Mexico City: Nuevomar, 1984), pp. 65-94.
2. John Wesley, "Sermon on the Mount, Discourse VIII," in *The Works of the Rev. John Wesley, A.M.*, ed. Thomas Jackson, 3rd ed., 14 vols. (London: Wesleyan Methodist Book Room, 1872; reprinted Grand Rapids: Baker Book House, 1979), V:366. Unless otherwise indicated, all subsequent references to Wesley's writings will be to this edition of his *Works*, cited in parentheses in the main body of the text by volume and page number(s).
3. It is astonishing in the light of this and similar passages that Wellman J. Warner, in *The Wesleyan Movement in the Industrial Revolution* (New York: Macmillan, 1930; reprinted Russell & Russell, 1967), could still speak of the "wholeheartedness with which [Wesley's Methodism] approved economic enterprise and the pursuit of gain" (p. 138), or suppose that economic success could be viewed unambiguously as a mark of divine approval for Wesley's Methodism (p. 161). Warner may be right in attributing these views to Methodists after the time of Wesley, but there is no possibility of attributing these views to Wesley himself.
4. The "Index of Scriptural References" provided by Albert C. Outler in his edition of Wesley's sermons lists 36 references to I Tim. 6:9-10; see *The Works of John Wesley*, vol. 4: *Sermons IV, 115-51*, edited by Albert C. Outler (Nashville: Abingdon Press, 1987), p. 681. This does not include references to speaking on the texts in his *Journal* or allusions to them in his letters and essays.
5. See the sermon "Of Former Times," VII:165.

6. That liberation theology is above all a practical theology that is concerned to understand and transform the pastoral function of the Church is emphasized by a number of these theologians. See, for example, Juan Luis Segundo, *The Hidden Motives of Pastoral Action* (Maryknoll, N.Y.: Orbis Books, 1978), and José Míguez Bonino, *Doing Theology in a Revolutionary Situation* (Philadelphia: Fortress Press, 1975).

7. Wesley uses this term to refer to the whole spectrum of the biblical message from creation to eschatology. One of the decisive contributions of liberation theology is to anchor the view of solidarity with the poor, protest against injustice, and social transformation in just such an ample reading of the Bible. See chapter 9 below.

8. "On Family Religion," VII:84-85.

3. A Preferential Option for the Poor

1. The recognition of the danger of a merely sentimental attachment to the poor is a characteristic of the theology of liberation. See Gustavo Gutierrez, *We Drink from Our Own Wells: The Spiritual Journey of a People* (Maryknoll, N.Y.: Orbis Books, 1984), p. 16.

2. In the United States today, for example, almost daily there are stories of the terrible risks run by "illegal aliens" in their desperate quest for work—and the most gruelling sort of work at that. Astonishingly, many of the same people who claim that the poor are lazy seek to place even more obstacles in the way of those who stake their very lives in the search for honest employment.

3. Wesley was often pressed to pay off the debt incurred for the building or purchase of the many Methodist chapels that were an increasingly important feature of the movement. This exigency even led to the class meeting as the typical form of Methodist organization, as Wesley noted in his *Short History of the People Called Methodists*, XIII:310. But this activity is not referred to when Wesley deals with stewardship. It remains true that the taking of collections was generally related to the relief of the poor in contrast to the "subscription" that was used to pay off the debt.

4. One of Wesley's criticisms of the Moravians was the partiality of their compassion. He wrote, "I do not admire their confining their beneficence to the narrow bounds of their own society" (*Journal*, Nov. 28, 1750, II:214; see also *Journal*, Dec. 21, 1751, II:248).

5. For further discussion of this aspect of Wesley's ministry, see E. Brooks Holifield, *Health and Medicine in the Methodist Tradition* (New York: Crossroad, 1986).

6. Gutierrez notes: "There is no authentic evangelization that is not accompanied by action in behalf of the poor" (*We Drink from Our Own Wells*, p. 44). In this respect Wesley's position is even more consistent than that of Gutierrez since, for Wesley, it is not a matter of two actions in tandem but of even evangelization's being governed by the commitment to the poor.

7. Warner provides a helpful summary of the role Methodism played in fostering this movement (*The Wesleyan Movement in the Industrial Revolution*, pp. 333-36).

8. When, in 1976, the youths of Soweto in South Africa burned down the Shabeens (government sponsored speakeasies), protesting that these

saloons were providing the government with revenue while poisoning the bodies of the poor and so drugging their minds that they could not change their situation, they were making a decidedly Wesleyan point.

4. Protest Against Injustice

1. Wesley, for example, protests against the view of a certain Dr. Cadogen, who recommended total abstinence from wine, "But why should he condemn wine *toto genere*, which is one of the noblest cordials in nature?" (*Journal*, Oct. 9, 1771, III:443).
2. But see the reference to Wesley's mysterious offer to raise troops for the Crown in the Appendix, pp. 199-22.
3. For a description of the way in which Methodism, following the death of Wesley, turned its back on Wesley's social ethic in this as in other respects, see Bernard Semmel, *The Methodist Revolution* (New York: Basic Books, 1973), pp. 146-69.
4. The "honest Quaker" was Anthony Benezet, who wrote three attacks on the institution of slavery from 1762 to 1771. The anti-slavery position of the Quakers dates from as early as 1727. See Warner, *The Wesleyan Movement in the Industrial Revolution*, pp. 42-43.
5. *Thoughts Upon Slavery* (XI:59-79) contains large sections extracted from the book by Anthony Benezet that had earlier impressed him.
6. This is not clearly recognized by Leon O. Hynson in his celebration of the Wesleyan position on human liberty in *To Reform the Nation: Theological Foundations of Wesley's Ethics* (Grand Rapids: Francis Asbury Press, 1984).
7. For a brief description of the relationship between these forms of trade monopoly and their importance to England, see Franz Hinkelammert, "Las condiciones económico-sociales del Metodismo en la Inglaterra del Siglo XVIII," in *La tradición protestante en la teología latinoamericana*, ed. José Duqué (San José, Costa Rica: DEI, 1983), pp. 21-30. This economic analysis of theology is applied to our own context in Hinkelammert's "The Economic Roots of Idolatry: Entrepreneurial Metaphysics," in Pablo Richard et al., *The Idols of Death and the God of Life: A Theology* (Maryknoll, N.Y.: Orbis Books, 1983).
8. For an excellent analysis of liberation theology, see Rebecca Chopp, *The Praxis of Suffering* (Maryknoll, N.Y.: Orbis Books, 1986).
9. One of the weaknesses of Semmel's presentation of Wesley's political ethic is that he speaks of Wesley's horror of mob violence without recognizing the basis of this horror in Wesley's own experience. See Semmel, *The Methodist Revolution*, p. 63.
10. Indeed, a difference that separates the proponents of Marxist theory from those of liberation theology is that the former proclaim an abstract right of the oppressed to engage in armed struggle, but in practice oppose it wherever the interests of powerful Marxists are threatened, as in Hungary, Poland, or Afghanistan. Many liberation theologians oppose violence, but refuse to offer a blanket condemnation when the poor are driven to insurrection by the oppression of the powerful, whatever they may call themselves. Wesley will not embrace any theory of armed struggle, but he does not suppose that the poor may be justly condemned for actions to which they are driven by their oppressors.

5. Stewardship: The Redistribution of Wealth

1. Warner and Semmel are equally oblivious to this dimension of Wesley's thought.
2. It is a pity that Wesley did not see clearly the implication of this for the relation to Caesar, for there cannot be two owners, and if God truly is the sole proprietor, that leaves Caesar holding an empty bag!
3. In this Wesley stands in essential continuity with the teaching of the early Church. See, for example, the relevant sermons of Leo the Great in *The Nicene and Post-Nicene Fathers*, 2nd series, vol. XII (Grand Rapids: Eerdmans, reprint 1956). Especially important are the two sermons "On the Collection" (IX and X), but the sermons on fasting (XII, XVI, and XVII) are also relevant here, providing an early parallel to these elements of Wesley's teaching.
4. It must be clear that for this sort of evangelical economics, giving to the poor is not a matter of "charity" but of justice. This principle had already been clearly formulated by St. Gregory the Great in his *Pastoral Rule* when he wrote, "For when we administer necessaries to the indigent, we do not bestow our own, but render them what is theirs; we rather pay a debt of justice than accomplish works of mercy." See *The Nicene and Post-Nicene Fathers*, 2nd series, vol. XII (Grand Rapids: Eerdmans, reprint 1956), p. 47. Thus Warner (*The Wesleyan Movement in the Industrial Revolution*, pp. 209, 246) is correct when he distinguishes the Wesleyan ethic from the notion of charity, although he notes that the Methodists seemed to have lost sight of this after Wesley (p. 247). In this respect Semmel wrongly attributes to Wesley what became the misunderstanding of later Methodists (*The Methodist Revolution*, p. 80).
5. The text I have used is *Certaine Sermons or Homilies: A Facsimile Reproduction of the Edition of 1623*, with an introduction by Mary Ellen Richey and Thomas B. Stroup (Gainesville: Scholars Facsimiles and Reprints, 1968). All subsequent references to the texts of the Homilies will be taken from this edition, cited by page number in parentheses in the main text.
6. So, for example, Basil, in his sermon "I Will Pull Down My Barns," avers: "He who who strips another man of his clothing, is he not a robber; and he who does not clothe the naked when he could, should he not be called the same? The bread you hold in your clutches, that belongs to the starving. That cloak you keep locked away in your wardrobe, that belongs to the naked. Those shoes that are going to waste with you, they belong to the barefooted. The silver you buried away, that belongs to the needy. Whomsoever you could have helped and did not, to so many have you been unjust." *The Sunday Sermons of the Great Fathers*, trans. and ed. M. F. Toal (Chicago: Henry Regnery, 1954), p. 332.
7. Wesley's initially romantic estimate of the character and culture of the Native Americans was to be tempered by subsequent experience; see *Journal*, Dec. 2, 1737, 1:66-8; and *Original Sin*, XI:210-13. Still he continued to be impressed by and made frequent allusion to the simplicity of their lives; see, for example, "Sermon on the Mount, Discourse VIII," V:365.
8. See Thomas W. Madron, "John Wesley on Economics," in *Sanctification and Liberation*, ed. Theodore Runyon (Nashville: Abingdon Press, 1981), pp. 108-9.

9. The "communism" in view here is not, of course, that of State ownership, still less that of state tyranny, whether in Leninist, Stalinist, Maoist, or other forms. This Pentecostal communism corresponds to what Marx (in the following century) called "primitive communism," except that here it is not a case of original innocence but of regenerated love. See my "Was the Founder of Methodism a Communist?" *The United Methodist Reporter* (Oct. 21, 1988); and "Wesley's Preferential Option for the Poor," *Quarterly Review* 9/3 (Fall 1989): 10-19. Although the terms *primitive communism* and *pentecostal communism* are technically correct, I have yielded to *commun(al)ism* as a concession to the sensibilities of anxious readers.

10. John Wesley, *Explanatory Notes Upon the New Testament*, new edition in 2 vols. (London: Wesleyan Methodist Book Room, n.d.; reprinted Grand Rapids: Baker Book House, 1981); hereafter cited as *Notes*. This edition has no page numbers. As a consequence, the references here are to the chapter and verse of the NT text.

11. E. H. Sugden, in his notes to the sermon on "Scriptural Christianity," goes out of his way to contest Wesley's own view. Sugden's comment on Wesley's use of the example of Acts 2 and 4 is as follows: "It is to be observed in regard to the communion of the Church at Jerusalem, (1) that it was not compulsory. From Acts v, it is clear that both before and after the sale of his possessions, it was open to Ananias to do as he thought best with it; (2) that the realization of all their capital for immediate distribution was an economical mistake, however praiseworthy its motive; for in a very few years it became necessary for St. Paul to seek contributions all over the world for the poor saints at Jerusalem." See Sugden, *The Standard Sermons of John Wesley,* 2 vols. (London: Epworth Press, 1961), I:97-98).

   Here Sugden passes over in silence Wesley's own interpretation of Acts 5 and, moreover, leads the reader to suppose that this reference to Acts was an isolated aberration on Wesley's part. The condescending reference to a "praiseworthy motive" for the practice of the pentecostal community leaves out of account the fact that this motive was no other than the Holy Spirit. Finally the supposition that there was a connection between this practice and the subsequent collection for the poor in Jerusalem is not only without any textual support, but also trivializes the theological importance of that collection in Paul's own perspective.

12. Wesley does occasionally refer to property in connection with the idea of civil liberty (see XI:41-2, 81, 87, 92, 95, 137). However, while Wesley argues forcefully for liberty of conscience and especially freedom of religion, he does not make an independent case for civil liberty but rather accepts the definiton of Blackstone (XI:95), who emphasizes the freedom from arbitrary loss of life, freedom, and property. What is at stake here is that one should be protected from robbery, murder, or imprisonment, whether on the part of the State or of any other force. Wesley maintains that this is the liberty that the people of England have and of which the slaves are deprived (XI:81). The references to this civil liberty all occur in Wesley's political essays on the theme of liberty and the American rebellion (see *Thoughts Upon Liberty, A Calm Address to Our American Colonies, Some Observations on Liberty,* and *A Calm Address to the Inhabitants of England*). The right to property is by no means an absolute right. It is merely the right not to be deprived arbitrarily of property. For Wesley, this, of course, permits taxation by the State in accordance with the constitution (XI:89).

   These references to the civil liberty of property do not come into conflict

227

with Wesley's statements about stewardship, since Wesley in any case believes that the law of God takes precedence over any human law. Thus Wesley's acknowledgment of some property rights in the context of a discussion of political philosophy cannot be used to obscure the radicality of his theological judgment that the accumulation of excess property or the practice of excess expenditure is a robbery of God and the poor, and that as Christians we are empowered by the same grace that forgives us of sin in order to participate in the practice of pentecostal commun(al)ism for the sake of the poor.

Although Warner correctly notes that "clearly, an emphasis upon economic security as the condition of civil liberty was not intended as an argument for the existing social inequities" (*The Wesleyan Movement in the Industrial Revolution*, p. 107), he vastly overestimates the place of this alleged emphasis on "economic freedom" (pp. 106-7).

6. Actualization and Controversy

1. See my essay "The Origin of Methodism" in *Methodist History* (forthcoming).
2. See Letter to a Friend, Oct. 10, 1735, XII:39.
3. It is interesting to note that Wesley wrote no tract on abstinence from alcohol, but he did on tea. Had he written one on alcohol, presumably the same principles would have applied: It is an unnecessary expense, and the money saved should be given to the poor.
4. While Wesley's anthropology is not adequate for the twentieth century, it was considerably more social than that of the majority of his followers, then or now.
5. We should note that Methodists who do not accept Wesley's evangelical economics can scarcely take refuge in the complaint that all this is nothing but *adiaphora*, nothing but secondary. Although Wesley was indeed sometimes guilty of insisting on *adiaphora*, this by no means was in itself rejected by the Methodists from a superior vantage point of a concern for the central, as opposed to the peripheral concerns of the gospel. Methodism has been "distinguished" by its concern for *adiaphora*, as the various "abstinence" campaigns of nineteenth- and early twentieth-century Methodism demonstrate. The reasons for Methodism's refusal of evangelical economics must be sought elsewhere.
6. The view that Wesley accepted the given sociopolitical arrangements as being unalterable is clearly unsustainable.
7. Credit for this is normally given to Max Weber, *The Protestant Ethic and the Spirit of Capitalism* (New York: Scribners, 1958), and R. H. Tawney, *Religion and the Rise of Capitalism* (New York: Harcourt Brace, 1926).
8. It should be clear that whenever Wesley supposes that the Methodist project is in danger of failing it is because it is failing to actualize his teaching on economics. This will become more evident in chapter 8. Moreover, it is not the case that these are the musings of a tired old man. They come from the period of Wesley's greatest theological productivity.

7. Theological Basis of Wesley's Ethic

1. See "Conversión, hombre nuevo y compromiso" in Duqué, ed., *La tradición protestante en la teología latinoamericana*, p. 208.

2. See also the introductory article "Wesley and the Theologies of Liberation" by Theodore Runyon in his *Sanctification and Liberation,* esp. pp. 32ff.

3. But this change does not derive from Aldersgate, as some (for example, Hynson, *To Reform the Nation,* pp. 33-38) maintain, but rather it comes about as a result of a long process in the readjustment of Wesley's views, beginning some years before Aldersgate and continuing for about a decade following.

4. One of the strengths of Semmel's discussion of Methodism is the way in which it connects the social impact of Wesley's views with the Arminian theology of Wesley.

5. Although Wesley is in many ways the patron of an evangelical approach to theology, he was also quite critical of the so-called "Gospel preachers" of his own day for preaching a gospel without radical transformation. See, for example, Letter to Miss Bishop, Oct. 18, 1778, XIII:36; Letter on Preaching Christ, Dec. 20, 1751, XI:486-92; and *Thoughts Concerning Gospel Ministers,* X:455-57.

6. See Wesley's correlation of "roots" and "fruit" in "Upon Our Lord's Sermon on the Mount, Discourse IV," V:305ff.

7. This is the characteristic misinterpretation of E. P. Thompson; see his *The Making of the English Working Class* (New York: Random House, 1963.)

8. So, for example, the early sermons "Scriptural Christianity," V:37-52; or "The Witness of Our Own Spirit," V:134-43.

9. See "On Sin in Believers," V:144-55.

10. See his letter to his father of Dec. 10, 1734, cited in *Journal,* Mar. 28, 1739, I:177-85.

11. To be sure, the early Wesley did emphasize personal transformation. It is one of the characteristics of Wesley's later sermons (those not in the "Standard Sermons") that there is much greater emphasis on the transformation of society. See, for example, the sermons on "The Foundation of City Road Chapel," "The General Spread of the Gospel," and "The Signs of the Times."

12. The development of an evangelical economics for our own time or an economics of the gospel is the subject of an important new work by M. Douglas Meeks, *God the Economist: The Doctrine of God and Political Economy* (Minneapolis: Augsburg/Fortress, 1989).

8. Why Did Wesley Fail?

1. Such a discussion would involve an approach either through the question of the general adequacy of Wesley's own method of biblical interpretation, a much discussed issue, or would involve a direct approach to the Bible, and in particular the NT, in order to inquire into the economic views either explicit or implicit in the texts. This last is, I think, the more fruitful approach, since Wesley wished to be held accountable to the Bible as the norm of his teaching.

2. While it is the case that Wesley tended to think in terms of persons rather than in terms of social structures, this was true for his age in general. A reconsideration of evangelical economics for our time will have to take fresh insights concerning the character of human existence into account, just as Wesley was prepared to take into account the insights of the sciences of his own day in the development of his anthropological and cosmological categories.

3. Some attention is given to this theme by Semmel (*The Methodist Revolution,* pp. 110-45) and by Warner (*The Wesleyan Movement in the Industrial Revolution,* pp. 126-31 and 202-3). Warner's thesis is aptly stated as follows: "The uniqueness of the new movement as a programme of social reform was adulterated into a pale hue of respectability" (p. 273). Similar conclusions are demonstrated by John Kent in his essay "Methodism and Social Change in Britain," in Runyon, *Sanctification and Liberation,* pp. 83-101.

4. It is clear that it is precisely these texts that are used by Warner (*The Wesleyan Movement in the Industrial Revolution,* pp. 138-41) and Semmel (*The Methodist Revolution,* pp. 71-79) to come to their astonishing conclusion that Wesley was a prime supporter of the capitalist ethos. Warner even speaks of "the wholeheartedness with which it [the Methodism of Wesley] approved economic enterprize and the pursuit of gain" (p. 138). While Warner and Semmel think of this as a positive effect of Wesley, the same position is taken by John C. Cort in *Christian Socialism* (Maryknoll, N.Y.: Orbis Books, 1988), to dismiss Wesley's economic views as being reactionary, despite the fact that the passages cited with so much approval from the early Church theologians are repeated nearly verbatim in Wesley's sermons. It is obvious that there has come to be a traditional "reading" of Wesley as proto-capitalist, which is accepted by interpreters of opposed ideological commitments. Yet, it is a view of Wesley that manages to ignore Wesley's actual teachings on the subject.

5. Among a host of texts that could be cited here, we may mention the *Journal* entries for Oct. 12-21, 1760; July 11, 1764; Oct. 20, 1764; June 28, 1765; Nov. 20, 1767; and so on. Essays that contest the distorted reading of the three rules include *Thoughts Upon Methodism* and the various essays on dress. Sermons include "On Riches," "The Danger of Riches," "The Danger of Increasing Riches," "The Spread of the Gospel," "Obedience to Pastors," "God's Vineyard," and "Causes of the Inefficacy of Christianity." In every case, Wesley refers to the three rules. In no case does he argue at all for gaining. In every case, he insists that the whole point is the third rule (giving). That is, Wesley only refers to these rules in order to insist on giving, never once to speak of gaining. Thus Wesley's repeated references to this threefold rule show not that Wesley thought that his authoritative teaching had been given in that sermon, but that that sermon was the regular cause for the distortion and evasion of his teaching.

6. This is true even for the otherwise excellent discussion of Wesley's social ethic by Manfred Marquardt in *Praxis und Prinzipien der Sozialethik John Wesleys* (Göttingen: Vandenhoeck & Ruprecht, 1977). While Marquardt recognizes (against Semmel) that Wesley's economic ethic is incompatible with capitalism (see pp. 43-46), he nevertheless makes his task unnecessarily difficult by permitting the sermon on "The Use of Money" to dictate his outline of Wesley's economic ethic (p. 39). Such a decision cannot derive from the place of this sermon in the thought of Wesley, but only from its place in the conservative Methodism of the nineteenth century—that is, from the attempt not to follow but to ignore Wesley's characteristic teachings on economics.

7. See Albert C. Outler's discussion of the complicated history of Wesley's sermon corpus in his Introduction to *The Works of John Wesley,* vol. I: *Sermons, 1–33* (Nashville: Abingdon Press, 1984), pp. 29-55.

8. There were, of course, other charges made against Wesley—for example, that he was a papist or an antinomian. The former was used to incite popular opposition on the basis of supposed disloyalty to the crown (see the Appendix). But the strictly theological charges (antinomianism) against Wesley never seem to have played a role in stirring up mob violence against the Methodists.
9. See Wesley's *An Earnest Appeal to Men of Reason and Religion*, VIII:51ff.
10. See, for example, his sermons on "Salvation by Faith," "Justification by Faith," "The Marks of the New Birth," and "The New Birth."
11. Article XXXVIII of The Articles of Religion of the Church of England, in Philip Schaff, ed., *The Creeds of Christendom, With a History and Critical Notes*, 3 vols. (New York: Harper and Bros., 1877), III:513.
12. See Madron in *Sanctification and Liberation*, ed. Runyon, pp. 108-9, 230-31.
13. Thus Warner (*The Wesleyan Movement in the Industrial Revolution*, p. 156) cites the 1760 tract by Alexander Jephson, *A Friendly and Compassionate Address to All Serious and Well-disposed Methodists*, which sought to dissuade them from "their notion of the community of Christian men's goods." From the date of the work, it is probable that Jephson was alarmed at Wesley's *Notes*. So far from dissuading Wesley of this doctrine, Wesley actually comes to insist more and more on it in the later sermons.
14. See Warner, *The Wesleyan Movement in the Industrial Revolution*, p. 156.
15. The Articles of Religion of the Methodist Church, Article XXIV, as found in *The Book of Discipline of the United Methodist Church, 1988* (Nashville: The United Methodist Publishing House, 1988), p. 67.
16. It seems highly improbable that Wesley let the offending Article stand in his own revision of the Articles of Religion. It need only be noted in this connection that the Coke who later urgently denied Wesley's own teaching on this subject is the same one who was entrusted with carrying Wesley's edition of the Articles to the Americans.
17. *The Book of Discipline, 1988*, p. 73. This Confession of Faith is now an element of the official theology of The United Methodist Church.
18. The mark of a Wesleyan view of stewardship is that it is a trust from God *for the poor*. This is completely missing from the Social Creed, the Social Principles, and the Confession of Faith.
19. The assessment of Warner (*The Wesleyan Movement in the Industrial Revolution*, p. 281) is sobering: "Wesley saw that the triumph of the Christian ethic was bound up with its ability to create desires beneficent to society. For the same reason he realized that there were certain kinds of inequalities which were fatal to its social programme. His successors failed to grasp these fundamentals. They compromised. They courted respectability. They chose the easier task, as though a mystical intensity could compensate for the loss of moral imperatives." This assessment is just, save that Warner here as usual substitutes "society" for "the poor," thereby contributing to the de-radicalization of Wesley's views.

9. The Relevance of Wesley

1. See Wesley's *Thoughts Upon Methodism*, XIII:258-61.
2. The question of idolatry has become one of the main themes of liberation theology. See Pablo Richard et al., *The Idols of Death and the God of Life: A Theology* (Maryknoll, N.Y.: Orbis Books, 1983).

3. For Wesley's critique of these "gospel preachers" see "Thoughts Concerning Gospel Ministers," X:455-56, and "Letter on Preaching Christ," XI:486-92.
4. However, the ferment in lands where Marxism is the reigning ideology holds some promise of reversing these distortions. Unfortunately, in the West this ferment is usually evaluated in terms of greater reliance on private property and market forces rather than in terms of human dignity and care for the poor.
5. See *The Book of Discipline, 1988,* paragraph 73.
6. It is true that Wesley launched a building campaign. He attempted, as we do not, to reduce the impact of this expense by insisting that churches be built as cheaply as possible. Still one of the reasons for the failure of Wesley to persuade Methodists of the main tenets of evangelical economics was the economic pressure of this acquisition of chapels.
7. The sermon "The Almost Christian" (V:17-25) is an illustration of the worst of the tendency to use a couple of words from the NT to develop a theme that has nothing whatever to do with the text.
8. One of the issues that is thought to be critical for our time is the alternative between State and private ownership of property, especially of the means of production. But as normally posed this is a false issue, since socialism no longer defines itself in terms of the state ownership of the means of production (see Cort, *Christian Socialism*), nor is capitalism typically defined as the untrammeled rights of private property. The question really becomes that of the appropriate mix, given existing conditions, of state ownership (as in the Post Office), public ownership by the society as a whole (as in some utilities), regulated monopolies (as in communications), worker ownership, public corporations, and individual and family ownership, to mention only some of the possible elements. But appropriate to what? What are the ends to be accomplished by this mix of elements? It is with this latter question that an evangelical economics is mainly concerned. While most ethical systems take the question of justice seriously, a Wesleyan social ethic will be found in the company of those who take solidarity with the poor and commitment to the welfare of the most vulnerable members of society as the most important test of social (and personal) justice in the economic sphere.
9. See, for example, the sermon "On the General Spread of the Gospel."
10. Especially in his *We Drink from Our Own Wells.* Indeed, it is also recognized by Tomas Borgé; see *Christianity and Revolution: Tomas Borgé's Theology of Life,* ed. Andrew Reding (Maryknoll, N.Y.: Orbis Books, 1987).

Appendix: Wesley on Politics

1. That Methodism after the death of Wesley emphasized loyalty to the Crown in a way that distorted Wesley's own political views is a point ably made by Warner, who speaks of the Methodists as priding themselves on their political "docility" (*The Wesleyan Movement in the Industrial Revolution,* pp. 130-31).
2. *Certaine Sermons and Homilies.* All page numbers refer to the above cited edition.
3. For Wesley's remarks both on this and on the new government of the former colonies, see the sermon "Of Former Times," VII:165.
4. Semmel (*The Methodist Revolution,* pp. 56-81) provides a good background

discussion of the ferment in England, though his account is somewhat marred by a one-sided presentation of Wesley's response. The discussion of that response is more balanced in Warner (*The Wesleyan Movement in the Industrial Revolution*, pp. 73-135).

5. One of the deficiencies of Semmel's discussion of Wesley's attitudes toward the prospect of rebellion is that he seems to be unaware of Wesley's sympathy with a protest against manifest injustice and fails to understand that Wesley's fear of mob rule was based not on antipathy to popular movements but on painful experience with mobs aroused by the wealthy and powerful to further their own ends against the Methodists.

6. Charles A. Beard, *An Economic Interpretation of the Constitution of the United States* (1913; reprinted New York: Free Press, 1986).

7. Wesley's reference to civil liberty with respect to property is not to be understood as denying the view of stewardship and community of goods, which he was defending in other contexts at the same time. He is accepting the frame of reference of his opponents, which emphasizes human liberty in these ways, but in order to show that they have all they can ask for already. This does not mean that Wesley thought nothing of the security of life and home, which was at the heart of civil liberty. One should not be deprived of these things without due process of law. But this was, for Wesley, adequately guaranteed by the existing constitution. Interestingly, he refuses to answer the hypothetical question: But what if things change? What if the constitution proves to be an inadequate safeguard? For Wesley, it was enough that for now there was no ground for complaint. He was, in this as in other matters, not a theoretician but a thoroughly practical thinker, with all the limits—and strengths that implies.

8. In many respects my conclusions are in material agreement with those of Hynson with respect to Wesley's support for human rights. There are, however, differences, not only in the way of arriving at these conclusions, but also with respect to significant nuances in evaluating Wesley's position. Although Hynson does emphasize the support given by Wesley to the idea of liberty, he does not adequately distinguish between what for Wesley is fundamental (freedom of conscience) and the less well developed view of civil liberty. Even more important, he does not seem to realize the place that the criterion of the poor plays in Wesley's thought generally, including Wesley's political thought.

9. Another of the defects of Hynson's view of Wesley on human rights is that he seems to be unaware of the way in which talk of liberty and rights does regularly mask these interests. In this, Wesley is more "contemporary" than many of his interpreters.

10. It is noteworthy that Methodist theologians have played a significant role in the development of such a theology of liberation. The development of libertation theology owes much to José Míguez Bonino, especially *Doing Theology in a Revolutionary Situation* and *Toward a Christian Political Ethic* (Philadelphia: Fortress Press, 1983). Among the younger theologians, we should mention Elsa Tamez, *Bible of the Oppressed* (Maryknoll, N.Y.: Orbis Books, 1982); the collection of essays edited by Tamez and Saul Trinidad, *Capitalismo: Violencia y anti-vida: La opresión de las mayorías y la domesticación do los dioses* (San José, Costa Rica: CSUSA, 1978); and Victorio Araya, *God of the Poor* (Maryknoll, N.Y.: Orbis Books, 1987). Essays by these and other Methodist theologians of liberation, like Emilio Castro and Mortimer Arias, are found in *La tradición protestante en la teología latinoamericana:*

Primer intento: La lectura de la tradición metodista, ed. José Duqué (San José, Costa Rica: DEI, 1983). Many of these essays are available in translation in *Faith Born in the Struggle for Life,* ed. Dow Kirkpatrick (Grand Rapids: Eerdmans, 1988).

These contributions are based on a long, though often obscured, tradition of Latin American Methodism. Methodist participation in the revolution of Mexico has been demonstrated by Jean-Pierre Bastien in *Protestantismo y sociedad en México* (México City: CUPSA, 1983); and in *Los Disidentes: sociedades protestantes y revolución en México 1872–1911* (México City: El Colegio de México, 1989). And the role of the Methodist preacher and revolutionary Rubén Jaramillo in the middle decades of this century are well known to all but Methodists in Mexico; see Rubén Jaramillo, *Autobiografía y asesinato* (México City: Nuestro Tiempo, 1967).

LaVergne, TN USA
01 September 2009
156546LV00002B/130/A

5297035R0

Made in the USA
Lexington, KY
25 April 2010